Reflections on the Commemoration of the First World War

D1521944

The First World War's centenary generated a mass of commemorative activity worldwide. Officially and unofficially; individually, collectively and commercially; locally, nationally and internationally, efforts were made to respond to the legacies of this vast conflict. This book explores some of these responses from areas previously tied to the British Empire, including Australia, Britain, Canada, India and New Zealand. Showcasing insights from historians of commemoration and heritage professionals, it provides revealing insider and outsider perspectives of the centenary. How far did commemoration become celebration, and how merited were such responses? To what extent did the centenary serve wider social and political functions? Was it a time for new knowledge and understanding of the events of a century ago, for recovery of lost or marginalised voices, or for confirming existing clichés? And what can be learned from the experience of this centenary that might inform the approach to future commemorative activities? The contributors to this book grapple with these questions, coming to different answers and demonstrating the connections and disconnections between those involved in building public knowledge of the 'war to end all wars'.

David Monger is Senior Lecturer in History at the University of Canterbury, New Zealand. He is the author of *Patriotism and Propaganda in First World War Britain: The National War Aims Committee and Civilian Morale*, co-editor of *Endurance and the First World War: Experiences and Legacies in New Zealand and Australia* and has written several articles on aspects of First World War history.

Sarah Murray is Curatorial Manager at Canterbury Museum, New Zealand. She specialises in the history of the First World War and public history. Sarah is the author of *A Cartoon War: The Cartoons of the New Zealand Free Lance and New Zealand Observer as Historical Sources, August 1914–November 1918*, co-editor of *Endurance and the First World War: Experiences and Legacies in New Zealand and Australia* and has both published articles and curated exhibitions on the First World War.

Routledge Studies in First World War History

Series Editor: John Bourne
The University of Birmingham, UK

The First World War is a subject of perennial interest to historians and is often regarded as a watershed event, marking the end of the nineteenth century and the beginning of the 'modern' industrial world. The sheer scale of the conflict and massive loss of life means that it is constantly being assessed and reassessed to examine its lasting military, political, sociological, industrial, cultural and economic impact. Reflecting the latest international scholarly research, the Routledge Studies in First World War History series provides a unique platform for the publication of monographs on all aspects of the Great War. Whilst the main thrust of the series is on the military aspects of the conflict, other related areas (including cultural, visual, literary, political and social) are also addressed. Books published are aimed primarily at a post-graduate academic audience, furthering exciting recent interpretations of the war, whilst still being accessible enough to appeal to a wider audience of educated lay readers.

Also in this series

Military Service Tribunals and Boards in the Great War
Determining the Fate of Britain's and New Zealand's Conscripts
David Littlewood

The Royal Flying Corps, the Western Front and the Control of the Air, 1914–1918
James Pugh

The Great War and the British Empire
Culture and Society
Edited by Michael J.K. Walsh and Andrekos Varnava

Aerial Propaganda and the Wartime Occupation of France, 1914–18
Bernard Wilkin

Reflections on the Commemoration of the First World War
Perspectives from the Former British Empire
Edited by David Monger and Sarah Murray

https://www.routledge.com/history/series/WWI

Reflections on the Commemoration of the First World War

Perspectives from the Former British Empire

**Edited by
David Monger and
Sarah Murray**

Routledge
Taylor & Francis Group

LONDON AND NEW YORK

First published 2021
by Routledge
2 Park Square, Milton Park, Abingdon, Oxon OX14 4RN

and by Routledge
52 Vanderbilt Avenue, New York, NY 10017

Routledge is an imprint of the Taylor & Francis Group, an informa business

British Library Cataloguing-in-Publication Data
A catalogue record for this book is available from the British Library

Library of Congress Cataloging-in-Publication Data
Names: Monger, David, editor. | Murray, Sarah, editor.
Title: Reflections on the commemoration of the First World War :
perspectives from the former British Empire / edited by David
Monger, and Sarah Murray.
Other titles: Perspectives from the former British Empire
Description: Abingdon, Oxon ; New York : Routledge, 2021. |
Series: Routledge studies in first world war history | Includes
bibliographical references and index.
Identifiers: LCCN 2020029850 (print) | LCCN 2020029851 (ebook) |
ISBN 9780367898731 (hardback) | ISBN 9781003021629 (ebook)
Subjects: LCSH: World War, 1914–1918—Great Britain—
Colonies—Anniversaries, etc. | World War, 1914–1918—
Monuments—Great Britain—Colonies. | War memorials—India. |
War memorials—Australia. | War memorials—New Zealand. |
War memorials—Canada.
Classification: LCC D680.G7 R44 2021 (print) |
LCC D680.G7 (ebook) | DDC 940.4/609171241—dc23
LC record available at https://lccn.loc.gov/2020029850
LC ebook record available at https://lccn.loc.gov/2020029851

ISBN: 978-0-367-89873-1 (hbk)
ISBN: 978-1-003-02162-9 (ebk)

Typeset in Times New Roman
by codeMantra

Contents

Figures

Tables

Contributors

Bryce Abraham is a historian of heroism, war and society, and honours and awards. His PhD, conferred by the University of Newcastle, Australia, examined the shifting constructions of Australian military heroism from Sudan to Vietnam (1885–1975), with an emphasis on the associated constructs of masculinity and the award (and non-award) of the Victoria Cross. He is presently Assistant Curator, Private Records at the Australian War Memorial in Canberra. You can find his work in *Wartime*, the *Bulletin of the Auckland Museum* and featured on *The Dead Prussian Podcast*.

Sarah Cook is a Senior Archivist at Library and Archives Canada (LAC). She has worked in various aspects of the archival profession at LAC, from appraisal and disposition to how we make this content available to researchers. She has published and given scholarly papers in the fields of film, archives and Canadian military history, as well as curated several web exhibitions and digital tools.

Tim Cook is a historian at the Canadian War Museum, where he has curated over a dozen exhibitions. He has authored 13 books and over 60 peer-reviewed articles. He is a director for Canada's History Society, and a member of the Royal Society of Canada and the Order of Canada.

Santanu Das is a Senior Research Fellow at All Souls College, University of Oxford, where he is the Professor of Modern Literature and Culture. He is the author of *Touch and Intimacy in First World War Literature* (2006) and the editor of *Race, Empire and First World War Writing* (2011) and the *Cambridge Companion to the Poetry of the First World War* (2014). His most recent book *India, Empire and First World War Culture: Literature, Images, and Songs* (2018) won the Hindu Non-fiction Prize in India. He is currently editing the *Oxford Book of First World War Colonial Writing*.

Xavier Fowler completed his PhD at the University of Melbourne in 2018, studying sport and its relationship with social conflict in Australia during the First World War. He currently teaches twentieth century history at Deakin University.

Louisa Hormann MA(Dis), first began centenary museum work in 2014, undertaking a summer scholarship updating records for First World War collections and research at the Museum of New Zealand Te Papa Tongarewa. Louisa completed her Master's thesis in History and Postgraduate Diploma in Museum and Heritage Studies at Victoria University of Wellington in 2016. She joined the archive and research team at the Air Force Museum of New Zealand in 2017 and is the 2019–2021 Emerging Museum Professionals representative on the Museums Aotearoa Board. Her research interests include the social history of twentieth century conflict, Holocaust displacement, and the representation of marginalised histories in museums.

Rowan Light is an Honorary Academic at the University of Auckland, where he was awarded his doctorate in 2019 for his thesis 'Mobilising Memory: Anzac Commemoration in Australia and New Zealand, 1965–2015'.

Margaret Lovell-Smith is an independent historian whose research interests include the nineteenth century women's movement, women's biography and local history. She is the lead researcher for the 'Voices Against War' project and wrote many of the articles for the voicesagainstwar.nz website. She is currently co-writing a book about Canterbury's peace and anti-militarist movement before and during the First World War. Previous publications include *Easily the Best: the Life of Helen Connon 1857–1903* (2004), *Hurunui Heritage: the Development of a District 1950–2000* (2000), *The Enigma of Sister Mary Leo* (1998) and *The Woman Question – Writings by the Women Who Won the Vote* (1992).

David Monger is Senior Lecturer in History at the University of Canterbury, New Zealand. He is the author of *Patriotism and Propaganda in First World War Britain: the National War Aims Committee and Civilian Morale*, co-editor of *Endurance and the First World War: Experiences and Legacies in New Zealand and Australia* and has written several articles on aspects of First World War history.

Sarah Murray is Curatorial Manager at Canterbury Museum, New Zealand. She specialises in the history of the First World War and public history. Sarah is the author of *A Cartoon War: The Cartoons of the New Zealand Free Lance and New Zealand Observer as Historical Sources, August 1914–November 1918*, co-editor of *Endurance and the First World War: Experiences and Legacies in New Zealand and Australia* and has both published articles and curated exhibitions on the First World War.

Acknowledgements

Many thanks to the Canterbury100 collaborative whose cooperation, support and hard work was behind the *Reflections: On the Commemoration of World War One* conference. Held at Tūranga City Library in November 2018, the conference was the impetus for this volume and we would like to acknowledge not only the team who brought the conference to fruition but also all those who participated in it. Our particular thanks to Louisa Hormann and Simon Moody of the Air Force Museum of New Zealand; Joanna Szczepanski from Canterbury Museum; Kate Odgen and Kathryn Hartley from Christchurch City Libraries; the team from South Canterbury Museum; Joanna Condon and Rowan Light from the University of Canterbury and the teams at Te Rūnanga o Ngāi Tahu, Selwyn Library and Waimakariri District Libraries. Our thanks also to Daniel Steel and Tom Gilmour for volunteering their time to assist the smooth running of the conference. We would also like to extend our warmest thanks to all those who presented at the conference; it was no easy task to select from amongst the high calibre papers those to include in this volume. We are most grateful to the Canterbury History Foundation, Canterbury Museum, Museums Aotearoa and New Zealand Micrographic Services Ltd for their generous financial support of the conference and the wider kaupapa of the Canterbury100 group.

We would like to thank Tanushree Baijal, Rob Langham, Max Novick and the team at Routledge for commissioning this volume and for carefully guiding it through to publication. We would like to acknowledge the anonymous reviewer of the manuscript whose helpful suggestions undoubtedly much improved the book. Our thanks also to Daniel Steel for his meticulous work on the index for this volume.

Our contributors deserve warmest thanks for their responsiveness, care and commitment to this project. Your speedy responses and thoughtful chapters have made this project a real pleasure. Colleagues at the University of Canterbury and Canterbury Museum, notably Joanna Szczepanski and Neeha Velagapudi, have enthusiastically supported this work and are much appreciated.

Finally, our thanks to our families and friends for their support particularly Dominic, Sophia and Heather.

David Monger and Sarah Murray
Christchurch, May 2020

Introduction

Assessing the centenary of the First World War

David Monger and Sarah Murray

In late November 2018, an international conference entitled *Reflections on the Commemoration of World War One* took place at Tūranga, the central library of Christchurch, Aotearoa New Zealand. The event was organised by Canterbury100 – a collaborative group involving the region's major cultural and heritage institutions, which led Canterbury's contribution to the wider WW100 programme established by the New Zealand Government to coordinate its centenary activities – as the culmination of its centenary work.[1] The conference brought together an international array of researchers addressing long-term and contemporary commemoration of the First World War. Reflecting Canterbury100's collaborative, multi-institutional approach, the conference aimed to unite the expertise of academic researchers and heritage professionals, and both 'outside' observations and 'inside' reflections on commemoration and centenary activities. The chapters of this book represent a small sample of the insights provided at the conference and, likewise, give both inside and outside perspectives. In doing so, they demonstrate once more that lessons continue to be learned (and, sometimes, not to be learned) about the historical and contemporary significance of the First World War.

Canterbury100

One hundred years after the First World War, museums and cultural institutions played a significant role in reflecting on the personal and national impact of the conflict. Like many other countries, New Zealand's commemoration of the First World War balanced a national approach to commemoration with local and community activities on a regional stage. In Canterbury, a region on the east coast of New Zealand's South Island, a series of devastating earthquakes in 2010 and 2011 disrupted planning for the centenary. The recovery from these seismic events diverted much of the time, energy and resources of Canterbury's heritage institutions. By 2013, as the region's recovery was underway, a meeting of heritage staff brought together several of the larger and many of the smaller institutions to discuss their plans for the upcoming centenary. Following this meeting, the Canterbury100 group formed to offer a collaborative network for centenary activity that would provide a focus for the community in the early years of the centenary, with the hope that individual institutions would be allowed more space and time to develop their own centenary plans later. Canterbury100 immediately set to work on three areas of activity. The first focus was the design and development of an exhibition with touring elements. Opening in August 2014 at the Air Force Museum of New Zealand, an institution relatively unscathed by the earthquakes, the exhibition provided a summary of the First World War as well as a selection of stories from modern day Cantabrians about their families' stories from the war. Shortly after the opening of the exhibition, Canterbury100 launched its second major event; an event day to provide expert advice and information on First World War history. The group welcomed hundreds of visitors with their stories and objects and provided each visitor with background information to the artefacts in their care, ideas of where to find further information and the opportunity to share their story. These stories were shared on a website developed by Canterbury100 to capture and communicate community stories and aspects of material culture relating to the conflict. This latter focus drew on the group's awareness of the importance of creating legacy work with relevance beyond the centenary. In fact, one of the group's aims was to establish networks and relationships that would endure after the centenary.

After the initial activity in 2014 and 2015, Canterbury100 continued regular meetings to share information on progress with each organisation's plans and to identify ways of working together. Individual members of the group opened their own commemorative exhibitions, ran public programmes and delivered commemorative events. In the case of Canterbury Museum, for instance, the exhibition *Canterbury and World War One: Lives Lost, Lives Changed* opened on 1 December 2017, running until 11 November 2018. Due to a desire to continue to offer access to these stories thereafter, it then opened as an online exhibition. During the centenary, Canterbury Museum offered several talks, including programmes each Anzac Day, developed education lessons and digitised First World War collections to add to its online collections access portal.[2]

By 2017, Canterbury100 identified the need to mark the end of the centenary period and reflect on achievements, challenges and failures not only of the group but also of the way in which the centenary itself had been understood, presented, engaged with and commemorated. As a result, the group decided to observe the conclusion of the centenary period with a conference that brought together museum professionals, historians, librarians, academics, students, film-makers, artists, writers, researchers and government sector contributors to reflect on the war's commemoration.

The papers presented at the conference, and the selection that appears as chapters in this book, demonstrate both inside and outside perspectives about the historical and contemporary commemoration of the First World War. In some ways, these pieces show a divergence between insider and outsider viewpoints. At the end of the centenary, academics frequently suggest that little progress or innovation has been achieved in enhancing public understanding of the war's complexities whereas GLAM (Galleries, Libraries, Archives and Museum) sector views suggest awareness of the need to challenge existing narratives, implying a sector already actively responding to modern scholarship and, particularly in their exhibitions, delivering innovative new material. In many ways, these perspectives point to the continued need for closer interaction between academics and GLAM professionals in future. One hundred years on, lessons for future activity can still be learnt, not only about the First World War itself but about the ways in which all those keen to understand and explain the past might better comprehend each other's approaches and contributions. Those preparing for the historical acknowledgement of other momentous past events can benefit from understanding how and why centenary efforts followed the paths they did. Meanwhile, the range of new perspectives suggested by this collection's authors demonstrates the continued need to study, engage and reflect on historical and contemporary understandings of the First World War.

Centenary scholarship, commemoration and the centenary in perspective

In Part I, historians provide 'outsider' perspectives on the war's commemoration. Our contributors discuss some of the purposes the centenary commemorations have served within Britain, India, Australia and New Zealand. In Chapter 1, Santanu Das suggests British politicians and groups of varying perspectives used the centenary to promote social cohesion and community-building through a 'sanitised' emphasis on multiculturalism. While rightly making or endorsing efforts to recognise often overlooked South Asian contributions to the war, he suggests, critical historical responses were ignored and critical contemporary voices largely dismissed, as commemoration largely became celebration. Chapter 2, by Bryce Abraham, highlights a sanitising impulse in a different way in considering Australian conceptions of heroism during the centenary period, away from previously stressed martial valour and towards 'humanitarianism, selflessness and sacrifice'. Abraham ties this to the development of a 'new nationalism' since the 1980s, uncomfortable with the violence and trauma associated with war. Heroes responsible for saving lives have thus, he argues, replaced those skilled at taking lives in much commemorative activity. Similarly stressing the impact of 'new nationalism' in Chapter 3, Xavier Fowler finds a more martial tone in Australian professional sport's appropriation of Anzac Day to suit its own, commercial, myth-making. Like Das's concerns about multicultural commemoration, Fowler sees the sporting community's embrace of the war as valorising martial activity while ignoring problematic or contradictory elements of sport's wartime history. Finally, in Chapter 4, Rowan Light discusses the extremely successful New Zealand exhibition,

Gallipoli: the Scale of Our War. Once again, nationalism is a prominent theme in Light's chapter, emphasising the extent to which this centenary exhibition revived attempts begun in the 1980s to build a 'New Zealand story' around the Gallipoli campaign. For Light, like the other contributors to Part I, therefore, centenary commemorations provided a useful vehicle to address perceived 'contemporary needs... and... political and cultural agendas', rather than to ensure a more thorough and complex understanding of the war and those affected by it. For the authors, familiar, comfortable clichés were usually more likely elements of centenary commemorations than challenging new perspectives.

Such assessments find many echoes in wider contemporary scholarship. The onset of what a previous volume on the war's commemoration described as 'the centenary to end all centenaries' added a mass of new scholarship to an already rich field.[3] Studies of grief and commemoration are substantial parts of the war's modern social and cultural history, and classic works like Jay Winter's *Sites of memory, sites of mourning* have been required reading in university courses on the war for a generation.[4] Rather than re-tread well-worn paths in outlining the major works of this scholarship, this introductory section provides an overview of a body of new, openly accessible, scholarship related to commemoration and the centenary which is a product of the centenary itself. *1914–1918-online. International Encyclopedia of the First World War* was launched in October 2014 as a 'collaborative project by the largest network of WW1 [sic] researchers worldwide, spanning more than 50 countries'.[5] Overseen by an international team of editors, it continues to expand and evolve as new articles are added and existing ones modified. Its aim in 2014 was to adjust the 'general public's understanding of the First World War[, which] continues to be shaped by the Western Front, images of endless trenches, positional warfare, and the industrial battles of attrition'. By providing a transnational and comparative approach, which the editors considered 'not new to scholars' but not yet 'part of the wider public's common knowledge':

> The encyclopedia intends to summarize the latest knowledge of international experts and make it accessible to a general audience to a degree that is more comprehensive than has been the case so far. In this way, it aims to make a contribution to a post-national and global understanding of the First World War that includes the culture of remembrance.[6]

The memory of the war was identified specifically as a core focus of the encyclopaedia's mission. It is unsurprising, therefore, that commemoration features heavily in its content. On 7 October 2019, the encyclopaedia hosted 1,414 published articles. Of these, a search showed that more than a third, 546, contained the word 'memorial', while 248 used the word 'commemoration'. Three major themes, 'Bereavement and mourning', 'Centenary' and 'Commemoration, Cult of the Fallen' incorporated several dozen individual articles which, alongside a few others (such as accounts of individual memorials) provided a sample of 58 articles (Table 0.1). A survey of these is neither exhaustive nor complete (there were, e.g., 36 yet to be published articles listed for the 'Centenary' theme, including the thematic overview article, beyond the 14 already published). Nonetheless, it reveals some common features in existing scholarly commentaries.

This similarity is partly explained by the brief provided to contributors. Section editors commissioned authors to write specific topics, and outlined issues to address.[7] The encyclopaedia contains a 'Call for Papers' section listing as yet unwritten topics and provides guidance on expected content

Table 0.1 1914–1918 Online articles surveyed

Bereavement and mourning theme (11)	*Centenary theme (14)*	*Commemoration, cult of the fallen theme (16)*	*Miscellaneous (17)*
Bereavement and Mourning [BM] *[Thematic Survey]*	Centenary [C] (Armenia)	Commemoration, Cult of the Fallen [CCF] *[Thematic Survey]*	Anzac (Australia)
BM (Africa)	C (Belarus)		Bean, Charles
BM (Australia)	C (Bulgaria)	CCF (Canada)	Cenotaph
BM (Belgium)	C (Canada)	Commemoration and Remembrance (USA)	Langemarck Myth
BM, Commemoration, Cult of the Fallen (France) [combined article]	C (Computer Games)	CCF (Africa)	Mémorial Interallié
	C (Israel and Palestine)	CCF (Australia)	Memory of the War: Popular Memory 1918–1945, 1945 to the Present *[Thematic Survey]*
BM (Germany)	C (Italy)	CCF (Belgium)	
BM (Great Britain)	C (Russia)	CCF (East Central Europe)	Recording the Experiences of War: Personal Accounts of World War I (USA)
BM (New Zealand)	C (Singapore)	CCF (Germany)	
BM (Ottoman Empire and Middle East)	C (Slovenia)	CCF (India)	Remembrance Day 11 November 1922 – Today (France)
	C (Turkey)	CCF (Indochina)	
BM (South East Europe)	C (United Kingdom)	CCF (Newfoundland)	Stab-in-the-Back Myth
BM (USA)	C (USA)	CCF (New Zealand)	Tannenberg Myth
	C (Visual Arts)	CCF (Russian Empire)	Thiepval Memorial
		CCF (South East Europe)	Tomb of the Unknown Soldier (Rome)
		CCF (Union of South Africa)	Tomb of the Unknown Soldier (Warsaw)
		CCF (Switzerland)	War Cemeteries (Germany)
			War Memorials (Germany)
			War Memory, Commemoration (Ottoman Empire/ Middle East)
			Ypres, Menin Gate

and length. Michal Kšiňan and Bruce Scates, for instance, asked potential authors of 'Centenary (Austria)' to address contemporary events, commenting, among other things, on 'political, cultural and social trends in commemorative activities and practices'; on whether activity was state or popularly driven and on the extent of public interest and whether centenary activities 'create[d] any changes in memory'.[8] Each of these issues features fairly prominently in the surveyed articles. Thus, the editors' didactic aims, discussed previously, shaped content produced by authors, though they, nonetheless, took diverse approaches to similarly themed topics. What emerge as major recurring considerations for the authors are (Figure 0.1): emphasis on the politicised nature of commemoration and the centenary; often in relation to this, emphasis on commemoration's effect on national identities; identification of the war as a disruptive moment for traditional grieving and commemorative processes; common references to sacrifice and the figure of the unknown soldier; some discussion of perceived shifts in interest levels at different times and occasional comments on the repetition of clichés or, less commonly, on new innovations.

Much the most common feature of the *1914–1918-online* sample is the identification of political influence over commemoration. This, unsurprisingly, is noted as a dramatic issue in places where the war's memory carries significant diplomatic implications, as with Turkey's ongoing refusal to acknowledge the Armenian Genocide, which is highlighted in several

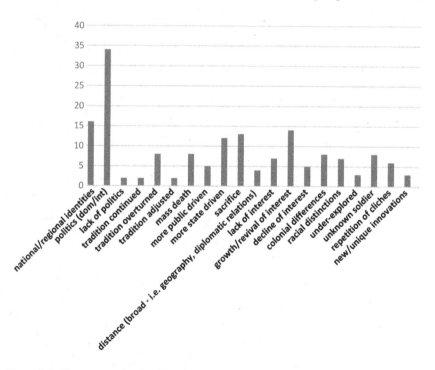

Figure 0.1 Themes emphasised in *1914–1918-Online* articles.

articles, with diverging interpretations. Nazan Maksudyan's account of Turkey's centenary activities, for instance, censures Turkey's government for shifting its 1915 commemoration of the battle of Gallipoli from 18 March, where it had 'always been observed', to 24–25 April, where it would overshadow Armenia's Genocide Remembrance Day. By contrast, Pheroze Unwallah, while also asserting a 'clear Turkish state campaign to use Gallipoli... to overshadow the genocide centennial', rejected the suggestion that attention to 24 April was new, arguing this had occurred 'for many years' and citing his own attendance at such an event in 2007.[9] Israeli, Palestinian and international attempts to address legacies of the 1917 Balfour Declaration – endorsing a national home for Jews in Palestine – and the conquest of Palestine itself, Roberto Mazza argues, also produced dramatic political claims. Despite Israeli and Australian Prime Ministers, Benjamin Netanyahu and Malcolm Turnbull, linking a re-enactment of the battle of Beersheva to the foundation of Israel, Mazza suggests the political grandstanding was more important to international media than to local people, who showed little interest in the event.[10] While the stakes may be highest in these examples, however, scholars considering several nations likewise highlight both the international and domestic political considerations frequently governing official centenary efforts. Oxana Sergeevna Nagornaja, for example, notes the 'patriotic turn' initiated on 'instructions from the head of state', Vladimir Putin, after around 2010 which resurrected the First World War as a 'forgotten war', obscured by the Second, and used it to project 1914–1918 as part of a long heritage of Russian 'patriotic' wars. While encouraging Russians to reflect more favourably upon the war, Nagornaja suggests these efforts were also retorts to the exclusion of Putin from 'all-European mourning festivals' in light of the military situation in Ukraine. Hence, she argues, Kaliningrad, Russia's enclave in Europe, became a considerable site of commemorative activity, allowing leading Russians a presence in Europe during the centenary. The revival of interest in the war, thus, was largely because it could provide a 'useful past'.[11] In Bulgaria, while the public and political parties generally showed little interest in the centenary, Gueorgui Peev notes public censure of any study of controversial topics, and the continuation of diplomatic disputes with Macedonia over the destruction of a commemorative plaque. Once again, the war became 'useful', here, as 'yet another episode in the extended confrontation between the two countries over historical memory'.[12]

However, the 'usefulness' of the First World War past for nations in the 2010s was not confined to international diplomacy. Commemoration, by nations seeing themselves as victorious, defeated, or neutral alike, frequently provided a vehicle for promoting national identities and pride. In Canada, Geoffrey Bird suggests, centenary efforts were complicated by overlap with the 150th anniversary of the foundation of the Dominion of Canada. Both those celebrations and the centenary efforts, he suggests, featured a predictable emphasis on nation-building, centred particularly around the Canadian capture of Vimy Ridge in 1917 – a feat that, as Sarah Cook's chapter in this volume demonstrates further, has long been a cornerstone of Canadian commemorative attention. Bird stressed the need for nations to 'remember well', suggesting Canada had done so to some extent, via genuine efforts at 'reconciliation' of the wartime experiences of Canada's minority populations. While some criticised a perceived emphasis on positive stories, however, the Department of Canadian Heritage concluded that 80% of Canadians agreed that commemorative activity had helped build 'a sense of pride and belonging to Canada'.[13] Previous commemoration of Canada's war sometimes included negative interpretations, while, in Newfoundland, a separate iconic battle, Beaumont Hamel, was used as a symbol of difference by those who opposed integration into Canada.[14] However, comparing Bird's article with Jonathan Vance's account of commemoration since the war's end suggests basic continuities in Canadian convictions that the war was a national landmark,[15] in marked contrast to the neighbouring USA, where centenary efforts attempted to resurrect a 'forgotten' war in the hope of pointing to a moment of national emergence.[16]

If the centenary was differently 'useful' in Russia, Canada and the USA, elsewhere scholars suggest a more mixed impact. In the United Kingdom, Lucy Noakes suggests, state efforts to find '"national moments"... to strengthen community ties and a sense of national identity' were not wholly successful.[17] Despite the wish of some historians and Conservative Ministers to celebrate the UK's victory as well as remembering its dead, she argues, well-entrenched ideas of futility, waste and mass death dominated the centenary, alongside a continued focus on male soldiers at the expense of other experiences. Meanwhile, attitudes to commemoration remained 'deeply political' with debates over the wearing of poppies as symbols of remembrance highlighted not only by Noakes (who notes the controversy caused by Northern Irish and Serbian footballers refusing to wear shirts with poppies) but also by Santanu Das's contribution to this collection. Both, in different ways, note the efforts of the extreme right in UK politics to co-opt the poppy in the service of their own political ends.

Scholars of Indian commemoration note the atypicality of western commemorative styles such as memorials and monuments in India, while also highlighting the racial discrimination that operated in the post-war period, when individual Indian graves (unlike British ones) were not recorded.[18] As Manfred Hettling and Tino Schölz note, this was a widespread issue. The 'cult of the dead' that became archetypical in western commemoration of the war was difficult to transfer to European nations' colonial subjects, partly because this approach clashed with traditional cultural rituals around death, and partly because colonial powers did not make the same effort to recognise individual Indian and African soldiers as they did Europeans. While 5,000 Indian troops who died at Neuve Chappelle were individually recognised on a monument, for example, their counterparts who died at Basra were not,[19] and similar distinctions are noted for several formerly colonised populations.[20] The omission of black service and death in

South African commemoration until the 1990s, and the racial discrimination shown towards black US citizens in early efforts to support pilgrimages to overseas sites, meanwhile, differently affected the meaningfulness of commemoration in these multiracial nations.[21]

Politics and national identities, then, are stressed by many scholars as being at the core of understanding commemoration and centenary efforts. Even a nation that remained neutral, Switzerland, apparently saw value in using the war's memory to frame Swiss identities, in the process smoothing over the differing experiences and identities of Swiss people.[22] Postcolonial societies, and those of defeated nations, sometimes struggled with the war's meaning, with different political interpretations often placed on the war over time by competing nationalist and other groups.[23] Only one chapter discussing national commemoration – regarding Slovenia, a nation whose people had sometimes fought in the Austro-Hungarian armies, and which was subsequently absorbed into Yugoslavia – suggested that current interest in the war was 'free from ideological discourse and political attention'. Even this was noted in contrast to the still highly political legacies of the Second World War.[24] As noted earlier, chapters in Part I of this collection, by Das, Abraham, Fowler and Light all explore aspects of these fundamental features of the war's centennial. Abraham's account of the portrayal of Australian war heroism highlights a fundamental shift in emphasis in Australian commemoration and engagement with conflict. Pointing to the award of a Victoria Cross for Australia to Corporal Ben Roberts-Smith for his service in Afghanistan in 2010, Abraham notes the 'sanitised' public commentary on his deeds, which stressed protection of mates over the violent deeds necessary to deal with three machine-gun posts. Roberts-Smith also appears in Fowler's account of the associations between sport and Anzac Day in modern Australia, having promoted a rugby league 'Anzac Cup' fixture on the basis that sportsmen dutifully volunteered for armed service after 1914. Fowler's account of Australian sports' questionable associations with (or exploitation of) Anzac Day and the 'Anzac spirit' points to some of the distaste that has emerged in Australia at the excessive exploitation of Anzac commemoration for other purposes. Such concerns are also highlighted by Joan Beaumont, who critiques the commercialisation of commemoration through examples of supermarket appropriation of Anzac to sell food and the excessive advertising placed within a commemorative television series of Gallipoli.[25]

If a new Gallipoli-centred initiative fell flat in Australia, the same cannot be said of New Zealand, where the exhibition *Gallipoli: The Scale of Our War* drew more than 2.5 million visitors by 24 April 2019.[26] For Light, the exhibition was both 'unprecedented' and 'unique', yet derived substantially from reinterpretations undertaken, as in Australia, primarily in the 1980s. Post-centenary comments about the public's knowledge of the war, he notes, still focus on established clichés, and he suggests the exhibition served primarily to re-entrench Gallipoli's supposed centrality to the 'New

Zealand story'.[27] Reinforcement of existing perspectives is another observation made several times in *1914–1918 Online*. Besides Beaumont, Bird, Noakes and Vance's articles, discussed earlier, Peev bemoaned the failure of scholars to 'open new questions' during Bulgaria's centenary, while Barbara Bracco suggests Italian centenary efforts often featured a 'victim paradigm' focused on the suffering caused by the war.[28] Once more, she traces this to the 1980s. Multiple authors also highlight the frequent references to 'sacrifice', mass death and the figure of the Unknown Soldier as a focal point for remembrance. Stéphane Tison explains these features as connected phenomena. Confronted with the shock of mass death, numerous societies (especially, but not exclusively, those of victorious nations) chose to acknowledge this as a sacrifice on their behalf, in which the 'soldier defending their national land, or forging a nation through their sacrifice became a sort of quintessential expression of citizenship, achieved in the trenches and inspiring generations to come'. Dutiful sacrifice was then, often, embodied by a single figure, an unknown soldier, entombed in numerous places including the UK, France, the USA, Belgium, Romania, Yugoslavia, Austria, Bulgaria, Greece, Hungary, Poland, Italy and Germany in the first decades after the war.[29] Other nations, such as Australia (1993), Canada (2000) and New Zealand (2004) later recovered their own unknown soldiers as apparently indispensable components of appropriate commemoration. In Belgium, public desire for the tomb of an unknown soldier in the 1920s overrode state hopes for a broader memorial, embodying both military and civilian deaths, to capture the 'specificity of Belgian "martyrdom and heroism"'.[30] In some other places, unknown soldiers' burial sites became further places for political contests; over competing ideologies in France; as venues for fascist appropriation in Germany and Italy, or as a symbol of resistance to Soviet rule in Poland.[31] Such disputes, already underway within parents' living memory of the wartime dead, foreshadowed the subsequent use and re-use of the war and its commemoration by subordinate nationalities during and immediately after the Cold War, or by political opportunists during the centenary, as discussed earlier.[32]

Centenary projects

While academic assessments provided in *1914–1918-online* tend to stress the limited innovation or novelty of centenary efforts, practitioners of public-facing projects, including those featured in Part II of this collection, often saw themselves as challenging dominant perceptions. Tim Cook's exploration of Canadian soldiers' oral culture tackles issues such as the sanitisation noted by Das and Abraham in Part I, and in other commentators' accounts, by re-emphasising the value of slang, irreverent songs and swearing. His account also questions common assumptions of futility, victimhood and disillusionment. Both Louisa Hormann's chapter on recovering the history of New Zealand's First World War airmen and Margaret Lovell-Smith's account of critical voices against the war stress their aim to bring less well-known aspects of New Zealand's First World War experience to public attention. Meanwhile, Sarah Cook's examination of a lost Canadian film of the unveiling of the Vimy Memorial in the 1930s extends the observations of Bird and Vance, noting that, even if the film survived in its entirety, it would probably not resonate with modern Canadian audiences. Hence, if Vimy remains central to Canadian conceptions of the war, its meaning has evolved over time. Considering such transitions complicates ready assumptions of apparently unshifting clichés. As both the *1914–1918-online* articles, and the chapters in this collection, suggest, while recurrent familiar topics are clearly present, the emphases behind these topics shift over time.

The centenary of the First World War generated abundant commemorative activities and, while academics engaged in debate and published new research, museums, art galleries and governments invested heavily in commemorative exhibitions and activities. The variety of events was staggering, with new or rejuvenated exhibitions; digitisation and digital projects; education programmes; artistic interpretations (including artworks, performances and plays as well as movies, documentaries and television programmes); publications (both academic and popular); memorialisation (including new or restored memorials, national ceremonies and commemorative events); public talks; conferences and an extensive selection of pilgrimages, tours and trails of battlefields, memorials and places. These initiatives took place around the globe and were driven by a wide array of organisations including schools, sporting groups, community groups and heritage organisations.

In the century since the First World War, a variety of narratives gained currency in terms of the portrayal and understanding of the conflict, both in academic contexts but also in the ways in which heritage institutions appreciated and represented the war. In Britain, stories of tragedy, together with the futility and loss of the war remained prominent with remembrance activities shaped around themes of loyalty, duty and sacrifice.[33] In Canada, which also marked 150 years since the creation of the Dominion of Canada during the centenary of the war, stories of national identity as well as lasting tragedy were prominent.[34] In Chapter 5, Tim Cook suggests it is timely to reconsider the dominant historiography of loss and suffering and move to allow aspects of culture to demonstrate the nuanced ways in which troops coped with and endured the war. Cook explores Canadian soldiers' culture through slang, swearing and song both during the war and on their return to Canada, outlining the ways in which voice culture expressed masculinity and identity as well as its role in coping. His chapter navigates the complexity of soldier's voice culture on its return from the front to Canada and considers how this played an active role in the remembrance of the conflict.

Remembrance of the conflict, whilst taking place on a global stage, was also specific to each nation and, in part, served to reinforce existing narratives. This was particularly the case in the commemoration of the anniversary of specific military campaigns. New Zealand's remembrance of Gallipoli mirrored Canada's commemoration of the Battle of Vimy Ridge and Britain's tributes to the Battle of the Somme.[35] Sarah Cook's 'Reclaiming Salute to Valour', Chapter 8 of this collection, considers film's commemorative role in marking the unveiling of Canada's memorial to the Battle of Vimy Ridge. Piecing together snippets of information from the archival record, due to the original film's loss in a devastating fire, her contribution demonstrates the role of government and veteran agencies in directing the process of commemoration and remembrance.

Although, in most countries, heritage commemorations tended to focus on specific battles rather than a complete or critical reflection on the larger story of the war, many projects challenged accepted narratives. In Britain, for instance, the experiences of minority groups or those whose stories had remained silent, such as troops and labourers from around the Empire, refugee experiences or the stories of the home front, were included in Heritage Lottery Fund community heritage projects; almost 100 million pounds of funding which encouraged a broader perspective on the war.[36] Similarly, in Belgium, the *In Flanders Fields* museum exhibitions deliberately presented the stories of women, children and other under-represented groups.[37] In Turkey, official commemorative activities brought aspects of the Muslim experience to light although, as outlined earlier, experiences of the Armenian Genocide remained hidden.[38] In Chapter 6, Louisa Hormann reflects on the challenges of curating an exhibition on an unknown subject, New Zealand's war in the air, during a period of commemoration. Charting the development of the exhibition and its content, Hormann demonstrates how the centenary offered an opportunity to expose hidden stories from the period and to challenge existing narratives. Furthermore, her work stands as an important reflective piece on curatorial practice, an example of thoughtfully engaging with a commemorative exhibition to provide lessons for future commemorations.

Similarly, Margaret Lovell-Smith's Chapter 7 explores a regional commemorative project, "Voices Against War," that brings to light the stories of Canterbury men, women and organisations that do not fit neatly within the prevailing narrative of the conflict. Her work uncovers and recovers anti-war history through the voices of dissenters and peace advocates that were previously silent, using archives and family sources. Her work is part of a trend to encourage varied perspectives, ensuring the relevance of commemoration to marginalised or silenced community groups. Thanks to the centenary, access to these groups' stories has been enhanced by significant investment in digitised material. The expansion of valuable online resources such as the Auckland War Memorial Museum's Cenotaph, a database of New Zealanders who served in all conflicts, was mirrored around the world.[39] Library and Archives Canada scanned the personnel files of those who served in the conflict; its largest ever digitisation project.[40] Europeana provided access to digitised items from European museums, libraries and archives including almost 400,000 First World War items.[41]

The commitment to commemorate the First World War's centenary required sustained effort and energy at local, national and international levels. In New Zealand, a survey at the end of 2018 found that 93% of New Zealanders took part in the centenary in some form or other, with visits to exhibitions the most common experience.[42] Nationally, commemoration was dominated by two exhibitions; the Museum of New Zealand Te Papa Tongarewa's eight million dollar *Gallipoli: The Scale of our War* exhibition and the ten million dollar (plus an additional ten million dollar cost to decommission the display) *Great War* exhibition, curated by filmmaker Sir Peter Jackson.[43] Other New Zealand events ran on a considerably more modest scale with regional museums committing tens or hundreds of thousands of dollars to commemorative exhibitions and smaller museums even less. In the main, most commemorative exhibitions and events were national or local in focus. Only a few, like the *Flowers of War* project crossed international boundaries.[44]

While the chapters in Part I provide salutary warnings about the extent to which centenary commemorations were often directed towards particular agendas and could obscure and simplify the full complexity of wartime experience, those in Part II demonstrate the very real efforts of those involved in public commemorative activity to highlight the obscure and restore silenced voices. This divergence suggests the centenary may not mark the end of the First World War's hold on professional and public historical interest. Rather the lessons of the centenary period, however chronologically defined in different places, may inspire new efforts to combine the expertise of different sectors of historical knowledge, whether in the interests of deepening understanding of the war itself, or of fostering closer collaboration in the presentation of other elements of our shared past.

Notes

1 Reflecting the limited resources that characterised these activities, the group's website was archived in 2019: https://web.archive.org/web/20190119063256/http://canterbury100.org.nz/.
2 Canterbury Museum, 'Canterbury and World War One: Lives Lost, Lives Changed'.
3 Mycock, Sumartojo and Wellings,'Centenary'.
4 Winter, *Sites of Memory*.
5 http://www.1914-1918-online.net/
6 Daniel et al., 'Introduction'.
7 This was David Monger's experience in being invited to write several articles for the encyclopaedia.
8 https://encyclopedia.1914-1918-online.net/call-for-papers/centenary_austria. This page was accessed on 6 December 2019. Since these documents disappear from the website once an article is under way, an archived version of the call may be found at: https://web.archive.org/web/20191205032241/https://encyclopedia.1914-1918-online.net/call-for-papers/centenary_austria.

9 Maksudyan, 'Centenary (Turkey)'; Unwalla, 'Mourning (Ottoman Empire/Middle East)'. For additional comments, see Adjemian, 'Centenary (Armenia)'; Anderson, 'War Memory'.
10 Mazza, 'Centenary, Israel/Palestine'.
11 Nagornaja, 'Centenary (Russia)'.
12 Peev, 'Centenary (Bulgaria)'.
13 Bird, 'Centenary (Canada)'.
14 Cadigan, 'Commemoration (Newfoundland)'.
15 Vance, 'Commemoration (Canada)'.
16 Wilson, 'Centenary (USA)'.
17 Noakes, 'Centenary (United Kingdom)'.
18 Chhina and Chhina, 'Commemoration (India)'.
19 Hettling and Schölz, 'Bereavement and Mourning'.
20 Owino, 'Mourning (Africa)'; Blackburn, 'Centenary (Singapore)'; Chetty and Ginio, 'Commemoration (Africa)'; Jennings, 'Commemoration (Indochina)'.
21 Chetty and Ginio, 'Commemoration (Africa)'; de Vries, 'Commemoration (South Africa); Hulver, 'Mourning (USA)'; Trout, 'Commemoration (USA)'.
22 Kuhn and Ziegler, 'Commemoration (Switzerland)'.
23 E.g. Chhina and Chhina, 'Commemoration (India)'; Rossol, 'Commemoration (Germany)'; Jalonen, Richter and Szlanta, 'Commemoration (East Central Europe)'.
24 Svoljsak, 'Centenary (Slovenia)'.
25 Beaumont, 'Commemoration (Australia)'.
26 'Te Papa extends Gallipoli exhibition to Anzac Day 2022', press release, 24 April 2019: https://www.tepapa.govt.nz/about/press-and-media/press-releases/2019-media-releases/te-papa-extends-gallipoli-exhibition-anzac.
27 For related discussion of the centrality of Anzac Day as an element of New Zealand identity, see Harris, 'Commemoration (New Zealand)'.
28 Peev, 'Centenary (Bulgaria)'; Bracco, 'Centenary (Italy)'.
29 Tison, 'Commemoration, Cult of the Fallen'.
30 van Ypersele, 'Mourning (Belgium)'.
31 Dalisson, 'Remembrance Day (France)'; Goebel, 'War Memorials (Germany)'; Salvante, 'Tomb, Rome'; Thakur-Smolarek, 'Tomb (Warsaw)'.
32 In addition to works already named, see Zamoiski, 'Centenary (Belarus)'; Grawe, 'Langemarck Myth'; Brandt, 'War Cemeteries (Germany); Cohen, 'Commemoration (Russian Empire)'; Šarenac, 'Commemoration (South East Europe)'.
33 Pennell, 'Taught to Remember'; Noakes, 'Centenary (United Kingdom)'.
34 Bird, 'Centenary (Canada)'.
35 Bird, 'Centenary (Canada)'; Noakes, 'Centenary (United Kingdom)'.
36 Noakes, 'Centenary (United Kingdom)'.
37 Gough, *Centenary (Visual Arts)*.
38 Maksudyan, 'Centenary (Turkey)'.
39 Auckland War Memorial Museum, 'Cenotaph'.
40 See, for example https://www.warmuseum.ca/event/vimy-beyond-the-battle/; https://www.warmuseum.ca/witness/; and https://www.bac-lac.gc.ca/eng/discover/military-heritage/first-world-war/personnel-records/Pages/personnel-records.aspx.
41 Europeana Collections, https://www.europeana.eu/portal/en/collections/world-war-I, accessed 1 December 2019.
42 WW100 Programme Office, 'WW100 First World War Centenary Programme Final Report'.
43 WW100 Programme Office, https://ww100.govt.nz/te-papa-and-weta-workshop-open-ground-breaking-gallipoli-exhibition; Stewart, 'Sir Peter Jackson's Great War exhibition canned'.
44 Flowers of War, http://flowersofwar.org/.

Bibliography

Adjemian, Boris. "Centenary (Armenia)." In *1914–1918-online. International Encyclo-pedia of the First World War*, edited by Ute Daniel, Peter Gatrell, Oliver Janz, Heather Jones, Jennifer Keene, Alan Kramer, and Bill Nasson [all subsequent references to this encyclopedia given as *1914–1918-online*]. Berlin: Freie Universität Berlin, 2019. https://encyclopedia.1914-1918-online.net/article/centenary_armenia.

Anderson, Kyle J. "War Memory, Commemoration (Ottoman Empire/ Middle East)." In *1914–1918-online*. Berlin: Freie Universität Berlin, 2018. https://encyclopedia.1914-1918-online.net/article/war_memory_commemoration_ottoman_empire_middle_east.

Auckland War Memorial Museum. "Cenotaph." https://www.aucklandmuseum.com/war-memorial/online-cenotaph.

Beaumont, Joan. "Commemoration, Cult of the Fallen (Australia)." In *1914–1918-online*. Berlin: Freie Universität Berlin, 2016. https://encyclopedia.1914-1918-online.net/article/commemoration_cult_of_the_fallen_australia.

Bird, Geoffrey. "Centenary (Canada)." In *1914–1918-online*. Berlin: Freie Universität Berlin, 1919. https://encyclopedia.1914-1918-online.net/article/centenary_canada.

Blackburn, Kevin. "Centenary (Singapore)." In *1914–1918-online*. Berlin: Freie Universität Berlin, 2019. https://encyclopedia.1914-1918-online.net/article/centenary_singapore.

Brandt, Susanne. "War Cemeteries (Germany)." In *1914–1918-online*. Berlin: Freie Universität Berlin, 2014. https://encyclopedia.1914-1918-online.net/article/war_cemeteries_germany.

Cadigan, Sean T. "Commemoration, Cult of the Fallen (Newfoundland)." In *1914–1918-online*. Berlin: Freie Universität Berlin, 2016. https://encyclopedia.1914-1918-online.net/article/commemoration_cult_of_the_fallen_newfoundland.

Canterbury Museum. "Canterbury and World War One: Lives Lost, Lives Changed." https://worldwarone.canterburymuseum.com/.

Chetty, Suryakanthie and Ruth Ginio. "Commemoration, Cult of the Fallen (Africa)." In *1914–1918-online*. Berlin: Freie Universität Berlin, 2015. https://encyclopedia.1914-1918-online.net/article/commemoration_cult_of_the_fallen_africa.

Chhina, Rana and Adil Chinna. "Commemoration, Cult of the Fallen (India)." In *1914–1918-online*. Berlin: Freie Universität Berlin, 2018. https://encyclopedia.1914-1918-online.net/article/commemoration_cult_of_the_fallen_india.

Cohen, Aaron. "Commemoration, Cult of the Fallen (Russian Empire)." In *1914–1918-online*. Berlin: Freie Universität Berlin, 2014. https://encyclopedia.1914-1918-online.net/article/commemoration_cult_of_the_fallen_russian_empire.

Dalisson, Rémi. "Remembrance day: 11 November 1922-Today (France)." In *1914–1918-online*. Berlin: Freie Universität Berlin, 2015. https://encyclopedia.1914-1918-online.net/article/remembrance_day_11_november_1922-today_france.

Daniel, Ute, Peter Gatrell, Oliver Janz, Heather Jones, Jennifer D. Keene, Alan Kramer and Bill Nasson. "1914–1918-online. International Encyclopedia of the First World War. Introduction." In *1914–1918-online*. Berlin: Freie Universität Berlin, 2014. https://encyclopedia.1914-1918-online.net/article/Introduction.

de Vries, Jacques Jean Pierre. "Commemoration, Cult of the Fallen (Union of South Africa)." In *1914–1918-online*. Berlin: Freie Universität Berlin, 2018. https://encyclopedia.1914-1918-online.net/article/commemoration_cult_of_the_fallen_union_of_south_africa.

Flowers of War. http://flowersofwar.org/.

Goebel, Stefan. "War Memorials (Germany)." In *1914–1918-online*. Berlin: Freie Universität Berlin, 2015. https://encyclopedia.1914-1918-online.net/article/war_memorials_germany.

Gough, Paul. "Centenary (Visual Arts)." In *1914–1918-online*. Berlin: Freie Universität Berlin, 2015. https://encyclopedia.1914-1918-online.net/article/centenary_visual_arts.

Grawe, Lukas. "Langemarck Myth." In *1914–1918-online*. Berlin: Freie Universität Berlin, 2019. https://encyclopedia.1914-1918-online.net/article/langemarck_myth.

Harris, Margaret. "Commemoration, Cult of the Fallen (New Zealand)." In *1914–1918-online*. Berlin: Freie Universität Berlin, 2014. https://encyclopedia.1914-1918-online.net/article/commemoration_cult_of_the_fallen_new_zealand.

Hettling, Manfred and Tino Schölz. "Bereavement and Mourning." In *1914–1918-online*. Berlin: Freie Universität Berlin, 2019. https://encyclopedia.1914-1918-online.net/article/bereavement_and_mourning.

Hulver, Richard Allen. "Bereavement and Mourning (USA)." In *1914–1918-online*. Berlin: Freie Universität Berlin, 2015. https://encyclopedia.1914-1918-online.net/article/bereavement_and_mourning_usa.

Jalonen, Jussi, Klaus Richter and Piotr Szlanta. "Commemoration, Cult of the Fallen (East Central Europe)." In *1914–1918-online*. Berlin: Freie Universität Berlin, 2014. https://encyclopedia.1914-1918-online.net/article/commemoration_cult_of_the_fallen_east_central_europe.

Jennings, Eric Thomas. "Commemoration, Cult of the Fallen (Indochina)." In *1914–1918-online*. Berlin: Freie Universität Berlin, 2015. https://encyclopedia.1914-1918-online.net/article/commemoration_cult_of_the_fallen_indochina.

Kuhn, Konrad and Beátrice Ziegler. "Commemoration (Switzerland)." In *1914–1918-online*. Berlin: Freie Universität Berlin, 2016. https://encyclopedia.1914-1918-online.net/article/commemoration_switzerland.

Maksudyan, Nazan. "Centenary (Turkey)." In *1914–1918-online*. Berlin: Freie Universität Berlin, 2019. https://encyclopedia.1914-1918-online.net/article/centenary_turkey.

Mycock, Andrew, Shanti Sumartojo and Ben Wellings. "'The centenary to end all centenaries:' The Great War, Nation and Commemoration." In *Nation, Memory and Great War Commemoration: Mobilizing the Past in Europe, Australia and New Zealand*, edited by Shanti Sumartojo and Ben Wellings, 1–24. Bern: Peter Lang, 2014.

Nagornaja, Oxana Sergeevna. "Centenary (Russia)." In *1914–1918-online*. Berlin: Freie Universität Berlin, 2019. https://encyclopedia.1914-1918-online.net/article/centenary_russia.

Noakes, Lucy. "Centenary (United Kingdom)." In *1914–1918-online*. Berlin: Freie Universität Berlin, 2019. https://encyclopedia.1914-1918-online.net/article/centenary_united_kingdom.

Owino, Meschack. "Bereavement and Mourning (Africa)." In *1914–1918-online*. Berlin: Freie Universität Berlin, 2017. https://encyclopedia.1914-1918-online.net/article/bereavement_and_mourning_africa.

Peev, Gueorgui. "Centenary (Bulgaria)." In *1914–1918-online*. Berlin: Freie Universität Berlin, 2018. https://encyclopedia.1914-1918-online.net/article/centenary_bulgaria.

Pennell, Catriona. "Taught to Remember: British Youth and First World War Centenary Battlefield Tours." *Cultural Trends*, 27, 2. 2018: 83–98.

Rossol, Nadine. "Commemoration, Cult of the Fallen (Germany)." In *1914–1918-online*. Berlin: Freie Universität Berlin, 2014. https://encyclopedia.1914-1918-online.net/article/commemoration_cult_of_the_fallen_germany.

Salvante, Martina. "Tomb of the Unknown Soldier, Rome." In *1914–1918-online*. Berlin: Freie Universität Berlin, 2016. https://encyclopedia.1914-1918-online.net/article/tomb_of_the_unknown_soldier_rome.

Šarenac, Danilo. "Commemoration, Cult of the Fallen (South East Europe)." In *1914–1918-online*. Berlin: Freie Universität Berlin, 2014. https://encyclopedia.1914-1918-online.net/article/commemoration_cult_of_the_fallen_south_east_europe.

Stewart, Matt. "Sir Peter Jackson's Great War Exhibition Canned and Building Returned to University," 2018. https://www.stuff.co.nz/entertainment/arts/105980484/sir-peter-jacksons-great-war-exhibition-canned-and-building-to-return-to-university.

Svoljsak, Petra. "Centenary (Slovenia)." In *1914–1918-online*. Berlin: Freie Universität Berlin, 2018. https://encyclopedia.1914-1918-online.net/article/centenary_slovenia.

Thakur-Smolarek, Keya. "Tomb of the Unknown Soldier, Warsaw." In *1914–1918-online*. Berlin: Freie Universität Berlin, 2014. https://encyclopedia.1914-1918-online.net/article/tomb_of_the_unknown_soldier_warsaw.

Unwalla, Pheroze. "Bereavement and Mourning (Ottoman Empire/ Middle East)." In *1914–1918-online*. Berlin: Freie Universität Berlin, 2018. https://encyclopedia.1914-1918-online.net/article/bereavement_and_mourning_ottoman_empire_middle_east.

Trout, Steven. "Commemoration and Remembrance (USA)." In *1914–1918-online*. Berlin: Freie Universität Berlin, 2017. https://encyclopedia.1914-1918-online.net/article/commemoration_and_remembrance_usa.

van Ypersele, Laurence. "Bereavement and Mourning (Belgium)." In *1914–1918-online*. Berlin: Freie Universität Berlin, 2014. https://encyclopedia.1914-1918-online.net/article/bereavement_and_mourning_belgium.

Vance, Jonathan. "Commemoration and Cult of the Fallen (Canada)." In *1914–1918-online*. Berlin: Freie Universität Berlin, 2015. https://encyclopedia.1914-1918-online.net/article/commemoration_and_cult_of_the_fallen_canada.

Wilson, Ross. "Centenary (USA)." In *1914–1918-online*. Berlin: Freie Universität Berlin, 2019. https://encyclopedia.1914-1918-online.net/article/centenary_usa.

Winter, Jay. *Sites of Memory, Sites of Mourning: The Great War in European Cultural Memory*. Cambridge: Cambridge University Press, 1995.

WW100 Programme Office. "WW100 First World War Centenary Programme Final Report." Wellington, 2019.

WW100 Programme Office. https://ww100.govt.nz/te-papa-and-weta-workshop-open-ground-breaking-gallipoli-exhibition.

Zamoiski, Andrei. "Centenary (Belarus)." In *1914–1918-online*. Berlin: Freie Universität Berlin, 2019. https://encyclopedia.1914-1918-online.net/article/centenary_belarus.

Part I

Commemoration and the centenary in perspective

1 Colonial commemoration in a time of multiculturalism

South Asia and the First World War[1]

Santanu Das

On Sunday 28 October 2018, two weeks before the centenary of the Armistice, Trafalgar Square in London erupted into festivity: it was Diwali, the Indian festival of lights. But, the year being 2018, the Diwali festivities turned into something different. There were men dressed up as First World War sepoys, young boys on parade, and *khadi* poppies on sale. Sadiq Khan, the first Muslim Mayor of London, spoke movingly about the South Asian contribution to the First World War: one and half million men from undivided India (comprising today's Bangladesh, India, Pakistan and Myanmar, formerly Burma) were recruited, of whom over a million served abroad.[2] Khan's emphasis on the South Asian contribution was part of a two-fold shift that has been taking place over the last few years across Europe and particularly in Great Britain: a concerted effort to embed the memory of the First World War in a more multi-racial framework and employ it towards the vision of a more inclusive, multicultural society. What was new though in the aforementioned occasion was the *khadi* poppy which Sadiq Khan had donned. *Khadi,* the woven cotton fabric associated with anti-colonial nationalism in British India and particularly with Mahatma Gandhi, is here appropriated as a marker of military service under the Raj: war, empire, postcoloniality and multiculturalism are fused and confused as commemoration slips into celebration.

Sadiq Khan invoked the Mahatma but he was actually singing from the hymn-sheet of his fellow MP of South Asian origin and political opponent – the former Tory Minister Baroness Sayeeda Warsi. In 2013, in the lead-up to the centennial commemoration, Warsi had observed:

> Our boys weren't just Tommies; they were Tariqs and Tajinders too.
>
> A picture of a soldier in a turban is not what we immediately associate with the Great War. And yet so many men from so far away came to Europe to fight for the freedoms we enjoy today. Their legacy is our liberty, and every single one of us owes them a debt of gratitude.
>
> I will make it my mission to ensure that the centenary is a chance for everyone to learn about the contribution of the Commonwealth soldiers. After all, our shared future is based on our shared past.[3]

The previous year, in an article in *The Sun*, she had written:

> There were also black British Soldiers, like the iconic footballer Walter Tull, who died in 1918 as he helped his men retreat in heavy gunfire.
>
> These are the people we must remember – people who everyone in today's Britain can relate to.
>
> When I went head to head with BNP leader Nick Griffin on Question Time – the first time his party was given an airing on the Beeb – he was slapped down for stealing patriotism for his own racist ends.
>
> As the daughter of Pakistani immigrants, I proudly bang the drum for Britain's heritage, because it's mine too.
>
> After all, both my grandfathers fought with the Allies.
>
> I am also proud to serve in a government which respects our troops and resources them properly, honouring our Military Covenant.
>
> So two years from now, 100 years since the Great War began, let us all come together under one flag to remember what our heroes did for every single one of us.[4]

Warsi's recommendation, in her capacity as the Faith and Communities minister at the time, set the agenda for the 'Commonwealth' war commemoration in Britain. Warsi is to be commended for her efforts to bring recognition to these colonial soldiers airbrushed out of Eurocentric narratives of the war. Four million non-white men were recruited into the armies of Europe and the United States during the war, including two million Africans and 1.5 million Indians. Warsi's intervention was crucial at a time when, as she notes, the white supremacist British National Party (BNP) had been trying to hijack and whitewash First World War memory.[5]

The aforementioned speech, however, instrumentalises the past in complex ways. For the ethnic diasporic communities, the war contribution becomes a powerful way of seeking greater enfranchisement within and assimilation into British society. Imperial war service becomes a bulwark against racism and xenophobia as the status of the grandfather as a defender of Pax Britannia in its hour of need enables the 'daughter of immigrants' to 'proudly bang' the drum of her 'British identity'. Within the South Asian context, Warsi's reference to the Muslim 'Tariq' and the Sikh/Hindu 'Tajinder' is a shrewd and important recognition of the multi-religious, multi-ethnic and multi-lingual nature of the army of undivided India. And yet, if we press her rhetoric further, clear political agendas emerge. The emphasis is on 'bravery', the accent falls on 'sacrifice', the focus is on 'shared past' which, together with the term 'Commonwealth soldiers', erases the inequalities and asymmetries of empire. Indeed, 'shared' has become one of the most overused words in this centennial commemoration – 'shared past', 'shared experience', 'shared memory', to be put in the service of a 'shared future'.[6]

In Britain, the First World War centennial commemoration has been invented as the grand-stage to play the theme of multiculturalism and tied to an agenda of social cohesion and community building. While it has resulted in a powerful expansion of war memory and an extraordinary outburst of energy, it has also resulted in the sanitisation of the violence of both war and empire. Such a process in turn prompts broader questions: how do we recover difficult, marginalised pasts and what is the relationship between historical amnesia, centennial commemoration and present-day concerns? Whose remembrance are we talking about and how can we decolonise war commemoration? This chapter engages with some of these questions through a focus on the Indian contribution to the First World War; starting with the Indian war experience itself and the post-war moment to understand the war's contested legacies in the subcontinent.

Imperial war and post-war commemoration

Undivided India contributed the highest number of troops from any of the European colonies, dominions or protectorates. According to records of the time, the total number of Indian ranks recruited during the war, up to 31 December 1919, was 877,068 combatants and 563,369 non-combatants, making a total of 1,440,437; in addition, there were 122,000 men recruited in pre-war years. Between August 1914 and December 1919, India sent overseas for war purposes 622,224 soldiers and 474,789 non-combatants, to be pressed into one of the seven divisions that sailed to Europe, East Africa, Mesopotamia, the Sinai and Palestine, Suez, and Gallipoli.[7] Why did these men enlist? Most came from poor, non-literate backgrounds for whom the military was an age-old profession; different impulses – social aspirations, family and community traditions and ideas of honour or *izzat* – were fused and confused with expectations of economic reward in the form of cash or, more commonly, land.

If the idea of the *izzat*-fuelled, loyalist sepoy has now been debunked as a colonial construction, the idea of these men as mere 'mercenaries' speaks, on the other hand, to a post-nationalist moment.[8] As argued elsewhere, a more nuanced vocabulary is needed to understand the complex socio-psychological world of the sepoys in 1914 where financial incentive, ideas of *izzat* and varying degrees of ambivalence about their role in the colonial army were finely blended.[9] While many censored sepoy letters speak eloquently about loyalty to the 'Sarkar', some hint at a deeply conflicted relationship to such duty. Consider the following letter written on 18 March 1915 by Amir Khan, shortly after the battle of Neuve Chapelle, to his brother in Punjab:

The enemy is weakening. In the fighting of the 10th March, up to the 12th, according to my estimate, 5,525 Germans were taken prisoners of war, and 25 guns and machine guns... Our new army is collected in great numbers. Wherever he shows strength, our guns at once knock him flat. Please God, I speak with certainty, our King – God bless him – is going to win and will win soon...

[On a separate scrap of paper] God knows whether the land of France is stained with sin or whether the Day of Judgement has begun in France. For guns and of rifles, there is a deluge, bodies upon bodies, and blood flowing. God preserve us, what has come to pass! From dawn to dark and from dark to dawn it goes on like the hail that fell at Swarra [?] camp. But especially our guns have filled the German trenches with dead and made them brim with blood. God grant us grace, for grace is needed. Oh God, we repent! Oh God, we repent![10]

Such ambivalence, already present in wartime testimonies, became endemic to the memory of the First World War in India during the post-war years amidst the rising tide of nationalism.

On 4 August 1914, India was dragged into the war as part of the British empire. However, the Indian nationalists supported the war effort enthusiastically: the road to India's 'Home Rule', noted Mahatma Gandhi, lay in the fields of France and Flanders.[11] Yet, after the war, contrary to widely held expectations, Woodrow Wilson's doctrine of 'self-determination of nations' was extended only to the white dominions, causing widespread disillusionment across the non-white colonies, from India to Egypt.[12] In India, the war was instead followed by the draconian Rowlatt Act which extended the policies of wartime into peacetime, including the detention without trial of men suspected of anti-government activities. Such brazen violation of human rights, compounded with increases in taxes and ongoing inflation, caused widespread fury which blazed along the streets of Punjab, which had contributed more than half the number of Indian combatants. On 13 August 1919 in Amritsar, at the orders of General Dyer, soldiers opened fire on a large crowd of unarmed protesters gathered in a walled garden at Jallianwallah Bagh, killing at least 400 and wounding over 1,000 in one of the most infamous incidents of colonial atrocity.[13] Mahatma Gandhi, who had played a major role in recruiting the soldiers for the imperial war in 1918, now denounced them as 'hired assassins of the Raj', as he united Muslims and Hindus in the nation-wide Khilafat movement.[14] It was into this febrile climate in 1919, with the nationalist protests ablaze across the country, that the sepoys of the Raj returned to their country.

Yet, in an example of the complex and contradictory history of the country, on 19 July that year, Indian troops took part in the Victory Parade and Peace Pageant to the Cenotaph in London. Troops on parade were photographed, painted and flashed across the empire. And, in 1921, the Duke of Connaught laid the foundation stone in Delhi for the All India War Memorial (now known as the India Gate) designed by Edwin Lutyens. 'One way to adapt the notion of *lieux de memoire* in postcolonial scholarship', notes

Jay Winter, 'is to insist upon the hybrid character of colonial and postcolonial sites of memory. Each and every one is a palimpsest, an overwritten text'.[15] Indeed, was Lutyens' monument an ode to empire or to the Indians who died, or to both? Over time, the Delhi Gate has been so thoroughly assimilated into the fabric of the city that few know of its imperial war origins; instead, it now houses the 'Amar Jawan Jyoti' or the 'eternal flame' honouring the soldiers of the Republic of India killed in wars waged since the independence, military incursions or peacekeeping activities. In 2014, when I visited Bhondsi – a small village on the outskirts of Delhi, which heavily recruited during the First World War – I was taken to the local war memorial where the names of the First World War fallen were followed not just by those of the Second but those killed in subsequent wars: past and present, imperial and national histories touched and blended seemingly without friction.

In the immediate post-war years, sepoy names were emblazoned in official memorials and gravestones across the world, from the Menin Gate at Ypres, the Memorial to the Missing in Neuve Chapelle or the giant Commonwealth Memorial in Basra to sites scattered across British India.[16] Yet, the actual story inside India was very different. Financial compensation, it has been suggested, took the place of commemoration in India: no narrative space was created, at the national or public level, around the war's casualties or veterans.[17] The Amritsar massacre of 1919 pushed these men deeper and darker into the shadow. War service was viewed as little more than an 'occupational hazard', with the loss of a limb or an eye as the price.[18] Amnesia about India's war service set in so quickly within the country because its memory was so contested: the nationalist anti-colonial heroes wholly supplanted these men in public memory.[19]

But amnesia is not absence: memories persisted, stubbornly, silently, privately. A few years ago, in Kolkata, I interviewed the Punjabi novelist Mohan Kahlon who had lost his two uncles in Mesopotamia. He told me how his grandmother had gone mad with grief at the loss of her sons and their house in the village of Lyallpur in Punjab came to be known as 'pagalkhana' ('asylum'). Around the same time, I also interviewed, in Delhi, the family of Lieutenant Colonel Raj Singh Gursey.[20] His grandfather, Pat Ram, was also killed in the war but the memories were very different. Pat Ram had helped in the local recruitment campaign and received silver coins and cash for his efforts; at the time of Pat Ram's death, his wife was just 22 and she continued to draw war pension for another 54 years. She had the silver coins made into a necklace which she used to wear proudly and the family used the cash to buy land during the Partition. The two interviews epitomise the complex and contradictory relationship of the First World War to India and the multidirectionality of any memory. In my own family, one of my great uncles served as a doctor in France during the war years; his younger brother joined the Bengal anti-colonial revolutionaries in the post-war years and was beaten to death at Presidency Jail in Kolkata.[21] Even within the same family, there may not be a homogenous memory of the war: any com-memoration needs to include multiple narratives.

Contested memory, masala commemoration

It is not surprising that, a 100 years on, India is finally coming to terms with its role in the two world wars; the centenary has allowed some of these sub-terranean memories to emerge. Rana TS Chhina, a former Squadron Leader and the secretary of the United Service Institution of India, played a seminal role in trying to create this space, from collecting important war memora-bilia and penning commemorative volumes to representing the government at high-level delegations and collaborating on a range of projects, both in In-dia and abroad.[22] While Chhina is passionately interested in the First World War – both his grandfathers had served – his aim is to create a hub, as it were, for war remembrance more generally in the Indian public sphere.

There are two immediate problems. In the absence of institutions such as the Imperial War Museum or the Australian War Memorial, how is that space created, especially when most of the sepoys were non-literate and did not leave behind an abundance of testimonies and memoirs? Second, in a postcolonial nationalist state, how does one reinstate and commemorate these sepoys tainted with the label of 'imperial sentinels' or, perhaps worse, 'mercenaries'. The opening salvo was fired by an influential legal figure, Jus-tice Markandey Katju:

> The Indian soldiers [of the First World War] were really mercenaries and hirelings of the British and French ... The Indian troops fought as hired assassins to kill Germans for Anglo-French interests, not Indian interests. They may have been brave, but many hired assassins are also brave. Why then should we honour them?[23]

The phrase 'hired assassins' came from Gandhi and stuck, though one can-not overlook the bitter irony that these sepoys were recruited and sent to their deaths in 1914 by nationalists in the hope of political gain and then denied commemoration a 100 years later in the name of nationalism. In this context, these sepoys had to be first cleared of the taint of being 'mercenar-ies' and reclaimed as gallant and loyal exemplars of modern India for the work of commemoration to begin. 'Sacrifice' became the safest route to this recuperative strategy:

> It is a matter of great pride that the very significant Indian contribution to the war that changed the course of modern history is finally getting the recognition that it so richly deserves. The Indian soldier deserves an acknowledgement of his contribution, and a commemoration of his **sacrifice**, making clear his central place in history.
>
> (Rana Chhina, Secretary of USI)

Remembrance is our opportunity as a society to recognise the sacrifice made by all soldiers, on all our behalves, irrespective of their backgrounds. It is not about the politics of the conflict, it is about honouring the self-sacrifice of those who paid the ultimate price.
(Defence Advisor to the British High Commission,
Mark Goldsack)[24]

Over the last four years, there has been a significant reclaiming of the sepoys in India through a combination of activities, from high-profile events at the Delhi Gate, community projects and high-quality publications by the United Service Institute (USI) to renewed academic interest and a steady stream of articles in the national press.[25] Rana Chhina, the Secretary of the USI and a retired Squadron Leader – both of his grand-fathers fought in the First World War, has played a central role in securing recognition of the Indian soldiers through organising, co-ordinating and facilitating various commemorative activities, both in India and abroad. One of the major developments was the procurement by the Indian Government of the official War Diaries of the Indian regiments from the National Archives in London and the erection of commemorative plaques in the hometowns of all the men who received Victoria Crosses in the First World War.[26] Both the Indian Prime Minister, Narendra Modi, and Prince Charles have made trips to Neuve Chapelle War Memorial; Prince William and his wife Kate Middleton laid wreaths at the Delhi Gate. The marigold, a flower associated with religious rituals, has been chosen, in place of the poppy, as the symbol of commemoration. Some of the most meaningful collaborations have been transnational, such as the 'Unremembered' project: in a coordinated event, schoolchildren in Leicester and Delhi held placards bearing the names of hitherto anonymous porters and labourers at the same time and connected via virtual reality.[27]

Much of the commemorative zeal around the Indian sepoy had come, paradoxically, from Great Britain. More than a decade before the centenary years, the erection of the Memorial Gates at Hyde Park Corner and its unveiling by Queen Elizabeth II in 2002 to commemorate the South Asian, African and Caribbean contribution to the two world wars, with a special 'Chattri' memorial with the names of the Indians VCs inscribed on its dome, was an important step.[28] The main impetus came, however, in 2014, with a cash allocation of 19 million pounds by the government and another 50 million pounds by the Heritage Lottery Fund.[29] Between 2014 and 2018, there has been an avalanche of commemorative programmes and activities from various organisations, including the BBC (which announced 2,500 hours of First World War programmes),[30] the Foreign and Commonwealth Office, the Imperial War Museum, Tate Britain, the Ministry of Defence, the arts commission 1914–1918 NOW and innumerable community groups across the country. What seemed to have been forgotten was that this hysterical commemoration was unleashed at a time of savage cuts to the National

Health Service, arts and disability welfare, the introduction of the 'hostile environment' policy,[31] and an unprecedented rise in homelessness and people relying on food-banks.[32] A prominent strand within this commemorative fest was the remembrance of the colonial non-white contribution with a focus on the theme of 'connected communities' and 'shared histories'. With a series of terrorist attacks happening during the centennial years – in Paris (2015), Belgium (2016) and London (2017) – war commemoration, especially Warsi's attempt to diversify war memory and include immigrants as well, was no doubt a ploy towards countering the indoctrination of British Asian Muslim youths by stressing the role of their grandfathers in the War.[33]

One of the most important legacies of the centenary will be a greater challenge to the colour of war memory. Within this reassessment, the story of the South Asian soldiers has enjoyed reasonable visibility, from radio and television programmes such as *The World's War: Forgotten Soldiers of Empire* (BBC 2), *Soldiers of the Empire* (Radio 4) and the radio play 'Subterranean Sepoys' (Tara Arts) to films such as *Farewell, My Indian Soldier* and *Red Pepper, Black Pepper*, to exhibitions, light and sound shows and concerts at the Brighton Pavilion, dance-theatre ('The Troth' based on the First World War Hindi story 'Usne Kaha Thah'), ballet (such as Akram Khan's *Xenos*) and creative re-enactments; in addition, mostly funded by the Heritage Lottery Fund, there has been a host of community projects led by citizen-historians, such as 'Whose Remembrance?', 'We Were There too', 'Empire, Faith and War', 'Beyond the Western Front', 'Salt of the Sarkar', 'Unknown and Untold'.[34] What was extraordinary was the sheer energy around these events, involving and attracting diverse communities and audiences, and showcasing remarkable creativity. A classic example is the project 'Empire, Faith and War', curated by the United Kingdom Punjab Heritage Association and focussing on the Sikh contribution. This exhibition, in 2014, unearthed and displayed, for the first time, a remarkable variety of Indian war artefacts, hosted a series of cultural programmes and organised a series of academic events.[35] These public-facing activities were often accompanied by the recovery of fresh primary material, such as diaries, objects, albums and memoirs and a simultaneous process of dissemination through online sources, such as the project website, YouTube videos, twitter, blog posts and Facebook accounts. If *The Battle of the Somme* (1916) was one of the most watched film during the war years,[36] online media has played a similarly vital role in their centennial upheaval.

However, some of the most moving centennial commemorative projects in the age of digital technology were solidly physical and *in situ* with an inviolate link to actual sepoy presences. In the same year the foundation stone of the India Gate was laid in Delhi, the Prince of Wales unveiled the *Chattri* (meaning umbrella or pavilion) Memorial at Patcham on the South Downs in Sussex – the cremation site of 53 Sikh and Hindu sepoys who died in the hospitals in Brighton.[37] With the passage of time, the memorial fell into neglect and disrepair, and even served as a target for rifle-practice by troops during the Second World War. In the 1990s, it came to the attention of a local Sikh teacher Davinder Dhillon who formed the 'Chattri Memorial Group' dedicated to its revival and upkeep.[38] On 26 September 2010, a memorial tablet bearing all 53 names was unveiled by the Commonwealth War Graves Commission (CWGC) and, today, it is the site of a highly popular annual commemoration ceremony. A very similar story is to be found in relation to the Muslim burial ground at Horsell Common, at Woking, Surrey. Commissioned by the War Office, it was completed in 1917, with elaborate Islamic designs incorporating a domed archway and minaret, in keeping with the architecture of the neighbouring Shah Jahan Mosque; during the war, it received some 17 bodies, with another ten during the Second World War.[39] Post-First World War neglect, in this case, was compounded with post-Second World War racist vandalism, with the gravestones desecrated; in 1968, the bodies were exhumed and transferred to the Brookwood cemetery in order to protect them. As with the Chattri group, the local people rallied together, a grant from the Heritage Lottery Fund was organised in 2012 for restoration, and the grounds were finally re-opened in 2015, with an Islamic style 'peace-garden' as its centre, and extensive coverage on various media channels.[40]

What is common to and heart-warming about all three projects – 'Empire, Faith and War', the Chattri Group and Woking Peace Garden – is the enthusiasm and initiative of the local community. Each was informed by a genuine interest to recover the stories of the First World War sepoys and use them to shore up a sense of a 'shared past' between South Asia and Britain. The move was warmly welcomed by both the political community and the public at large, both committed to a vision of a more inclusive multicultural Britain. The sepoy made the '[u]ltimate sacrifice for a cause he didn't even understand' noted Zafar Iqbal, a galvanising force for the restoration of the burial ground. These men, we are told, demonstrate that 'there's no conflict between being Muslim and being British'.[41] In a similar vein, several prominent historians and politicians issued a request for a plaque to commemorate Khudadad Khan, the first Indian sepoy to win a Victoria Cross in the First World War:

> It is important today that all of our children know this shared history, of contribution and sacrifice, if we are to fully understand the multi-ethnic Britain that we are today. The gallant Sepoy Khan embodies that history.[42]

What we have here is at once a demand for recognition that is long overdue and an instrumentalisation of the past in terms that are deeply problematic. The word 'sacrifice' translates very differently in the colonial context. In a context where many sepoys did not even know what they fought for, faced institutional racial discrimination (the senior-most Indian officer was inferior in rank to the junior-most British officer) and were largely coerced in

1917 and 1918, the whole idea of 'sacrifice' for the empire sounds rather tenuous. Yet, the irony remains that, as in India, it is the rhetoric of 'sacrifice' that grants the sepoys a place in British public memory.[43]

Diversification versus decolonization

The centennial commemoration of the South Asian troops starkly reveals the chasm between diversification and decolonisation. Many of the projects, under the guise of racial and ethnic diversity, can become an ideological smokescreen, with little attention to what political functions they are made to serve. If, during the First World War, British politicians and journalists could not get enough of the romanticism and exoticism of Indians, Africans and West Indians coming to fight for Great Britain, the same images were splashed across the pages a 100 years later to mark the centenary, without any investigation of the racial politics of these photographs, or of the empire for which they were staged.[44] As Richard Smith has convincingly argued with reference to the West Indian contribution, 'the centenary commemorations in Britain also highlight a significant and troubling continuity' with the imperial war.[45] The underlying principle of social cohesion, while itself important and well-intentioned, has come in the way of any fruitful critique or serious discussion of the politics of race and empire; more insidiously, such commemorative practices can easily slip into an exercise in post-imperial nostalgia as well as a part-legitimisation, part-celebration of militarist culture. At a special commemorative service organised at Glasgow Cathedral in August 2014 to mark the 'Commonwealth' contribution, the following piece from Pericles' Funeral oration during the Peloponnesian War, was recited and broadcast:

> So they gave their bodies to the Commonwealth
> And received praise that will never die.[46]

On 10 November 2018, at the concert of the British Legion, India was the one 'Commonwealth' nation singled out as a sari-clad actress Nina Wadia gave a rendition of the Indian political leader and poet Sarojini Naidu's strangely war-like poem 'The Gift of India':

> And your love shall offer memorial thanks,
> To the comrades who fought in your dauntless ranks,
> And you honour the deeds of the deathless ones,
> Remember the blood of thy martyred sons.[47]

The elite nationalist Naidu's highly aestheticized imperial-heroic verse was worlds away from what the wives and mothers of the men who had gone to battle actually felt or sung – 'The war pains me like hot sand in a cauldron/ Every household now has widows'.[48] Such sentiments, wholly undermining the rhetoric of sacrifice or martyrdom, were nowhere evident in the centennial discourse for obvious reasons.

Instead, the Indian sepoy, the African *askari* or the West Indian soldier is always invariably a colonial hero, as if heroism and gallantry were the only ticket to remembrance; their contradictory motives and ambivalent responses are flattened into a paean of loyalty and service. Such loyalist and uncritical proclamations, according to some community leaders, are good for brown or black self-esteem in multicultural societies; the irony is that this often *is* the case. In many of the community centenary meetings, the descendants of these veterans turn up with the medals of a grandfather or a great-uncle and their 'glorious service' to Britain in its 'hour of need'. Such a narrative, informed by communal warmth and family pride, are important processes in establishing the 'British identity' of these ethnic groups who otherwise feel deeply disenfranchised; as discussed earlier, via the quotation from Sayeeda Warsi, it can be an important tool against racism and xenophobia. Understandably, ethnic community groups insist on telling 'positive' stories, even if it involves conscious sanitisation.[49] While we need to be sensitive and respectful, there must also be a space for critique. For the 'positive' element often gets out of hand and becomes an endorsement, verging on celebration, of military and imperial culture: politically, this unreconstructed heroism at once feeds into ethnic nationalism and British loyalism, in a context when 'Britishness' gets equated with a ring-wing ideology while the liberal left-wing tradition of dissent and pacifism gets largely overlooked.

Should the past, in all its racist injustices and asymmetries, be raked up or laid to rest, especially when there is already so much social tension? Would the past not be better served if it is narrated for a peaceful and harmonious future? Such presentist arguments, while seductive and to an extent even effective in the short term, are deeply spurious and ultimately damaging in their selective appropriation of the past; second, multiculturalism, in order to be robust, needs to interrogate the past and work through difficult, even painful, histories rather than papering over them. Of course, there are, indeed, heart-stirring tales of bravery, attested by the 11 Victoria Crosses won by South Asian soldiers, but most Indians and Africans, like their European counterparts, would have shivered like leaves and soiled their trousers as shells exploded around them; their letters and voice-recordings testify not to this absurd heroic image but to Wilfred Owen's exposure of the old lie: 'Dulce Et Decorum Est': they were only too human in inhuman circumstances. An heroic-martial celebratory narrative of the 'multicultural contribution' does not just give the lie to history but is being used, in a racialized variation of Michael Gove's infamous article from 2014, to undermine the lessons learnt from the anti-war poets and the denunciation of war in the 1960s and 1970s.[50] While a militaristic rhetoric about the First World War is now largely alien to British cultural memory of the war, it is here being imported under the guise of cultural and ethnic 'diversity': it is indeed a sad day for both Britain and India if their 'shared' past has to be founded on the violence and death they together inflicted on the 'enemy'.

Occasionally, there was a backlash, particularly in an area where the problem is most delicate: the indoctrination of British Muslim youth in the 'values' of Britain. It was decided by the government that narratives of South Asian loyalty and valour during the war would help to counter possible *jihadist* tendencies among British Muslim youths, as if it would counter the immediate social contexts – the then Home Secretary, Theresa May's, hostile environment policy, rise of Islamophobia and the continued British presence in Iraq and Afghanistan – which would have contributed to such disaffection. A crude version of this was the creation of the 'Poppy *hijab*' in 2014 by Tabinda-Kauser Ishaq, a 25-year old British Muslim student at the London College of Fashion, meant to symbolise 'Britain's diverse and shared history and the coming together of people from all backgrounds to remember in this centenary year'; it was sold by the Royal British Legion in 2015 for the first time.[51] Surprisingly, it was a sell-out success, hailed by many as 'wonderful and inspired', till British Asian activist and journalist Sofia Ahmed lashed out at the initiative, exposing its racist and pro-war politics:

> Marketing the poppy as a stance against extremism suggests that refusing the symbol is tantamount to 'extremism'... Buy a £22 hijab to prove that you're not a terrorist, wannabe 'jihadi bride' – planning on running off to Syria to find your ISIS prince in blood-stained camouflage...
>
> I also take issue with the fact that a symbol of my religion is being appropriated as a marketing tool for empire. My hijab is a visual sign of my religiosity and devotion to Allah and not a walking talking billboard on which to showcase my patriotism and undying loyalty to Britain. No other religious group is pressured to prove their allegiance in the same way. Somehow I don't think we'll be seeing budding Jewish designer marketing a poppy kippa anytime soon...
>
> Refusing to wear the poppy is not an 'extremist Muslim' stance, It's an ideological position based on anti-war sentiment...
>
> I'm a prime target for these initiatives, coming from a 'Martial Race' as I do. My great, great grandfather was awarded an 'order of merit' and given title of 'Subedar Major' for his 'bravery' during the first world war. However, the fact that he was probably fighting on the Mesopotamian campaign against the Muslim Ottoman empire, doesn't exactly fill me with ecstatic pride. It actually makes me a bit nauseous to think about what 'brave' act he must have carried out to be given the highest military award in the land...
>
> If there's one thing I am sure of, it is that given Britain's never ending lust for war in Muslim lands, and the use of the poppy campaign to garner support and sympathy for the military, my grandfather and those countless other Muslim men who took part in the world wars,

would turn in their graves at the sight of their grandchildren wearing that hijab.[52]

As Chris Allen, a researcher at the University of Birmingham on Islamophobic hate-crime, noted in response to the *Sun*'s images of women in poppy-*hijabs* on its front-page, these re-appropriations of the *hijab* can be little more than proxies for anti-Muslim bigotry: 'The wearing – or not wearing – of a patriotic hijab becomes a shrouded loyalty test'.[53] But Sofia Ahmed goes further. Hers is a double-resistance to the poppy – both to the imposition of the markers of a specifically British war memory on South Asian war experience as well as to 'poppy fascism' with its discriminatory bias in this case; it is in fact reminiscent of the British novelist Virginia Woolf's *Three Guineas* (1938), one of the greatest pacifist-feminist texts. Written in the long shadow of the First World War and in the context of rising fascism, Woolf here examines the connections between militarism, patriarchy, class and empire, often referring to the embellishments of army uniform as sustaining a particular version of masculinity.[54]

What these centennial projects reveal is a tension between an ethical use of memory – where the past is investigated in all its messiness and moral complexity – and a more instrumental use driven by definite agendas where the past needs to be shaped in the image of the present for a particular vision of the future. These two points of view, in turn, instead open up broader and more fundamental questions about the very function of commemoration: why do we commemorate the war dead? According to the political philosopher Cecile Fabre, we commemorate the war dead to reconnect the younger generation with the past, to pay our debts to the men (and women) who gave up their lives and finally to prevent future wars.[55] Fabre's observations raise specific political and moral questions for our present-day multicultural societies as well as philosophical issues underpinning any desire for peace. If commemoration of a particular group inevitably involves renewed othering and denigration of the 'enemy', how do we then, in the context of what I have been discussing, remember an Indian under-age sepoy, forcibly recruited, who ends up killing a Turkish or German soldier so as to be truthful and respectful to the memory of all three groups and find a common commemorative ground? Diversification of war memory is the first important, but relatively easy, step towards a more thoroughgoing decolonisation which, according to Immanuel Kant, was essential for 'perpetual peace'.[56] The centenary years have achieved the first step of challenging the colour of war memory but diversification, as has been argued previously, is not decolonisation, nor is the latter a question of race only: what lies ahead is the much more difficult task of purging slavish commemorative ceremonies of its militarist tendencies. Indeed, can we summon up the strength and the courage to remember and commemorate the war dead without any sanitisation of the violence they both inflicted and received, can we respect but not endorse the cause for which they fell, and instead open up a space for reflection and critique for the plural narratives and contested memories of the war?

Notes

1 I am very grateful to the two editors – David Monger and Sarah Murray – for reading the chapter with an exceptional degree of care and for their astute advice.
2 'Thousands Honour WW1 Troops at Diwali Festival', https://www.forces.net/news/thousands-gather-honour-wwi-troops-diwali-festival. All URLs are correct as of 10 October 2019.
3 'Baroness Warsi kick-starts campaign to remember Commonwealth Servicemen of the First World War', 16 April, 2013, https://www.gov.uk/government/news/baroness-warsi-kick-starts-campaign-to-remember-commonwealth-servicemen-of-the-first-world-war. Also see 'Special Report: Centenary of World War I', *The Independent*, 23 June 2013, https://www.independent.co.uk/news/uk/home-news/special-report-the-centenary-of-wwi-tommies-and-tariqs-fought-side-by-side-8669758.html.
4 'My boys weren't just Tommies', The Sun, 16 October 2012, https://sayeedawarsi.com/2012/10/16/the-sun-our-boys-werent-just-tommies-they-were-tariqs-and-tajinders-too/.
5 For the controversy around BNP leader Nick Griffin and the First World War, see the article 'Schoolboy confronts Griffin at the Memorial', *The Independent*, 7 November 2009. Griffin reluctantly agreed to a request by the 13-year-old schoolboy William Robey to be photographed next to the memorial for Pathan Indians at Menin Gate but became aggressive and acrimonious when challenged about his party's racist manifesto about wanting a predominantly white Britain and selective appropriation of history which went against the complex past, as inscribed on the memorial. Griffin started shouting at Robey who was asked to get his 'facts straight'. https://www.independent.co.uk/news/uk/politics/schoolboy-confronts-griffin-at-memorial-1816564.html.
6 David Cameron announces 50 million funding', *The Guardian*, 11 October 2012, https://www.theguardian.com/politics/2012/oct/11/david-cameron-fund-world-war-one-commemorations
7 The aforementioned figures are from *Statistics of the Military Effort*, 777. This number is in addition to soldiers already in the British Indian army at the time of the outbreak of the war, estimated at 239,561 (777). Also see Das, *India, Empire and First World War Culture*, 406–07, with which this essay shares some research material.
8 See the section on 'Mixed Motives: Livelihood, Tradition and Incentives', in Das, India, *Empire and First World War Culture*, 79–87; also see Ahuja, 'Corrosiveness of Comparison', 136.
9 Das, *India, Empire and First World War Culture*, 87.
10 Amir Khan. 129th [Baluchis], British Library, L/MIL/5/825/2, 141-2. The letter is included in David Omissi's fine anthology *Indian Voices*, x.
11 Mahatma Gandhi, Letter to V.S. Srinivasa Sastri, 18 July 1918, in Gandhi, *Collected Works*, 489.
12 See the chapter on 'The Impact of WW1' in Aydin, *The Politics of Anti-Westernism*, 93–125.
13 Wagner, *Amritsar 1919*.
14 Quoted in Bose, *His Majesty's Opponent*, 51. The Khilafat was an all-India Muslim movement, closely connected with Indian nationalism, to pressurise

the British government to recognise and preserve the authority of the Ottoman Sultan as the Caliph. See Minaut, *The Khilafat movement*, as well as her recent article on the subject: 'Khilafat Movement', https://encyclopedia.1914-1918-online.net/article/khilafat_movement.
15 Winter, 'In Conclusion: Palimpsests', 167.
16 See Chhina, *Last Post*.
17 Chhina and Chhina, 'Commemoration: Cult of the Fallen (India)', https://encyclopedia.1914-1918-online.net/article/commemoration_cult_of_the_fallen_india.
18 Shashi Tharoor, 'Why the Indian Soldiers of WW1 are forgotten', http://www.bbc.co.uk/news/magazine-33317368.
19 See Chandra, *Essays on Indian Nationalism*; for critique and revision, see Bose and Jalal, *Modern South Asia*.
20 Interview with Mohan Kahlon in Kolkata, 18 December, 2014; interview with Colonel Raj Singh Gursey, New Delhi, 22 January, 2015.
21 Interview with Indrani Haldar, in Kolkata, 20 December, 2014.
22 https://www.rediff.com/news/interview/world-must-remember-indian-heroism-in-wwi/20181207.htm. Also see Chhina, *The Last Post*.
23 Katju, *The Indian Express*, 11 December 2014.km, https://indianexpress.com/article/india/india-others/indian-soldiers-in-first-world-war-were-hired-assassins-of-british-justice-markandey-katju/.
24 Both the extracts are quoted in 'India and the UK commemorate fallen soldiers in World War I', https://www.gov.uk/government/news/india-and-uk-commemorate-fallen-soldiers-in-world-war-1. My emphasis.
25 Many of the articles, published in leading national dailies such as *The Times of India, Hindustan Times, The Telegraph* and *Indian Express*, are listed under the 'Indian Media' section of the excellent website on 'India and the Great War', maintained by the United Services Institute, http://indiaww1.in/indianmedia.aspx. The website also hosts videos, images, bibliography and a brief but incisive summary of the main events. Also see the war centennial issue of the popular national English magazine *India Today* in 2014.
26 This was again achieved through the efforts of Rana Chhina. For a report, see https://www.gov.uk/government/news/india-and-uk-commemorate-fallen-soldiers-in-world-war-1.
27 'The Unremembered: World War One's Army of Workers', https://www.big-ideas.org/project/the-unremembered/.
28 The creation of the Memorial Gates, through the initiative of Baroness Shreela Flather, among others, can be found in the webpage dedicated to it, with various useful links to the various commemorative events and speeches, including those by the former Prime Minister, John Major, https://memorialgates.org/index.html. Also refer to the webpage of the Memorial Gates Trust, http://www.mgtrust.org/.
29 https://www.gov.uk/government/news/19-million-package-to-mark-armistice-centenary.
30 'BBC announces 2,500 hours of First World War Programmes', *The Telegraph*, 16 October 2013.
31 The Immigration Act of 2014, receiving Royal assent on May 14, 2014, was designed to prevent landlords from renting accommodation to illegal immigrants, bar them from obtaining driving licences, and facilitating investigation into sham marriages. This was part of the 'Hostile Environment Policy' which was introduced by the then Home Secretary, Theresa May, with the remark: 'The aim is to create, here in Britain, a really hostile environment for illegal immigrants', see https://www.legislation.gov.uk/ukpga/2014/22/contents/enacted.

Also see *A Guide to the Hostile Environment* (2019) edited by the civil rights group *Liberty*, https://www.libertyhumanrights.org.uk/policy/policy-reports-briefings/guide-hostile-environment-border-controls-dividing-our-communities-%E2%80%93.

32 The Trussell Trust, the largest foodbank in the UK, handed out 1.2 million food packets in 2016–2017, compared to 41,000 in 2009–10, see https://fullfact.org/economy/how-many-people-use-food-banks/.

33 This was particularly the case with the 'poppy hijab' discussed later in the chapter.

34 For a report on a workshop that got together many of the project members and stakeholders working in the area, see 'South Asians and the First World War: Reflections', https://blogs.kcl.ac.uk/english/2016/07/06/south-asians-and-the-first-world-war-reflections. For some of the most important productions and projects, see *The World's War: Forgotten Soldiers of Empire*, presented by David Olusoga and shown on BBC 2 in August 2014, https://www.bbc.co.uk/programmes/b04dh242; 'Subterranean Sepoys', a radio play by Avin Shah, was available on Tara Arts from February to October 2014, https://www.tara-arts.com/whats-on/subterranean-sepoys-2014; 'Whose Remembrance' was an AHRC-funded Connected Communities project led by Suzanne Bardgett at the Imperial War Museum from 2013 to 2014, https://www.iwm.org.uk/research/research-projects/whose-remembrance; and 'Empire, Faith and War' was a series of seminars and events organised by the UK Punjab Heritage in 2014–15, http://www.empirefaithwar.com/page-2. The section on 'Uncovering Hidden Histories of the First World War' on the Heritage Fund Lottery website givers one a sense of the impulses behind the massive funding made available https://www.heritagefund.org.uk/blogs/uncovering-hidden-stories-first-world-war http://www.chattri.org/.

35 http://www.empirefaithwar.com/page-2.

36 Twenty million people or nearly half the population of Britain saw the film when it was first released in October 1916. See Marcus, 'First World War Film', 115.

37 See Visram, *Asians in Britain*, x.

38 The annual gathering of the Chattri has now vastly expanded in scope. See the website http://www.chattri.org/ for a full account of the activities of the group.

39 For a list of the names of the soldiers buried and general context, see https://www.exploringsurreyspast.org.uk/themes/places/surrey/woking/woking/woking_muslim_burial_ground/.

40 The BBC documentary *Britain's Muslim Soldiers* charts the story of the restoration of the burial ground and was aired on 3 January 2016, https://www.bbc.co.uk/mediacentre/proginfo/2016/01/britains-muslim-soldiers. Some of the details are archived at http://www.horsellcommon.org.uk/sites/the-peace-garden. Also see Santanu Das, https://www.independent.co.uk/news/world/world-history/are-faith-specific-war-memorials-the-best-way-to-remember-the-fallen-a672 7821.html.

41 Quoted from the BBC documentary *Britain's Muslim Soldier* (2015).

42 http://www.britishfuture.org/articles/news/remembering-khudadad-khan-31st-october-2014/. Also see 'The Soldier who embodied multi-ethnic war effort'.

43 A classic example is the 2013 article in the *Observer*, referred to earlier, on Sayeeda Warsi's efforts to diversify war memory. Warsi habitually falls back on the rhetoric of sacrifice: 'We have a duty to remember their bravery and commemorate their sacrifices', https://www.independent.co.uk/news/uk/home-news/special-report-the-centenary-of-wwi-tommies-and-tariqs-fought-side-by-side-8669758.html. The same is largely true of Indian media. See, for example, the article 'More martyrs to be immortalised' in the local *Pune Mirror* on 5 December 2014: 'The stone walls in the Khadki cemetery have the names of soldiers who

sacrificed their lives in 1914–18 war', https://punemirror.indiatimes.com/pune/civic/More-martyrs-to-be-immortalised/articleshow/45377966.cms. The language of sacrifice goes back to war time, as powerfully argued by David Monger, among others. See his chapter on 'Patriotisms of Duty: Sacrifice, Obligations and Community' in *Patriotism and Propaganda in First World War Britain*, 169–97.

44 Olusoga, *The World's War*, x.

45 Smith, 'Multicultural First World War', 347–63.

46 The special service at Glasgow Cathedral was attended by Prince Charles, UK Prime Minister David Cameron, First Minister Alex Salmond and Commonwealth heads of government, as well as UK and Irish politicians. The First Minister noted that 'as the curtain falls on 2014 Commonwealth Games, we acknowledge the countries of the Commonwealth we fought alongside during the Great War and it is fitting that this service in Glasgow Cathedral should focus on the contribution of these nations', https://www.bbc.co.uk/news/uk-scotland-28620000.

47 Naidu, 'India's Gift', *Broken Wing*, x. In this 'Festival of Remembrance', held at the Albert Hall on 10 November 2018 and attended by Queen Elizabeth II, members of the public, including the then British Prime Minister Theresa May, held up pictures of their ancestors who had served in the war, https://www.bbc.co.uk/uk-46165002.

48 Quoted by Amarjit Chandan, 'World War I and Its Impact on Punjabis', http://apnaorg.com/articles/amarjit/wwi.

49 I have in mind two such gatherings in the House of Commons in 2014, convened respectively by Sayeeda Warsi and Diane Abbott, when the descendants arrived with various pieces of war memorabilia and started airing their views. Even though I disagreed, I could not help admiring the intensity of their investment in these often-celebratory stories.

50 In a well-publicised article published on 2 January 2014 entitled 'Why does the British Left Insist on belittling True British Heroes', https://www.dailymail.co.uk/debate/article-2532930/MICHAEL-GOVE-Why-does-Left-insist-belittling-true-British-heroes.html, Michael Gove, the then Education Secretary, blamed *Blackadder* and the First World War poets for 'left-wing myths' about the war. The article was widely critiqued as having confused rival interpretation of history with 'myths'. See 'Michael Gove Criticises Blackadder Myths', The Telegraph, 3 January, 2014.

51 'Poppy Headscarf', 31 October 2014, http://www.britishfuture.org/articles/news/poppy-headscarf-centenary-victoria-cross-muslim-soldier/; 'Why British Muslims need a poppy hijab' in *The Telegraph*, 10 November 2015, https://www.telegraph.co.uk/women/womens-life/11985648/World-War-One-Remembrance-Day-British-Muslims-must-wear-poppy-hijab.html.

52 The article 'Why I won't be wearing the Poppy hijab' was first published on the online platform Media Diversified on 5 November 2014, https://mediadiversified.org/2014/11/05/why-i-wont-be-wearing-the-poppy-hijab and an amended version was published on 4 November 2015 as 'No, I won't wear the Poppy-hijab', *The Independent*, 4 November, 2015, https://www.independent.co.uk/voices/no-i-wont-wear-the-poppy-hijab-to-prove-im-not-an-extremist-a6720901.html.

53 'Split UK opinion over poppy hijab', *Al-Jazeera*, 9 November 2014. Also see 'The poppy hijab is just Islamophobia with a floral motif', http://theconversation.com/the-poppy-hijab-is-just-islamophobia-with-a-floral-motif-33692.

54 Wilson, 'Attacking Hitler in England', 36–47.

55 Fabre, *Cosmopolitan Peace*. Also listen to her podcast 'Remembering War', https://podcasts.ox.ac.uk/remembering-war.

56 Kant, *Perpetual Peace*, x.

Bibliography

Ahuja, Ravi. "The Corrosiveness of Comparison." In *The World in World Wars. Experiences, Perceptions and Perspectives from the South*, edited by Heike Liebau, Katrin Bromber, Dyala Hamza, Katharina Lange and Ravi Ahuja, 131–66. Brill: Leiden, 2010.

Aydin, Cemil. *The Politics of Anti-Westernism in Asia.* New York: Columbia University Press, 2007.

Bandyopadhyay, Sekhar, ed. *Nationalist Movement in India: A Reader.* Delhi: Oxford University Press, 2009.

Barrett, Michele. "Subalterns at War: First World War Colonial Forces and the Politics of the Imperial War Graves Commission." In *Can the Subaltern Speak?: Reflections on the History of an Idea*, edited by R. C. Morris, 156–76. New York: Columbia University Press, 2010.

Bose, Sugata. *A Hundred Horizons: The Indian Ocean in the Age of Global Empire.* Cambridge, MA: Harvard University Press, 2006.

Bose, Sugata. *His Majesty's Opponent: Subhas Chandra Bose and India's Struggle against Empire.* Cambridge, MA: Harvard University Press, 2011.

Bose, Sugata and Ayesha Jalal. *Modern South Asia: History, Culture, Political Economy.* New York: Routledge, 1998.

Bose, Sugata, and Kris Manjapra, eds. *Cosmopolitan Thought-Zones: South Asia and the Global Circulation of Ideas.* London: Palgrave, 2010.

Chandra, Bipan. *Essays on Indian Nationalism.* Delhi: Haranand Publications Pvt Ltd, 1993.

Chhina, Rana. *Last Post: Indian War Memorials around the World.* Delhi: United Services Institute, 2014.

Chhina, Rana and Adil Chhina. "Commemoration: Cult of the Fallen (India)." https://encyclopedia.1914-1918-online.net/article/commemoration_cult_of_the_fallen_india

Das, Santanu. *India, Empire and First World War Culture: Writings, Images, and Songs.* Cambridge: Cambridge University Press, 2018.

Fabre, Cecile. *Cosmopolitan Peace.* Oxford: Oxford University Press, 2016.

Gandhi, M.K. *The Collected Works of Mahatma Gandhi.* Ahmedabad: Government of India, 1965.

Kant, Immanuel. *Perpetual Peace: A Philosophical Essay.* Trans. M. Campbell Smith with a preface by Robert Latta. New York: Garland Publishing, 1972 [first published as 'Zum Ewigen Frieden. Ein Philosophischer Entwurf' in 1795].

Liberty. *A Guide to the Hostile Environment.* London: Liberty, 2019.

Marcus, Laura. "The Great War in Twentieth-Century Cinema". In *Cambridge Companion to the Literature of the First World War*, edited by Vincent Sherry, 280–301. Cambridge: Cambridge University Press, 2005.

Minaut, Gail. *The Khilafat Movement: Religious Symbolism and the Political Mobilization of India.* New York: Columbia University Press, 1982.

Monger, David. *Patriotism and Propaganda in First World War Britain: The National War Aims Committee and Civilian Morale.* Liverpool: Liverpool University Press, 2012.

Naidu, Sarojini. *The Broken Wing: Songs of Love, Death and Destiny 1915–1916.* London: William Heinemann, 1917.

Olusoga, David. *The World's War.* London: Head of Zeus, 2014.

Omissi, David, ed. *Indian Voices of the Great War: Soldiers' Letters, 1914–1918.* London: Macmillan, 1999.

Roy, Franziska, Heike Liebau and Ravi Ahuja, eds. *"When the War Began, We Heard of Several Kings": South Asian Prisoners in World War I Germany.* Delhi: Social Science Press, 2011.

Smith, Richard. "The Multicultural First World War: Memories of West Indian Contribution in Contemporary Britain." *Journal of European Studies*, 45, no. 4 (October 2014): 347–63.

Statistics of the Military Effort of the British Empire During the Great War, 1914–1920. London: His Majesty's Stationary Office, 1922.

Visram, Rozina. *Asians in Britain.* London: Pluto Press, 2002.

Wagner, Kim. *Amritsar 1919: An Empire of Fear and the Making of a Massacre.* London: Yale University Press, 2019.

Wilson, Peter. "Attacking Hitler in England: Patriarchy, Class and War in Virginia Woolf's Three Guineas." In *Classics of International Relations: Essays in Criticism and Appreciation*, edited by Hennik Bliddal, Casper Sylvest and Peter Wilson, 36–47. London: Routledge, 2013.

Winter, Jay. "In Conclusion: Palimpsests." In *Memory, History and Colonialism: Engagement with Pierre Nora in Colonial and Postcolonial Contexts (London Bulletin Supplement)*, edited by Indra Sengupta, 167–73. London: German Historical Institute, 2009.

2 Resurrecting heroes … or reinventing them?

Interpretations of the heroic in Australian First World War centenary commemorations

Bryce Abraham

During the advance on the Hindenburg Line in August and September 1918, Staff Sergeant Thomas (Frank) Cahir of the 9th Australian Field Ambulance was tasked with supervising the evacuation of the wounded to the east of Bray in northern France. The advance was part of the Hundred Days Offensive that would end the First World War. As British Empire and American forces made advances around Bray, Cahir had on more than one occasion moved across the ground just behind the main battle – sometimes under rifle and machine gun fire and the threat of gas attack – to maintain contact with the Regimental Aid Posts and ensure the efficient evacuation of casualty cases. For his efforts Cahir was praised for setting 'an example of endurance, cheerfulness, and soldierly qualities'.[1]

Almost a century later, and 89 years after Cahir's death, the Governor-General of Australia approved the retrospective award of the Distinguished Service Medal to Cahir in recognition of his services at Bray and elsewhere on the Somme from March to September 1918.[2] The Distinguished Service Medal is a modern decoration, created under the Australian Honours System in 1991 to recognise 'distinguished leadership in action'.[3] It is, roughly speaking, equivalent to the British Military Cross or (now defunct) Military Medal. This was not the first time the Distinguished Service Medal had been awarded for services rendered decades earlier. The award to Cahir was, however, the first time that a decoration had been granted under the contemporary Australian Honours System for the First World War. Media reports at the time of the award remarked that an administrative 'oversight' was to blame for Cahir not being recognised in 1918.[4] Indeed, he had been recommended for, but not awarded, the Distinguished Conduct Medal.[5] This was not entirely unusual. The process for honours and awards was rigorous, if occasionally inconsistent and subjective, and recommendations were often downgraded to a lesser honour or rejected outright.[6] At the time of the war Cahir's actions did not meet the appropriate standard for recognition.

Reflecting on Australia's early centennial commemorations of the First World War, historian Henry Reynolds wrote that an 'emphasis on individual valour and sacrifice crowds out the whole field'.[7] Reynolds' observation remained pertinent to Australian public and private commemorative initiatives during the centenary period. The phenomenon is in part explained by the rise of new nationalism and family history over recent decades, which has seen the First World War popularly understood and explored in Australia through a familial, localised and nationalist lens; one that tends to stress narratives of heroism, suffering and sacrifice. One need not look far for examples, but the most prominent include the grassroots campaign to have Sir John Monash, the citizen-soldier who commanded the Australian Corps on the Western Front in 1918, posthumously promoted to field marshal.[8] Or initiatives like the Roll of Honour projection program, which each night projects names of Australia's war dead onto the façade of the Hall of Memory at the Australian War Memorial.[9]

This chapter explores conceptions of heroism, commemoration and sacrifice in Australia during the war years and the centenary. Contemporary commemorations reflect modern ideals of heroism that centre on noble sacrifice, victimhood, and the saving of life – qualities inherent in Cahir's retrospective award. Yet the perceptions of heroism that shaped the fighting fronts and broader society up to 1918 were far more violent, aggressive and tactical in nature. The Cahir and Monash examples, as well as the programs fixated on the war dead, are part of a pattern that emerged during Australia's centenary commemorations not to resurrect the heroic narrative and understandings of heroism that existed during the First World War, but to reinvent them. In drawing upon a rich body of scholarship on recent war memory and commemoration in Australia, this chapter sheds fresh light on the shifts in Australia's heroic wartime narrative and illuminates some of the issues inherent in contemporary societies reflecting on – and misremembering – their history.

Heroism in the trenches, 1914–1918

On the outbreak of war, an almost sentimental Victorian approach to warfare permeated the British Empire. The small professional force that Britain initially deployed to France and Belgium in 1914 had been shaped by the conflicts of the late-nineteenth century and was unprepared for the war of attrition that followed.[10] This sentimental Victorian legacy also influenced early wartime notions of heroism. Men such as Lance Corporal William Fuller of the British Army's Welsh Regiment, one of the war's earliest recipients of the Victoria Cross (VC) – the premier award for martial heroism in the British Empire – were recognised for heroics reminiscent of the conflicts of a bygone era. In September 1914, Fuller advanced one hundred yards to retrieve a mortally wounded captain from the battlefield.[11] Having done so, he dashed back to collect the officer's rifle to, as Max Arthur puts it, 'prevent it falling into enemy hands'.[12] The retreat from Mons in August and September 1914 garnered a string of VCs embodying such heroic ideals. Actions that demonstrated perseverance against an overwhelming enemy force, the saving of life, and preventing the capture of military hardware were rewarded during this period.[13]

These were all types of heroism that had come to dominate the heroic paradigm within the British Empire in the late-nineteenth century. Saving life under fire is one, in particular, to note as dashing or galloping out onto a battlefield to rescue stranded comrades governed perceptions of heroism by the turn of the century.[14] The reason that 'humanitarian' acts came to dominate awards was grounded in both British racial ideals and pragmatism. Most obviously, a soldier captured or killed sapped the strength of the fighting force. But conflict with non-European forces also highlighted different cultural approaches to warfare. Britain fought dozens of wars on the periphery and frontier regions of the empire in the Victorian period, most often against non-white opponents, and ideas of Orientalism and racial hierarchies came to permeate British society and its perceptions of the racial 'other'.[15] With this came the realisation that certain peoples (such as the Zulus) showed little mercy to the living or dead, at least by European understandings. Abandoning a comrade to the whims of a 'native' force was thus a reprehensible act for the proud white Briton.[16]

By 1916, however, empire conceptions of heroism were in transition. Through the early period of the war, the French, British and empire forces had waged a largely defensive war on the Western Front. Political dissatisfaction with the conduct of the British Expeditionary Force and tensions between command and senior cabinet ministers, however, saw Field Marshal Sir John French replaced by General Sir Douglas Haig as British commander-in-chief on the Western Front in December 1915.[17] Haig considered humanitarian heroism to be out of step with modern European warfare. He argued that humanitarian acts sapped the fighting strength of frontline units, detracted from the primary task, and often resulted in 'unnecessary loss of life'.[18] He was also under pressure to vindicate his appointment and reorient the British Expeditionary Force to an offensive footing. As Keith Jeffery has argued, with the possibility of a peace settlement increasingly unlikely from late 1916, the only avenue that remained to secure victory or ensure defeat was a decisive campaign on the Western Front.[19] Encouraging aggressive and tactical actions – what can be considered 'war winning' heroics – while deterring acts that detracted from the fighting strength provided one means to do this.

Accordingly, in August 1916, instructions handed down by Haig's General Headquarters shifted the criteria for the VC. The relaying memorandum sent to units of the Australian Imperial Force (AIF) declared that from now on:

> the V.C. will only be given for acts of conspicuous gallantry which are materially conductive to the gaining of a victory. Cases of gallantry in life saving, of however fine a nature, will not be considered for the award of the V.C.[20]

In essence, the highest award for heroism would only be given to feats that directly contributed or led to a tactical victory. The instruction was clarified a month later when Haig had his Military Secretary, Major-General William Peyton, circulate a supplementary directive. 'In future', Peyton wrote, 'the Victoria Cross or other immediate reward will not be given for the rescue of wounded, excepting to those whose duty it is to care for such cases'.[21] Haig was determined that the British honours system be responsive to the demands of the modern battlefield. In doing so, he successfully engineered a break from lingering Victorian conceptions of heroism and reshaped the heroic paradigm within the British Empire.[22] From late 1916 onwards, British award bestowals were typified by the rushing of machine gun posts, the consolidation of ground, and the death or capture of enemy combatants. To give one example, Second Lieutenant George Ingram of the 24th Battalion AIF was awarded the VC for leading his men to neutralise a series of gun emplacements, a fortified quarry, and a heavily defended house to capture over a dozen German machine guns and more than 60 prisoners at Montbrehain in October 1918.[23] This proactive, aggressive form of heroism was not unique to the Western Front. With the movement of senior commanders and personnel between war fronts, Haig's paradigm of heroism filtered into other theatres, such as the Sinai and Palestine.[24]

Unsurprisingly, this version of heroism inherently favoured the principal combatants: the infantryman and machine gunner. These men came to be construed as the soldier archetype and epitomised ideas of British wartime masculinity because they were most afforded the opportunity to test their mettle in combat and 'coolness' under fire.[25] The interest afforded these men, however, alienated non-combatants and personnel that laboured behind the lines; men who, accordingly, tended to express occasional feelings of guilt or inadequacy. This sense affected two returned Australian soldiers interviewed by historian Alistair Thomson in the 1980s: Bill Langham, who served as an artilleryman on the Western Front, thought his job less gruelling than that faced by the infantry, while Percy Bird noted feelings of inferiority and shame following his redeployment as a clerk.[26]

Even stretcher-bearers, men (like Frank Cahir) who often laboured under fire, voiced doubts about the masculine legitimacy of their work.[27] Writing in 1915, Private Octavius Jocelyn Carr of the 1st Australian Field Ambulance lamented: 'Am almost wishing I was doing the real work of fighting as we seem to be the only hangers on to the army who do the real work'.[28] However, stretcher-bearers were often singled out by other soldiers for praise. As a Private Bishop reflected in July 1915: 'The chaps who deserve 'em [VCs] are our stretcher-bearers ... I reckon they earn a V.C. about a dozen times a day carrying in the wounded under fire. Never saw anything like it in my life'.[29] Such praise was not confined to the ordinary ranks, which demonstrates that the heroic paradigm endorsed by the military establishment did not always reflect what was socially or systematically revered.[30] Stretcher-bearers and medical personnel were also still able to be recognised for heroism under Haig's directive (remembering the caveat for 'those whose duty it is to care for such cases'). However, as A.G. Butler lamented in the official history of Australia's medical services in the war, the exception was widely misunderstood and often disregarded, particularly within the AIF.[31] By 1918, then, British Empire conceptions of heroism were firmly centred on the combatant and feats of aggressive, tactical heroics.

Propaganda and the promotion of aggressive heroics

This new tactical, aggressive paradigm of heroism did not exist in isolation on the war fronts. The influence of pervasive wartime propaganda saw it transported into the homes of, and become revered by, much of the Australian public. Propaganda was a significant aspect of the home experience for Australians, because military recruitment was based on voluntary enlistment and persuasion provided the key means through which to achieve mass social mobilisation.[32] The imagery of posters, text of pro-war articles in the press and the cry of government slogans induced men to enlist and reassured the public that the war was righteous and in Australia's interest. Early recruitment propaganda thereby appealed to a masculine sense of duty, loyalty and service. Other propaganda used guilt and shame as a motivator.[33] Such tactics were most prominent in atrocity propaganda, which highlighted real or imagined German atrocities against Belgian civilians and prisoners of war to demonise the Germans as an almost bestial and barbaric enemy.[34] Atrocity propaganda generated what historian Heather Jones has labelled 'war culture' in Britain and the Dominions, which in turn fostered a hatred for the enemy.[35] This hatred inspired an anti-German sentiment in Australia and made it easier for civic society to accept and revere violent heroics by empire combatants.[36]

Decorated 'war heroes' also became embroiled in the politics of recruitment and propaganda in Australia from 1917. A divisive conscription campaign, increasing devastation on the battlefield, and pressure to maintain reinforcements had led to a growing sense of war weariness for Australians at home. The situation sparked initiatives by the Australian government to stimulate enlistment and reinspire a sense of loyalty to the war effort. At the behest of the government men such as Albert Jacka, Arthur Blackburn and George Howell – each of whom had won the VC for violent acts of heroism – lent their likeness to propaganda posters, publicly advocated for the introduction of conscription, or appeared at recruiting rallies to stimulate enlistment.[37] The promotion of these heroic figures helped to sanitise battlefield violence, make the fighting fronts more palatable to the Australian public, and simultaneously glorify and normalise feats of aggressive wartime heroism.

Anzac and Australian national remembrance

Given the reshaping of heroism during the war years, the case of Frank Cahir and the broader pattern of Australian commemoration of 'heroes' a century later raises several questions about national remembrance of the First World War. How and why, for instance, was a stretcher-bearer retrospectively recognised for services that clashed with the dominant form of heroism that existed at the time of his actions? The answer lies in Australia's national narrative of the war. Australian conceptions of heroism, commemoration and understandings of war more broadly have fundamentally shifted over the intervening decades. Popular remembrance of the war in Australia is, much like that in New Zealand, grounded in nationalism and the mythology of the Anzac legend. The legend has manifested in different ways and assumed alternate meanings on each side of the Tasman, but in Australia it fills the role of a national foundation myth.[38]

By the outbreak of the war, the ideology of martial nationalism governed Western conceptions of nationhood. War became an intrinsic component of nationalism in Western Europe from the nineteenth century, as the aggressive imperialism, race patriotism and militarism of the time manufactured a sense that war provided the purest test of nationhood and manhood.[39] Such thinking was engrained in Anglo-Australia, but, as a settler-colonial society founded as a penal settlement, it lacked the requisite martial adventure to feel secure in its sense of nationhood. The frontier conflict with Aboriginal peoples was not perceived by settlers or their descendants to constitute war, as the conflict was irregular in nature and the scale of violence often concealed.[40] Federation in 1901 had also been a bureaucratic and bloodless affair, while a lack of romanticism and unease over controversial tactics meant the Boer War was unsuited for the purposes of a nation-building narrative.[41] The First World War instead filled this void. The gushing prose of British journalist Ellis Ashmead-Bartlett and the initiatives of Charles Bean as war correspondent and, later, Australia's official historian of the war, saw the invasion of the Gallipoli peninsula on 25 April 1915 as the 'birth place' of the Australian nation. Bean (among others) viewed the Anzacs as representative of an Australian national character: of a hardy people, shaped by the harsh Australian environment, who were loyal, capable in a crisis, and valued mateship.[42] The Anzac legend gained popular currency because, as historian Carolyn Holbrook points out, the glowing assessments that produced it were exactly what people wanted to hear.[43] The legend forged a national identity and provided the much-desired foundational myth, which afforded a sense of legitimacy to quash concerns over (white) Australia's origins as a British penal colony.

'Anzac' thus provides the prism through which Australians view their national identity and understand their martial history, to the extent that historian Ken Inglis has argued that the rituals, imagery and rhetoric of the Anzac legend constitute a 'civil religion' in Australia.[44] Reverence of the legend, however, has waxed, waned and shifted over the decades. Anzac fell into a dramatic decline in the 1960s and 1970s, a period that coincided with the maturation of the interwar generation and baby boomers (those with less tangible attachments to patriotic militarism and the world wars), the rise of the New Left protest movements, and increasing divisiveness over the Vietnam War.[45] The period also marked the decline of imperialism and British race patriotism in Australia, as Britain pulled away from the empire to prioritise engagement with Europe. For Australians, a people who had identified so intimately with the British race, Britain's decision to reorient its economic and strategic relationships precipitated what James Curran has labelled 'a crisis of national meaning'.[46] Anzac no longer defined national culture and identity, since the legend reflected increasingly antiquated British values of imperialism, racial science and militarism. This 'crisis' incited a period of introspection and a scramble for a new national sense of self.

The vacuum left by Anzac was not easily filled. Holbrook argues that the efforts of successive prime ministers, the Australia Council for the Arts, and generous investment in the arts and humanities failed to manufacture an adequate substitute.[47] Bill Gammage's *The Broken Years* (1974) and Patsy Adam-Smith's *The Anzacs* (1978) – influential social histories that personalised the service and sacrifice of Australia's soldiers – demonstrated a resurgent interest in war, but Peter Weir's 1981 film *Gallipoli* is generally considered the catalyst for Australia's new nationalism.[48] The film is surprisingly bereft of violence and battle scenes. Instead, the narrative follows two budding light horsemen through their journey to enlist and later as they are sent to fight on Gallipoli during the height of the campaign.

Weir's *Gallipoli*, and similar cinematic representations that followed, was so influential because of how it portrays Australians and the imperial relationship. The hardy, larrikin bushman of the ilk favoured by Bean makes a reappearance. This version of the Anzac is a striking contrast to representations of the British, who appear on screen as bungling, pompous and incompetent. The climax of the film is the disastrous charge at the Nek in August 1915; a clash Weir depicts as an instance of futility and needless sacrifice caused by inept and unsympathetic British officers. The representation is simplistic but, as film historian Daniel Reynaud argues, it glorified the Anzac legend in a new light and 'struck a responsive chord with the Australian public'.[49] Stuart Ward has furthered this argument to suggest that Weir's *Gallipoli* portrays Australian nationhood as born not in battle against the Ottomans or Germans, but as a reaction to obstinate British incompetence.[50] The influence of Weir's *Gallipoli* and similar popular culture and government initiatives saw Anzac reinvented to fit a new sense of Australian nationalism. Stripped of its imperial context, the legend was reformed into a foundational myth that symbolised increasing independence and scepticism of British imperialism.

Trauma, family history and the reshaping of the heroic narrative

The reshaping of the heroic narrative is a by-product of the revitalised Anzac legend. More specifically, though, it is connected to trauma theory and the rise of family history; both of which have been important in the resurgence of Anzac. Scholarly interest in war as a site of trauma and suffering, as well as clinical understandings of the physical and psychological effects of war, has assumed greater significance in recent decades. Since the 1970s, the psychiatric profession has sought to comprehend the traumatic effects of war on human psychology, which led to the seminal classification of post-traumatic stress disorder in the third edition of the *Diagnostic and Statistical Manual of Mental Disorders* published by the American Psychiatric Association in 1980.[51] War was, in both public and professional discourse, from then on increasingly understood to be a traumatic experience. Christina Twomey has connected this psychologising of war to understandings of Anzac, arguing that because of 'these changes to ideas about trauma and victimhood, the suffering of soldiers in war and the potential for them to be traumatised by it became a central trope in the public discussion of Anzac'.[52] War and Anzac were reconstrued not only to fit a new sense of nationalism but to conform to a narrative that emphasises conflict as a site of trauma and inherently construes the veteran as a victim.

The boom in family history since the 1980s has perpetuated the empathetic understanding of Australia's wartime past. Alistair Thomson observes that respondents to the contemporary incarnation of the Anzac legend are less inclined to engage in celebratory hero worship and more likely to pity the horrific experience of war.[53] Recent decades have seen a significant increase in the publication of wartime letters and diaries, as interest in genealogy has allowed family historians to explore and engage with the intimate and individual stories of their familial past.[54] Jay Winter argues that greater recognition of the traumatic effects of war facilitated this 'memory boom', as it sparked a curiosity to understand the history of that experience within families.[55] This has allowed family historians to draw a greater sense of self from the archival record. But they can also see their projects as being of national historical significance and their stories as deserving to be told. Holbrook suggests that the phenomenon often arises because family historians see evidence of suffering and war trauma within their forebear's experience.[56] Edward Lynch's wartime memoir *Somme Mud*, for instance, was published by the Lynch family in the lead up to the centenary because, as its editor Will Davies wrote, the account represents 'a literary time capsule' and offers a rare insight into the mateship, suffering and traumascape of war.[57] This is one of the more distinct legacies of the boom in family history: it has engendered a more intimate and individualistic understanding of war history.[58]

Trauma theory, the memory boom and understandings of veteran as victim have provoked a rethink as to what constitutes martial heroism in Australia. The original interpretation of the Anzac legend propagated a mythologising of the Australian soldier as a martial figure: one naturally skilled in combat and capable in war. The new nationalism of the 1980s, however, stripped Anzac of its militarism, while trauma theory rendered violence an uncomfortable facet of war. Former Australian Army officer Tony Vonthoff argues that the rise in victim narratives, coupled with the comparatively few Australian war deaths since Vietnam, has led to a popular disdain for martial violence and, thus, aggressive heroism. The result, Vonthoff suggests, is that individuals lauded for feats of violent, tactical courage – such as Albert Jacka, Arthur Blackburn and George Howell – have receded from popular memory, despite the esteem with which they were held in their own time.[59] That the number of monuments to, and books about, Australia's recipients of the VC have increased on a rather remarkable scale over the last two decades casts some doubt on Vonthoff's premise.[60] He does, however, have a point: the Australian media, and society more broadly, often downplay, disregard or sanitise the violence of the modern battlefield.[61]

Notions of humanitarianism, selflessness and sacrifice tend to be emphasised instead. This can be seen in the media reports on, and veneration of, contemporary martial heroes. Corporal Benjamin (Ben) Roberts-Smith, for example, was awarded the Victoria Cross for Australia (the successor to the VC in the Australian Honours System) for his heroism in rushing two machine gun posts and facilitating the demise of a third during an assault on a Taliban compound in Afghanistan in 2010.[62] His actions were reminiscent of First World War heroics, and, indeed, the media has attempted to connect Roberts-Smith with the 'Anzac tradition' and 'Anzac heroes' of old. News.com.au, for instance, compared the corporal to Albert Jacka, while Prime Minister Julia Gillard remarked that Roberts-Smith is now part of 'a greater tradition that binds all of us, a greater ... tradition called ANZAC'.[63] During this process, however, reports of Roberts-Smith's combat prowess have been sanitised. The violent and confronting nature of the battlefield have been moderated and his heroic image curated so that there has been minimal popular or media engagement with the aggressive nature of his deeds. Indeed, the combat fatigues Robert-Smith wore at the time of his heroic feat are on prominent display at the Australian War Memorial. His blood-stained running shoes, however, have been replaced by standard army boots.[64] There is an inherent assumption and acceptance that Roberts-Smith simply was heroic and that his feat was a selfless attempt to protect his 'mates'.[65] Understandings of war as traumatic have, thus, influenced Australian perceptions of war in such a way that these more comfortable and relatable virtues have come to dominate public understandings of martial heroism.

The emphasis on selflessness tends to conjure specific narratives of martial heroism: those of the compassionate soldier, the devoted carers for the sick and wounded, and self-sacrificing figures. Individuals, such as Gallipoli stretcher-bearer John Simpson Kirkpatrick, noted medical officers and prisoners of war Sir Edward 'Weary' Dunlop and Vivian Bullwinkel, and commander of the International Force East Timor (INTERFET) in 1999–2000, Sir Peter Cosgrove, have become well-known military figures because they represent the non-violent, selfless and humanitarian heroic narrative.[66] Attempts have even been made to incorporate Sir John Monash into this fold.

News reports towards the close of the centenary period ventured so far as to claim that the meticulous precision with which Monash planned battles were with a mind to minimising casualties.[67] This simplistic and ahistorical claim demonstrates the pervasiveness of the 'selfless' narrative.

The contemporary significance of humanitarianism, selflessness and sacrifice demarcates a reinvented and contemporary narrative of First World War heroism to which stretcher-bearers, like Frank Cahir, conform. That Cahir could be argued to be an archetype of this reshaped narrative is perhaps why he was such an attractive person to recognise almost a century later. Not only was he, as a stretcher-bearer, a selfless carer for the wounded, but he was also a victim of war. Cahir remained in Europe for three years after the end of the war, working with the Australian Graves Detachment to recover and bury the dead. In 1928, while working as a chemist's assistant in Melbourne, he poisoned himself. Cahir's death was ruled a suicide and attributed to his war service.[68]

Conclusion

Australian conceptions of martial heroism have experienced a dramatic shift since the First World War. Heroism during the war years was shaped by the demands of the battlefield and the British High Command. Victorian notions of bravery lingered until 1916, when by force and necessity it gave way to a paradigm of heroism that emphasised aggression, violence and tactical success. These were features of what can be considering 'war winning' heroics; acts that were intended to gain ground and reignite movement on the stagnant frontline of the Western Front. So doggedly did Sir Douglas Haig and his High Command pursue feats of aggressive, tactical heroics that, by 1918, ideas of heroism and masculinity in Australia were firmly centred on the combatant, almost to the exclusion of all others.

The violent and tactical paradigm, however, was not the version of heroism present in Australian First World War centennial commemorations. The reshaping of the Anzac legend to fit a new nationalism, coupled with the deeper understanding of war trauma and the boom in family history since the 1980s, have facilitated the rise of a heroic narrative that is at odds with that which existed during the First World War. The militarism and violence of the former have been stripped away to reveal a modern narrative that foremost values humanitarianism, selflessness and sacrifice. The shift to this form of martial heroism, one that prioritises more comfortable and relatable virtues, is understandable given the violent and confronting nature of war, and the detached manner in which the contemporary battlefield tends to be presented to the Australian public. It is, nevertheless, curious that the selfless and humanitarian narrative was incorporated into Australia's official centenary commemorations. The case of Frank Cahir, the campaigns to laud Sir John Monash, and the priority lent to individual tales of devotion and sacrifice represent a reinvention of the martial hero that existed between 1914 and 1918. The pattern is problematic, for it demon-strates an inadequate grasp of history and, at a national level, a disregard for the systems and processes in place a century ago. In attempting to reflect on its history, the Australian state overlooked more nuanced and critical means of engagement during the centenary period to instead insinuate a narrative of the First World War that embodies modern values.

Acknowledgements

This research was supported by an Australian Government Research Train-ing Program (RTP) Scholarship.

Notes

1 Recommendation for Staff Sergeant Frank Cahir, 15 September 1918, AWM28, 1/171 PART 2, Australian War Memorial, Canberra (hereafter AWM).
2 Paul Singer, 'Approved Gallantry Awards for Actions during World War I and II,' *Commonwealth of Australia Gazette*, no. C2017G00801, 17 July 2017.
3 Johnson, *Australians Awarded*, 115.
4 Ed Gardiner, 'Medal at Last for Preston Gallipoli Hero Frank Cahir,' *Herald Sun*, 18 October 2017, accessed 2 June 2019, https://www.heraldsun.com.au/leader/north/medal-at-last-for-preston-gallipoli-hero-frank-cahir/news-story/34d7e196c0b5643cb83608eef090762b; Madeline Slattery, 'Victorian WWI Dig-ger Awarded Posthumous Bravery Medal,' 9News.com.au, 18 October 2017, accessed 2 June 2019, https://www.9news.com.au/national/2017/10/18/21/24/victorian-wwi-digger-awarded-posthumous-bravery-medal.
5 Recommendation for Cahir.
6 For example, the AIF fielded at least 136 recommendations for the Victoria Cross during the First World War. Of that number, 63 received the award, 68 were downgraded to a lesser honour, and five received nothing at all. See Recom-mendation Files for Honours and Awards, AIF, 1914–18 War, AWM28, AWM.
7 Reynolds, *Unnecessary Wars*, 3.
8 See, for example: 'John Monash Should be Promoted to Field Marshal, Says Tim Fischer,' *Australian*, 28 July 2016, accessed 5 May 2019, https://www.theaustralian.com.au/news/nation/john-monash-should-be-promoted-to-field-marshal-says-tim-fischer/news-story/0c086c5a6ac63f06c67228d9f9187dba; Andrew Probyn and Matthew Doran, 'Sir John Monash Denied Field Marshal Promotion Despite Campaign Supported by Malcolm Turnbull,' *ABC News*, 18 April 2018, accessed 15 May 2019, https://www.abc.net.au/news/2018-04-18/sir-john-monash-denied-military-promotion-despite-campaign/9672990.
9 'Roll of Honour Name Projections,' Australian War Memorial website, accessed 15 May 2019, https://www.awm.gov.au/commemoration/honour-rolls/roll-honour-name-projections.
10 Strachan, *First World War*, 45.
11 'War Office, 23rd November, 1914,' *London Gazette*, 23 November 1914, 9663.
12 Arthur, *Symbol of Courage*, 193.
13 Smith, *Awarded for Valour*, 113.
14 Smith, *Awarded for Valour*, 96; Blanch and Pegram, *For Valour*, 4–28.
15 Said, *Orientalism*, 7–8, 31–73.
16 Smith, *Awarded for Valour*, 80–81.
17 Harris, *Douglas Haig and the First World War*, 184–85.

18 Major General William Peyton to Fourth Army Headquarters, 2 November 1916, AWM25, 391/2, AWM.
19 Jeffery, *1916*, 365–69.
20 Deputy Assistant Adjutant and Quartermaster General, 2nd Australian Division, to divisional sub-units, 29 August 1916, AWM25, 391/2, AWM.
21 Major General William Peyton to Second Army Headquarters, 29 September 1916, AWM25, 391/2, AWM.
22 D'Alton, 'Behind the Valour,' 125.
23 Bean, *Australian Imperial Force in France*, 1037–38; Recommendation for Second Lieutenant George Ingram, 27 October 1918, AWM28, 1/122 PART 2, AWM.
24 See Abraham, 'Valour in the Desert.'
25 Meyer, *Men of War*, 87–88.
26 Thomson, 'A Crisis of Masculinity?,' 137, 139.
27 See, for instance: Bassett, *Guns and Brooches*; and Harris, *More than Bombs and Bandages*.
28 Carr, quoted in Johnston, *Stretcher-Bearers*, 8–9.
29 Bishop, quoted in Alice Grant Rosman, 'South Australian Wounded in England,' *Advertiser* (Adelaide), 22 July 1915, 10.
30 Monash, for instance, wrote that 'the Stretcher-bearer service ... suffered exceedingly in its noble work ... and exposed itself unflinchingly to every danger.' Monash, *Australian Victories in France*, 287.
31 Butler, *Special Problems and Services*, 1045.
32 Beaumont, *Broken Nation*, 48–49, 103–09.
33 Robertson, 'Propaganda at Home (Australia).'
34 Robertson, 'Propaganda and "Manufactured Hatred,"' 246.
35 Jones, *Violence against Prisoners of War*, 38–39, 62–67.
36 Smart, '"Poor Little Belgium,"' 27–46; Saunders, '"The Stranger in Our Gates,"' especially 27–28, 35–36.
37 'Enlist in the Sportsmen's Thousand,' Sportsmen's Recruiting Committee, 1917, ARTV00026, AWM; 'Which? Man You Are Wanted!,' Sportsmen's Recruiting Committee, 1917, ARTV05005, AWM; Grant, *Jacka V.C.*, 25; Faulkner, *Arthur Blackburn, VC*, 120–29, 139; 'Sergt. Howell, V.C.,' *Western Champion* (Parkes, New South Wales), 13 June 1918, 23; Sergeant Howell, V.C. and M.M., *Lachlander and Condobolin District Recorder*, 5 June 1918, 4.
38 Scates, Frances, Reeves, et al, 'Anzac Day at Home and Abroad,' 523–31; Phillips, 'The Quiet Western Front,' 231–48.
39 Dawson, *Soldier Heroes*, 1; Berger, 'Introduction,' 5–6. See also McKenna, 'The History Anxiety,' 561–80.
40 Broome, 'Struggle for Australia,' 94–97; Connor, *Australian Frontier Wars*, 22; Inglis, *Australian Colonists*, 167.
41 Reynolds, *Unnecessary Wars*, 186–95; Holbrook, 'Nationalism and War Memory in Australia,' 220–21.
42 Holbrook, 'Nationalism and War Memory in Australia,' 222.
43 Holbrook, 'Nationalism and War Memory in Australia,' 222.
44 Inglis, *Sacred Places*, 458–71.
45 Twomey, 'Trauma and the Reinvigoration of Anzac,' 92–93; Holbrook, 'Nationalism and War Memory in Australia,' 227–28.
46 Curran, 'The "Thin Dividing Line,"' 469.
47 Holbrook, *Anzac*, 121–26.
48 Holbrook, *Anzac*, 137–42; Reynaud, *Celluloid Anzacs*, 183–84.
49 Reynaud, *Celluloid Anzacs*, 180. See also Bennett, 'Interpreting Anzac and Gallipoli,' 205–27.
50 Ward, 'A War Memorial in Celluloid,' 70–71.

51 Twomey, 'Trauma and the Reinvigoration of Anzac,' 105; Winter, 'Memory Boom in Contemporary Historical Studies,' 64.
52 Twomey, 'Trauma and the Reinvigoration of Anzac,' 106.
53 Thomson, *Anzac Memories*, 320.
54 Ziino, '"A Lasting Gift to His Descendants,"' 127; Holbrook and Ziino, 'Family History and the Great War,' 40.
55 Winter, 'Memory Boom in Contemporary Historical Studies,' 63–64.
56 Holbrook, 'Nationalism and War Memory in Australia,' 233.
57 Lynch, *Somme Mud*, x.
58 Holbrook and Ziino, 'Family History and the Great War,' 40–41.
59 Vonthoff, 'Military Heroism,' 35.
60 Stanley, 'Australian Heroes,' 202–06.
61 Brown, *Anzac's Long Shadow*, 4–5.
62 Blanch and Pegram, *For Valour*, 462; Masters, *No Front Line*, 338–41.
63 James Law, 'The Power of Ten,' *News.com.au*, 12 April 2015, accessed 12 September 2019, https://www.news.com.au/entertainment/tv/tv-shows/the-power-of-ten-the-heroes-ben-robertssmith-vc-looks-up-to/news-story/1e9c3b64bc9e282a16a6521652c44bf0; Gillard, quoted in 'Premier Pays Tribute to WA Hero,' *ABC News*, 24 January 2011, accessed 12 September 2019, https://www.abc.net.au/news/2011-01-23/premier-pays-tribute-to-wa-hero/1915586.
64 Brendan Nicholson, 'War Memorial Unveils Uniform of VC Feat of Corporal Ben Roberts-Smith,' *Australian*, 5 November 2013, accessed 20 October 2019, https://www.theaustralian.com.au/national-affairs/defence/war-memorial-unveils-uniform-of-vc-feat-of-corporal-ben-roberts-smith/news-story/af577f9e6ba5de85539054c71b092c40.
65 'Victoria Cross Winner Ben Roberts-Smith,' *Daily Telegraph* (Sydney), 24 February 2012, accessed 12 September 2019, https://www.dailytelegraph.com.au/victoria-cross-winner-ben-roberts-smith-a-doting-dad-deadly-warrior/news-story/e1b1e97819ee28e9325a41a17173a478?sv=86e0271670693ad9c052e73aa11f1f0f.
66 Vonthoff, 'Military Heroism,' 35–36.
67 See, for example, 'John Monash Should be Promoted to Field Marshal'; Greg Ray, 'The Centenary of the Battle of Hamel: From Weston to the Western Front,' *Newcastle Herald*, 4 July 2018, accessed 20 May 2019, https://www.theherald.com.au/story/5500859/from-weston-to-the-western-front/.
68 Geof Maslen, 'A Grim Duty on a Foreign Field,' *Sydney Morning Herald*, 30 November 2010, accessed 12 May 2019, https://www.smh.com.au/education/a-grim-duty-on-a-foreign-field-20101129-18dp0.html.

Bibliography

Abraham, Bryce. "Valour in the Desert: A Critical Examination of the Victoria Cross and Heroic Construct in the Palestine Campaign, 1916–1918." Honours thesis, University of Newcastle, 2014.

Arthur, Max. *Symbol of Courage: The Men Behind the Medal*. London: Pan Books, 2005.

Bassett, Jan. *Guns and Brooches: Australian Army Nursing from the Boer War to the Gulf War*. Melbourne: Oxford University Press, 1992.

Bean, Charles. *The Australian Imperial Force in France during the Allied Offensive, 1918*. Vol. 6 of *Official History of Australia in the War of 1914–1918*. Sydney: Angus & Robertson, 1942.

Beaumont, Joan. *Broken Nation: Australians in the Great War*. Crows Nest: Allen & Unwin, 2013.

Bennett, James E. "Interpreting Anzac and Gallipoli through a Century of Anglophone Screen Representations." In *A Companion to Australian Cinema*, edited by Felicity Collins, Jane Landman, and Susan Bye, 205–27. Hoboken: Wiley-Blackwell, 2019.

Berger, Stefan. "Introduction: Towards a Global History of National Historiographies." In *Writing the Nation: A Global Perspective*, edited by Stefan Berger, 1–29. New York: Palgrave Macmillan, 2007.

Blanch, Craig and Aaron Pegram. *For Valour: Australians Awarded the Victoria Cross.* Sydney: NewSouth Publishing, 2018.

Broome, Richard. "The Struggle for Australia: Aboriginal–European Warfare, 1770–1930." In *Australia: Two Centuries of War and Peace*, edited by Michael McKernan and Margaret Browne, 92–120. Canberra: Australian War Memorial, 1988.

Brown, James. *Anzac's Long Shadow: The Cost of Our National Obsession.* Collingwood: Redback, 2014.

Butler, A.G. *Special Problems and Services.* Vol. 3 of *Official History of the Australian Army Medical Services, 1914–1918.* Canberra: Australian War Memorial, 1943.

Connor, John. *The Australian Frontier Wars, 1788–1838.* Sydney: University of New South Wales Press, 2002.

Curran, James. "The 'Thin Dividing Line' Prime Ministers and the Problem of Australian Nationalism, 1972–1996." *Australian Journal of Politics and History* 48, no. 4 (2002): 469–86.

D'Alton, Victoria. "Behind the Valour: A Technical, Administrative and Bureaucratic Analysis of the Victoria Cross and the AIF on the Western Front, 1916–1918." MA thesis, University of New South Wales, 2010.

Dawson, Graham. *Soldier Heroes: British Adventure, Empire and the Imagining of Masculinities.* London: Routledge, 1994.

Faulkner, Andrew. *Arthur Blackburn, VC: An Australian Hero, His Men, and Their Two World Wars.* Kent Town: Wakefield Press, 2008.

Grant, Ian. *Jacka V.C.: Australia's Finest Fighting Soldier.* South Melbourne: Macmillan, 1982.

Harris, J. Paul. *Douglas Haig and the First World War.* Cambridge: Cambridge University Press, 2008.

Harris, Kirsty. *More than Bombs and Bandages: Australian Army Nurses at Work in World War I.* Newport: Big Sky Publishing, 2011.

Holbrook, Carolyn. *Anzac: The Unauthorised Biography.* Sydney: NewSouth Publishing, 2014.

Holbrook, Carolyn. "Nationalism and War Memory in Australia." In *Australia and the Great War: Identity, Memory and Mythology*, edited by Michael J.K. Walsh and Andrekos Varnava, 218–39. Carlton: Melbourne University Press, 2016.

Holbrook, Carolyn and Bart Ziino. "Family History and the Great War in Australia." In *Remembering the First World War*, edited by Bart Ziino, 39–55. New York: Routledge, 2015.

Inglis, Ken. *The Australian Colonists: An Exploration of Social History, 1788–1870.* Carlton: Melbourne University Press, 1974.

Inglis, Ken. *Sacred Places: War Memorials in the Australian Landscape.* Carlton South: Miegunyah Press, 1998.

Jeffery, Keith. *1916: A Global History.* London: Bloomsbury, 2015.

Johnson, Clive. *Australians Awarded: A Concise Guide to Military and Civilian Decorations, Medals and Other Awards to Australians from 1772 to 2013 with Their Valuations*. 2nd ed. Banksmeadow: Renniks Publications, 2014.

Johnston, Mark. *Stretcher-Bearers: Saving Australians from Gallipoli to Kokoda*. Port Melbourne: Cambridge University Press, 2015.

Jones, Heather. *Violence Against Prisoners of War in the First World War: Britain, France and Germany, 1914–1920*. Cambridge: Cambridge University Press, 2011.

Lynch, Edward. *Somme Mud: The War Experiences of an Infantryman in France, 1916–1919*. Edited by Will Davies. Milsons Point: Random House Australia, 2006.

Masters, Chris. *No Front Line: Australia's Special Forces at War in Afghanistan*. Crows Nest: Allen & Unwin, 2017.

McKenna, Mark. "The History Anxiety." In *The* Commonwealth *of Australia*. Vol. 2 of *The Cambridge History of Australia*, edited by Alison Bashford and Stuart Macintyre, 561–80. Port Melbourne: Cambridge University Press, 2013.

Meyer, Jessica. *Men of War: Masculinity and the First World War in Britain*. Basingstoke: Palgrave Macmillan, 2011.

Monash, John. *The Australian Victories in France in 1918*. 1920. Reprint, Collingwood: Black Inc, 2015.

Phillips, Jock. "The Quiet Western Front: The First World War and New Zealand Memory." In *Race, Empire and First World War Writing*, edited by Santanu Das, 231–48. Cambridge: Cambridge University Press, 2011.

Reynaud, Daniel. *Celluloid Anzacs: The Great War through Australian Cinema*. Melbourne: Australian Scholarly Publishing, 2007.

Reynolds, Henry. *Unnecessary Wars*. Sydney: NewSouth Publishing, 2016.

Robertson, Emily. "Propaganda and 'Manufactured Hatred:' A Reappraisal of the Ethics of First World War British and Australian Propaganda." *Public Relations Inquiry* 3, no. 2 (2014): 245–66.

Robertson, Emily. "Propaganda at Home (Australia)." In 1914–1918-online, *International Encyclopaedia of the First World War*, edited by Ute Daniel, Peter Gatrell, Oliver Janz, Heather Jones, Jennifer Keene, Alan Kramer, and Bill Nasson. Berlin: Freie Universität Berlin, 2015. doi: 10.15463/ie1418.

Said, Edward. *Orientalism*. London: Penguin Classics, 2003.

Saunders, Kay. "'The Stranger in Our Gates:' Internment Policies in the United Kingdom and Australia during the Two World Wars." *Immigrants & Minorities* 22, no. 1 (2003): 22–43.

Scates, Bruce, Rae Frances, Keir Reeves, et al. "Anzac Day at Home and Abroad: Towards a History of Australia's National Day." *History Compass* 10, no. 7 (2012): 523–31.

Smart, Judith. "'Poor Little Belgium' and Australian Popular Support for War, 1914–1915." *War & Society* 12, no. 1 (1994): 27–46.

Smith, Melvin Charles. *Awarded for Valour: A History of the Victoria Cross and the Evolution of British Heroism*. New York: Palgrave Macmillan, 2008.

Stanley, Peter. "Australian Heroes: Some Military Mates Are More Equal Than Others." In *The Honest History Book*, edited by David Stephens and Alison Broinowski, 196–210. Sydney: NewSouth Publishing, 2017.

Strachan, Hew. *The First World War*. London: Simon & Schuster, 2014.

Thomson, Alistair. "A Crisis of Masculinity? Australian Military Manhood in the Great War." In *Gender and War: Australians at War in the Twentieth Century*, edited by Joy Damousi and Marilyn Lake, 133–47. Cambridge: Cambridge University Press, 1995.

Thomson, Alistair. *Anzac Memories: Living with the Legend.* 2nd ed. Clayton: Monash University Press, 2013.

Twomey, Christina. "Trauma and the Reinvigoration of Anzac: An Argument." *History Australia* 10, no. 3 (2013): 85–108.

Vonthoff, Tony. "Military Heroism: An Australian Perspective." *Australian Defence Force Journal* 169 (2005): 33–39.

Ward, Stuart. "A War Memorial in Celluloid: The Gallipoli Legend in Australian Cinema, 1940s–1980s." In *Gallipoli: Making History*, edited by Jenny Macleod, 59–72. London: Frank Cass, 2004.

Winter, Jay. "The Memory Boom in Contemporary Historical Studies." *Raritan* 21, no. 1 (2001): 52–66.

Ziino, Bart. "'A Lasting Gift to His Descendants:' Family Memory and the Great War in Australia." *History and Memory* 22, no. 2 (2010): 125–46.

3 The first time he felt truly Australian

Anzac sport and Australian nationalism, 1995 – today

Xavier Fowler

Introduction

The resurgence of the Anzac legend in the Australian commemorative landscape has been nothing short of cultural phenomenon. Anzac, a derivation of the military acronym ANZAC (Australian and New Zealand Army Corps), connotes the concept that Australian soldiers possessed a set of venerable characteristics that made them ideal soldiers during the First World War. Not to be consigned to this moment in history, the qualities they exhibited were said to have revealed a distinctive Australian character and identity to the world.[1] As war correspondent and official historian, Charles Bean, proclaimed in 1924, 'it was on the 25th of April, 1915, that the consciousness of the Australian nationhood was born.'[2] Particularly since the 1980s, Australia becomes awash with commemorative activities and rituals each Anzac Day. Military services and parades, newspaper tributes, film and television productions, political speeches, pilgrimages to former battlefields and other commemorative activities, all seek to pay homage to its service personal both past and present.[3] By recognising the achievements of their ancestors as innately linked to the nation itself, contemporary citizens are encouraged to hold confidence in the worth of their shared identity.

Australia's cultural obsession with sport, too, has assisted in Anzac's proliferation of patriotic backslapping.[4] Eric Hobsbawm has commented on sport's powerful ability to generate partisanship, wherein even those who do nothing more than cheer from the sidelines act as 'symbols of their nation.'[5] This holds great sway in Australia, where sport's influence was so powerful it is believed to have soothed inter-colonial tensions and paved the way for political Federation in 1901.[6] Accordingly, the 'particular affinity' with which the contemporary sporting community has embraced Anzac sits comfortably with its connection to modern Australian nationalism.[7] In 2015, Kevin Sheedy, the father of the Australian Football League's (AFL) Anzac Day match, even designated the League as the 'vehicle' by which to educate the nation on its historical involvement in the war.[8] Through this popular commemorative tool, many have come to appreciate the central role sport played in creating the Anzac legend, the birth of the nation and the Australian identity.

The congratulatory tone of the occasion aside, the perceived connection between sport and Australia's experience of the First World War stands in stark contrast to the reality of the past. Sport during those tumultuous years possessed the ability to divide with as great a strength as it did to unite, offering a window into the kind of social conflict that characterised Australia's war. This chapter, therefore, contains a thorough comparison of the sporting community's contemporary efforts to integrate itself into the Anzac legend with the troubling impact sport had on national unity between 1914 and 1918. In doing so, it illuminates the potentially harmful consequences of leaving such ill-informed amalgamations unchecked, namely, the continued propagation of an archaic and narrow conceptualisation of the national identity. That modern Anzac sporting fixtures are organised with the sincerest of intentions is not disputed. Nevertheless, their inspection is crucial, given sport has become one of the primary means by which Australians access their memory of a war that has defined so much of what they understand about themselves and the nation they inhabit.[9]

Anzac day sport and 'New Nationalism'

Sport's relationship with Australia's commemoration of the First World War has followed a long, yet inconsistent, path since 1915. Athletic contests among soldiers were, among other things, a popular form of honouring fallen comrades during the war itself.[10] Instead of adhering to this precedent, however, the post-war period saw the emergence of competing interpretations of appropriate memorialisation. Several Australian states even went so far as to outlaw sport on Anzac Day in order to preserve the solemnity of the occasion. Pressure from ex-service organisations in search of a brighter commemorative day eventually overturned these laws, and by the 1960s, organised sport commonly featured on Anzac Day.[11] For example, the Victorian Football League (VFL) played 29 times on Anzac Day between 1960 and 1994.[12] Besides playing of the Last Post, however, these matches were rather routine affairs. Attendances were spasmodic, and the commemorative rituals and theatrics of later fixtures were, for the most part, absent.[13] Football's tentative forays into Anzac during these years, in fact, reflected wider society's apathy towards war commemoration, particularly in the aftermath of the Holocaust, the Vietnam War, the rise of the civil rights movement and the widening gap between baby boomers and the Great War generation.[14]

Yet, after going into what appeared to be a state of terminal decline, the 1980s spawned the 'second coming' of Anzac,[15] and with it the dawn of Anzac Day sport. The reason behind this resurgence has been debated by historians ever since. However, building on the work of Mark McKenna and Ken Inglis,[16] Carolyn Holbrook has compellingly argued that Anzac's revival rode the wave of 'New Nationalism' back to the shoreline of the national conscious. The slow disintegration of Australia's economic, political and cultural ties with Britain during the latter half of the twentieth century forced it into a state of radical introspection. From this emerged a new collective identity, one shed of its antiquated imperialist, militant, misogynistic and racist pillars in favour of a more cautious and inclusive nationalism, wary of its 'chest-thumping' variant.[17] Anzac proved surprisingly adaptable to this new mood. Bill Gammage's *The Broken Years* (1974) and Peter Weir's extraordinarily successful 1981 film, *Gallipoli*, highlighted the tragedy, sacrifice and, somewhat misleadingly in the case of the latter, progressive outlook of the original Anzacs. Australians were thus afforded the basis for a national myth they had been seeking since the decline of British race patriotism in the 1960s. Embraced by the public and politicians ever since, the dominant interpretation of Anzac in contemporary Australian society is closely attached to a form of subdued martial nationalism.[18]

With a more palatable basis of national identity established, the AFL's 1995 Essendon vs. Collingwood match sparked the turning point in sport's eventual integration into Anzac. The Keating government's 1995 'Australia Remembers' campaign, according to Melissa Walsh, fuelled the AFL's desire to establish a trademark fixture on Anzac Day.[19] Championed by Sheedy, the Essendon coach and former national service participant, a match was scheduled between the two clubs in order to honour Australian service personnel. The fixture struck a chord with a receptive public. Almost 95,000 spectators crammed into the Melbourne Cricket Ground (MCG), with 10,000 to 20,000 more locked outside the ground and forcibly dispersed by mounted police, where they moved to the Fitzroy gardens to listen to the game on their radios.[20] Impressed by the fixture's success, the AFL quickly moved to secure it permanently on its annual calendar. The Anzac Day match, or 'clash' as it would come to be known, has since retained all the structural rules and codes of conduct that govern regular matches, yet it is the accompaniment of idiosyncratic ceremonial activities and rituals that make the match a unique occasion. Many of these activities reflect a sombre memorialisation of the suffering experienced during wars in which Australia has participated. The two teams enter the playing field through a shared banner, prioritising the shared commitment to honouring the Anzac legend over the triviality of on-field rivalries. This is followed by the lining up of each team for a military procession, which includes the playing of the Last Post, the reciting of the Ode, and a minute's silence for the fallen, all customs borrowed from British and Australian military funeral traditions.[21]

The dawn of the millennium, however, proved to be a major turning point in the tone of the clash, from restrained solemnity to nationalistic spectacle, reflecting what McKenna has viewed as the wider transformation of Anzac Day toward a moment of 'celebratory' patriotism under the Howard government (1996–2007).[22] This form of Australian exceptionalism manifests itself most evocatively through the fashioning of modern footballers as the proud inheritors of the Anzac spirit. An example of this was the introduction of the Anzac Medal, awarded to the player who best exudes those qualities associated with the Anzacs, namely: skill, courage, sacrifice, teamwork and fair play.[23] The media eagerly contributes to this conceptualisation of the footballer as the reincarnation of its military forbearer. Robert Pascoe's research into press coverage of the Anzac Day clash highlights how tabloid papers such as the *Herald Sun*, with their reliance on sensationalist rhetoric, lavishly portray footballers as personifying the Anzac spirit.[24] Yet, even the understated coverage of *The Age* newspaper reveals that it, too, has succumbed to propagating hyperbolic comparisons. A 2001 match report described a valiant Collingwood that lost narrowly to rivals Essendon, through the lens of the Gallipoli story: 'Like the original Anzacs, it established a beachhead, but could not quite push on to a memorable victory.'[25]

Players and club officials soon became influenced by the martial rhetoric and symbolism of Anzac Day football. Though admissions are made of the incompatibility of war and sport, competitors regularly reveal a subliminal belief in their kinship with the original Anzacs. Coaches looking for motivational tools for their players fostered this mode of thought. Essendon captain, James Hird, spoke of Sheedy's ability to gather the 'ghosts of all the diggers [soldiers]' and bring them to the MCG.[26] His opposition coach, Mick Malthouse, adopted similar mechanisms, screening for his players Weir's *Gallipoli* and taking them to the Shrine of Remembrance before the 2000 clash.[27] Of course, their ability to live up to the legacy of Anzac was often determined by the result of the contest itself. After surrendering a 14-point lead late in the 2009 clash, an incensed Malthouse remarked that his club had 'let the Anzacs down'. In contrast, a victorious Essendon player beamed with pride in his team's determination to never give up on the contest, just like the Anzacs.[28] That both comparisons came in the immediate aftermath of the game's conclusion, wherein exhaustion erodes player inhibition and the directives of public relations departments, speaks to the sincerity with which they were delivered.

The amalgamation of soldier and football heroes has led promoters to declare the clash as emblematic of a distinctively venerable Australian identity. The game of Australian Rules football provides a palatable setting in which the ingredients of sport, war and nationalism are successfully conflated. Traditionally popular in Australia's southern and western states, an aggressive expansion policy implemented during the 1980s saw the game go truly national, with regular fixtures now played in all eight Australian states and territories.[29] Moreover, while its status as an exclusively Australian game prevents 'Aussie rules' functioning as a vehicle to gauge superiority over rival countries, its distinctiveness affords it claim to being truly representative of the national culture. This was on display in the lead up to the 2001 Anzac clash, when Collingwood President, Eddie McGuire, remarked 'they (war veterans) will see the reason why they fought so hard for the Australian culture with two great tribes going at each other.'[30] The inclusive spirit of New

Nationalism was also discernible in the ceremonial activities pre-game. After the 1995 and 1997 clashes were marred by incidents of racial vilification of Indigenous players, the AFL organised a procession of Aboriginal war veterans to march around the oval, wherein they received long-awaited recognition of their contribution to the defence of the nation.[31] In the space of only a few years, Anzac football had become not merely a 'vehicle' for honouring Australian service personnel and educating the nation about its military history but a celebration of Australia itself. As the journalist Mark Robinson remarked on Anzac Day 2002, '... it's not just a footy game. It's bigger than that. It's something that encompasses everything great about our country and its people.'[32]

Inspired by Anzac Day football's success other sporting competitions moved to get in on the act, with nationalism invariably swimming in its wake. Expressions of patriotism commonly associated with Anzac sport are, in fact, heightened when applied to nationally representative contests. It is in this international setting that the uniqueness of the Australian character can be displayed and tested against foreign competitors, just as it had during the war. In particular, the Australian men's cricket team under captain Steve Waugh embraced the nationalism inherent with Anzac. In 2001, it participated in what can only be described as a pilgrimage to the trenches of Gallipoli. While there, the team was photographed wearing Anzac-styled slouch hats and war medals, before it re-created the famous photo of Australian soldiers playing a cricket match on Shell Green. The players appeared overwhelmed by the emotional significance of the trip, with some describing it as life changing and others brought to tears.[33] Although the intense reaction of the team had much to do with the scale of life lost there, it was evident that tales of the distinguished performance of the Australian soldiers had also aroused the team members' patriotic sensibilities. Wade Seccombe expressed admiration for the soldiers who had 'forged our identity', while Ricky Ponting remarked the trip had made him 'feel proud to be Australian.' Reflecting on the experience, Waugh expressed hope his players would be inspired by the exceptionality of the national character established at Gallipoli for its upcoming tour of England:

> Everybody talks about the Anzac spirit. To me, it means being together, fighting together and looking after your mates. These are Australian values, which I want the Australian cricket team to always carry.[34]

The world of rugby also sought to fan the flames of patriotism, albeit under commercial motivations. In 1997, the newly created rugby Super League competition held an 'Anzac Test' between representative teams from New Zealand and Australia. Adopting a format that seemingly expressed the shared bond between soldiers from the Trans-Tasman region, marketing efforts instead utilised crude, albeit light-hearted, appeals to partisan loyalties, 'Australia is still in grave danger from our so-called neighbours.

The Kiwis were once our allies and now they're on the other side – at least for 80 minutes.'[35]

The power of this paradigm was so influential government institutions charged with promoting war memory appropriated it. In 2006, the Australian War Memorial, with funding from the Australian Sports Commission, created a travelling exhibition to tell the stories of the importance of sport to Australians serving overseas, as well as the wartime experiences of some of most loved sporting stars. The importance of honouring the connection between sport and war remained essential, according to the exhibition's webpage, for their amalgamation occupied an integral part of what it meant to be Australian:

> Qualities we associate with both sport and war – courage, teamwork, leadership, physical prowess, mateship, loyalty – are readily seen to be fundamental part [sic] of the "Australian identity"... Both activities have determined not just how Australians see themselves, but how the world sees them.[36]

Propelled by the amiable force of New Nationalism, sport's domination of Australia's memory of the First World War reached its zenith in 2015, the 100th anniversary of the Gallipoli landings. Coincidentally falling on a Saturday, the day provided fans with an orgy of Anzac-inspired sporting fixtures, including five National Rugby League (NRL) matches, two Super Rugby Union matches, two A-League soccer matches, the Tans-Tasman Netball Grand Final and numerous horseracing meets. The AFL, meanwhile, broadcast 12 straight hours of live football on paid and free-to-air television.[37] There are endless expressions of First World War memorialisation that arise each Anzac Day, however, it is sport that most successfully integrated itself into what Inglis describes as the 'civic religion' of Australia.[38] The patriotic connotations of these fixtures certainly peaked during the Howard years. Nevertheless, Anzac sport continued to provide assurance to Australians as to the worth of their national culture, identity and place in the world as they moved through the centenary years. As former Australian rules footballer, Jude Bolton, remarked on Anzac Day eve 2017, '[a] dawn service, through to Two-Up at a pub or RSL [Returned Service League] to a sporting match. It's very Australian.'[39]

Historical assimilation via 'selective memory'

Despite the popularity of these fixtures, questions have emerged about the sporting fraternity's legitimacy in assimilating itself so closely into Anzac Day and the Anzac legend. To validate sport's appropriation of such a culturally sacred entity,[40] athletes and administrators point to the special role sport played in supporting Australia's war effort, namely, its endless contribution of soldiers. In 2011, the NRL rolled out Victoria Cross recipient

Corporal Ben Roberts-Smith to promote that year's Anzac Cup. Smith sanctioned the match because, '[a]ll elite sportsmen used to volunteer because they thought it was their duty.'[41] These and other remarks are not entirely without substance. The premier NSW Rugby Union competition was forced to disband in 1915 when 97% of its players enlisted,[42] while 750 current and former VFL players and almost 3,000 Victorian cricketers joined the Australian Imperial Force during the conflict.[43] Furthermore, specially created Sportsmen's Recruiting Committees implored unenlisted men to 'show the enemy what Australian sporting men can do.'[44] Nor did the contribution of sport to the war effort stop once the men enlisted. It was also widely believed that Australia's proclivity towards games contributed to their famed prowess as soldiers. Reports from Gallipoli labelled Australian soldiers as 'a race of athletes', a title that helped to depict Australians as a unique, and superior, type of warrior.[45] In a less spectacular, yet more plausible sense, sport also became integral to keeping soldiers fit, building *esprit de corps* within units, and providing a release for tension while awaiting deployment to the frontline.[46]

Contemporary sports' impressive historical claim to Anzac Day, however, bases itself on a half-truth at best. Not only did Australian soldiers find their sporting skills counted for nought in the face of relentless artillery barrages and machine-gun fire, academic research has uncovered a significant amount of national division over the appropriateness of sport on the home front during the war. Civilian patriots and government officials complained that, rather than aiding soldiers' efforts, spectator sport distracted young men from enlisting while simultaneously consuming public finances better spent on the war effort. These criticisms usually emerged from the Protestant middle-class, who maintained stronger links with Britain and, therefore, had higher expectations of civic loyalty to Empire. Their sports, including tennis, golf and rugby union, had been largely abandoned by 1915 so that members could focus their attention on defence of the motherland. In contrast, the Irish-Catholic and working classes defended the continuation of spectator sports, such as prize fighting and rugby league, as a necessary distraction for a population overburdened by the pressures of total war. These two views, which reflected wider class and ethnic conflict, clashed with a severe ferocity during the war years.[47]

However, the game that provoked the most acute turmoil, ironically, was the one that makes the strongest contemporary claim over Anzac Day. The playing of Australian Rules football during the war incited considerable animosity toward the popular winter game.[48] One prominent private school educator proposed giving Iron Crosses to unenlisted footballers for their refusal to enlist, while recruiting agencies hung posters at the MCG asking crowds 'Will they never come?'[49] As citizens on either end of the social hierarchy played the game, the campaign against football also threatened to split it from within. The Western Australian Football League's attempt to disband competition almost ended in the Supreme Court after a challenge from several clubs.[50] Meanwhile, the VFL, forerunner competition to the AFL, incited considerable discord because of its determination to continue play during the war. It voted on three separate occasions on whether or not to suspend its fixtures, culminating in the decision by more than half its clubs to withdraw from the 1916 season. The League became embroiled in further controversy in 1917 after it was revealed that the remaining clubs failed to hand over promised profits to the patriotic fund. After several patrons violently attacked recruiting officers at matches the following weekend, the League not only faced the contempt of the patriotic press but also forcible curtailment by the State War Council.[51]

Despite Sheedy's designation of the Anzac clash as an educational 'vehicle' to help modern Australians understand their nation's experience of the war, the AFL has made little mention of its own scandalous history, even moving to cover up the stain of these events in order to protect the integrity of the Anzac fixture. In 1996, when the commercial potential of the clash was yet to be fully realised, the AFL commissioned a history of the competition entitled *100 years of Australian Football*. It spoke openly about the conflict between the VFL and the war effort, as well as the unpopularity of the game among patriots. This turmoil was framed within the wider context of the social division that gripped Australia during the war.[52] Twelve years later, and with the Anzac clash firmly established as a profitable cornerstone of the AFL calendar, it produced another history titled *The Australian Game of Football*. A celebratory publication released in conjunction with the game's 150th anniversary, it barely acknowledged the turmoil the game created during the war, instead rejoicing in its players' enlistment. The considerable outpouring of scorn against the game, meanwhile, was brushed aside as 'rare'.[53]

This careful management of football's wartime image fits neatly with Walsh's understanding of Anzac Day football as an exercise in remembrance that operates through 'strategic remembering and forgetting'. In this, Walsh refers specifically to the AFL's designation of the Anzac Day clash as a new tradition that begun in 1995, when in fact football had been played on Anzac Day long beforehand.[54] Yet the Anzac match as an example of 'strategic remembering and forgetting' can be seen to contribute to the AFL's, and for that matter wider Australian sport's, calculated decision to re-invent and manage its wartime image, one that aligns closely with popular conceptions of the Anzac legend and the war as a nation-making event. This process of selective memory has frustrated the historian Ian Syson, not only because of the AFL's desire to modify the past for the sake of cultural capital, but because it cowers at the opportunity to take pride in its predecessors' refusal to submit entirely to the bidding of Australia's Imperial overlords.[55] In many ways, the sporting community's distortion of the past mirrors Australia's general ignorance of the First World War as an event that tore at the social fabric of the country for the sake of a more comforting tale of triumphant nationalism.

The limits of New Nationalism

The infusion of sport, Anzac and a carefully doctored sense of Australian nationalism facilitates developments far more distasteful than mere historical misinterpretation. The New Nationalism that modern conceptions of Anzac bases its popularity upon sought to distance Australia from its traditional racist, militaristic and violent underpinnings. However, these anachronistic values have proved exceedingly hard to shake. Despite Inglis's assertion that multi-cultural participation with Anzac has been normalised,[56] a closer observation of Anzac's integration with sport reveals traces of its archetypically Anglo-centric foundations lingering below the surface of its more inclusive language. During the Australian men's 2001 cricket pilgrimage to Gallipoli, Patrick Farhart, the team's physio and son of Lebanese immigrants, conceded that the emotional visit generated his first occurrence of feeling 'truly Australian'.[57] Sport provided Farhart with a long-awaited sense of belonging to the country of his birth but could only do so through the 'Australian' prism of Anzac, and not on his own cultural heritage.

In fact, Anzac sport not only reveals enduring expectations of assimilation with Anglo-Australian identity, it also reinforces it. In the lead up to the 2002 Anzac Day match, it was reported that Collingwood footballer Alan Didak had supported Goran Ivanisevic in the 2001 Wimbledon tennis final against the Australian Pat Rafter, because of their shared Croatian heritage. In response, Mark Stevens of the *Herald Sun* reassured his audience that the young star would be 'charged with the Aussie spirit' come Anzac Day.[58] Didak's inclusion within the Australian identity came at the cost of conforming to a select expectation of what constitutes a true Australian, one that grants little allowance for dual loyalties or identity.[59] The expectation of adherence to this homogenised identity even facilitates a possessive element over Anzac Day, one that infers nation-based ownership of the occasion to the exclusion of all foreign entities. Collingwood's decision to invite Emirates Chairman Sheik Ahmed bin Saeed Al Maktoum to partake in the 2002 Anzac clash's pre-match entertainment proved a serious affront to Chief *Herald Sun* football writer Mike Sheahan. The offence occurred not only due to its commercial exploitation of Anzac but because the gesture symbolically handed the most sacred of national occasions to an outsider: 'Today is Anzac Day, and it belongs to Australia and Australians... there is nothing more Australian than Anzac Day. Nothing.'[60] The First World War may have been a global affair, but for those involved in Anzac sport, it is often remembered through a strictly national, usually Anglo, lens.

Nor has New Nationalism been entirely able to throw off Anzac's traditional affiliation with militancy. In the turbulence of the post 9/11 world, historians observed the incorporation of the Anzac legend into political rhetoric about the nation's involvement in modern conflicts. Addressing Australian troops at Baghdad airport on Anzac Day 2004, Prime Minister

Howard informed his audience they were the custodians of a long tradition of martial righteousness. 'You are seeking to bring to the people of Iraq', Howard proclaimed, 'the hope of liberty and freedom, and your example, your behaviour, your values, belong to the great and long tradition that was forged on the beaches of Gallipoli in 1915.'[61] There has been a significant level of apprehension about this kind of political rhetoric. Marilyn Lake and Henry Reynolds have expressed concerns that politicians, shielded by the inviolability of the Anzac legend, have become free to commit Australian troops to new conflicts without critical appraisal of their justification for doing so. They question whether Anzac has fostered a militarisation of Australian history and society that can, if deemed necessary, promote hyper-nationalism, possibly even jingoism.[62] Mervyn F. Bendle has brushed aside these concerns as merely the attacks of 'determined ideologues of the far-Left.'[63] Nevertheless, there is significant evidence to conclude an Anzac sport-induced level of passivity, and on occasion support, for Australia's most recent military excursion abroad.

In 2003, amidst the growing noise from the American government of the need to intervene militarily against Saddam Hussein's regime, AFL footballer Robert Murphy painted "No War" on his arm for the official team photo.[64] Murphy had wanted to make show of solidarity with the worldwide anti-war protests staged on 14 February.[65] While the matter went largely unnoticed at the time, the announcement that Australian Special Forces had begun operations in Iraq prompted the AFL to gag its players from making further statements on the war. Andrew Demetriou, the League's Operations Manager, announced: 'whatever players decide to do in their private lives, regarding the war or any other stand is fine, but they can't display it on the field.' Demetriou justified the decision on his belief that the sport and politics should be separate from one another. The football field, Demetriou explained, was 'almost sacred' and a place for people to 'forget about some of the troubled things that happen in the world.' Journalists queried why Demetriou supported other political protests in the sports arena, including the stand Zimbabwean cricketer's Andy Flower and Henry Olonga took against the oppressive tendencies of Robert Mugabe's regime, as well as Nicky Winmar's show of defiance against racial discrimination of Indigenous footballers, the latter of which Demetriou described as 'one of the most powerful things I've ever seen on a football field.' That the AFL's opening round was scheduled to promote World Harmony Day only added to the confusion surrounding the matter. Responding to these queries, Demetriou became noticeably defensive and attempted to shift moral outrage back onto the journalists, saying 'what you're trying to do is link it in some way, I almost find it distasteful.'[66]

While stopping short of declaring his own position on the war, Eddie McGuire proposed the League send a message of support to the Australian soldiers now committed to fighting. The motion was passed unanimously by every club President and CEO as well as the AFL Commission itself.

However, the failure to release this statement as promised prompted criticism from 3AW disc jockey, Neil Mitchell, who implied the AFL had not been proactive enough in supporting Australia's troops. Sensitive to this criticism, the League eventually released a carefully written statement wishing its soldiers a safe return, while never mentioning the words 'War' or 'Iraq'.[67] The AFL was clearly unwilling to make a strong statement and enter the debate over the wars justification. To support the invasion would alienate it from pro-war sections of the community and undermine the entire concept of its World Harmony round, yet to protest outright might bring about the more serious matter of estrangement from the Australian government, as well as the equally worrying public outrage for not supporting the latest generation of Anzacs. Such an act might even call into question the validity of its involvement with Anzac Day the following month. In the end, the only action guaranteed not to antagonise anyone was to display a neutral show of support for Australian troops abroad. If the AFL hoped to keep fans on side by doing so, then it would have felt vindicated by a *Herald Sun* poll, which found 77% of readers wanted the League to make a show of support to the troops by having goal umpires wave Australian flags, instead of their customary white ones.[68] Kevin Sheedy, meanwhile, took a strong stance against the anti-war camp, arguing that protesting the war and forsaking those sent to fight was one and the same: 'you support your country and the men and women that are over there... you don't not support them.'[69] Those who expressed anti-war statements, he believed, did so because of the absence of compulsory military service in the country, something he would change if given the opportunity.[70]

The rapid shift away from debating the war's justification toward supporting soldiers, [71] as though the two were mutually exclusive, encouraged some within the sporting community to move beyond a form of passive consent and towards outright support for the war itself. Popular depictions of sportsmen as the modern inheritors of the Anzac legend were evident in this. A special edition of the cricket magazine *Inside Edge* attempted to honour Steve Waugh by routinely equating him with the popular image of the Anzac soldier. Mention of his 'Anzac face' and the suggestion that Waugh 'could easily have been one of those Anzacs' are littered throughout the issue. The presence of such 'military allusions' was condoned by the magazine's editor Angus Fontaine, who placed 'the camaraderie he (Waugh) would bring to the trench', into the context of Australia's invasion of Iraq:

> So in the world going to hell in the quest for peace, does Steve Waugh playing his 157th Test on April 10 and so breaking the world record really matter? Certainly the answer must be yes... Just as he defied the odds to bring a nation to its feet on January 3, so too has he the power to lead us off the field... So, on Anzac day this year, salute our troops in Iraq but spare a thought for the other Waugh, who keeps fighting

harder, longer and straighter for Australia than anyone ever has. And feel safer for that at least.[72]

A clear merging of Australia's current sporting and traditional Anzac heroes is underway here, as is the assertion that such revered figures support the decision for Australia to partake in the controversial intervention against Iraq as a matter of national principle. The amiable veil of Anzac sport, meanwhile, assists in smoothing over the rougher edges of this otherwise bellicose message.

Numerous critics of Anzac Day sport have flinched at these comparisons of sportsmen and soldiers, arguing that they trivialise the sufferings of soldiers and their families in times when nations go to war.[73] However, another question remains: has Anzac's militarising influence left the sporting community vulnerable to partisan-motivated violence? Historian Jim Davidson believes so, claiming that 'young braves in national-colours, war paint, sporting flags and shouting abuse, quickly become the people who turned going to the beach at Cronulla into a riot.'[74] Such conclusions may be deemed melodramatic, yet, in recent years, there has been a marked increase in violence at Anzac Day football events. Though violence in the game has almost been eradicated since the 2000s, crowds witnessed a series of brawls between teams charged by the martial rhetoric of the press and motivational techniques of their coaches. The 2016 Anzac round alone produced 28 charges, resulting in tens of thousands of dollars in fines and two players suspended.[75] Instead of inciting outcry as counter to the commemorative purpose of the occasion, the violence received the approval of the popular television programme *AFL 360*, whose panellists Mark Robinson and Gerald Whateley described it as 'exciting'.[76] It was somewhat ironic, therefore, when Whateley offered sharp condemnation of Essendon supporters who booed Collingwood captain Scott Pendelbury upon his receiving of the Anzac Medal three years later:

> ... a lot of people who talk about it [Anzac], profess to be a part of it, don't honour that... Those people who booed didn't live those words, they didn't live the national character that we believe is part of Anzac, nor footy's place in it...[77]

To Whateley, the crowd's pledge to honour Australia's war veterans, and by extension the spirit of Anzac upon which the national identity rests, had given way to the more base impulse of sporting tribalism and the spectacle of the contest. Nevertheless, while hardly becoming, the crowd's behaviour was in actuality symbolic of Anzac's sports wider proliferation of partisanship, whether to the team or the nation. Indeed, those who booed were not acting counter to the spirit of Anzac and the 'national character'; they were evoking its dormant chauvinistic tendencies.

Conclusion

The incorporation of sport into Australia's commemoration of Anzac has gone from strength-to-strength since the 1990s. Riding the inclusive wave of war memory under New Nationalism, the AFL's Anzac Day clash has led a chorus of sporting organisations into paying homage to Australia's martial achievements, especially those forged during the First World War. In return, audiences are reassured about the worth of their national character. Whether on the playing or battlefield, the exceptionality of Australia and Australians is projected as evident and eternal. Though peaking in the early 2000s, the centenary years have done little to eradicate this. The amalgamation of sport, war and nationalism, however, is not only based on shaky historical foundations that distort people's understanding of the past, it also assists in the homogenisation and militarisation of the Australian identity. Because of this, there is a strong desire to do away with the concept of Anzac Day sport altogether. This, however, would create new complications. To refrain from playing sport on Anzac Day would continue to elevate Anzac to a level of religious significance, whereby its dominant status would render it safe from criticisms of propagating nationalistic myths and militaristic sentiments. Yet, to continue to saturate Anzac Day with sporting comparisons and metaphors only serves to exploit and undermine the horrific consequences of Australia's war-time history. The long-standing narrative of sport on Anzac Day, particularly its cathartic enjoyment by soldiers, reminds audiences of its merit as a commemorative tool. However, it remains essential that those involved are willing to frame the war as something larger than a banal tale of national achievement. It is important to keep a watchful eye on sport's incorporation into Anzac, just as it is equally important to monitor closely the infusion of patriotism into war memory of all nations. As Douglas Newton has recently remarked, 'The Great War should rattle our souls, not rouse our national self-esteem.'[78]

Acknowledgements

The author would like to thank the editors of Reflections for their insightful and constructive feedback.

Notes

1 For a discussion of the origins and development of Anzac's relationship with Australian nationalism, see Seal, *Inventing Anzac*. The contemporary conceptualisation of Anzac in Australia has largely neglected the New Zealand element in favour of a more exclusive national narrative. Pugsley, *The ANZAC Experience*, 20–21.
2 This date refers to the 1915 Gallipoli invasion, the first major land action undertaken by Australian soldiers during the war. It would henceforth become Anzac Day, the official day of national remembrance for those who have served

and perished in Australia's wars, conflicts and peacekeeping operations. Bean, *The Story of Anzac: From 4 May, 1915, to the Evacuation of the Gallipoli Peninsula*, 910.

3 For a wider discussion of the history of Anzac in Australia, see Holbrook, *Anzac: The Unauthorised Biography*; Inglis, *Sacred Places*; Lake and Reynolds, *What's Wrong with Anzac?*; Frame, *Anzac Day: Then & Now*.

4 For a history of Australian sporting culture, see Cashman, *Paradise of Sport*.

5 Hobsbawm, *Nations and Nationalism since 1870*, 143.

6 Mandle, "Cricket and Australian Nationalism in the Nineteenth Century," 224–45.

7 Holbrook, *Anzac: The Unauthorised Biography*, 1. Other examinations that have observed this trend include Inglis, *Sacred Places*, 563–5; Blackburn, *War, Sport and the Anzac Tradition*, 111–6.

8 Andrew Webster. 2015. "Kevin Sheedy says footy must always come second on Anzac Day." *Age* (Melbourne), April 24. https://www.theage.com.au/sport/afl/kevin-sheedy-says-footy-must-always-come-second-on-anzac-day-20150424-1ms655.html.

9 A television audience of 1.6 million people viewed the 2014 Anzac Day match, while the 2009 attendance doubled that of the Melbourne Shrine of Remembrance Dawn Service. Hawkins, *Consuming Anzac*, 102–03; John Elder. 2009. "It's a wonderful feeling, nearly 40,000 standing quietly at the Shrine of Remembrance." *Age*, April 26. 8; Andrew Petrie. 2009. "Dream result for lifetime Dons fan." *Age*, April 26. (Sport) 6.

10 Blackburn, *War, Sport and the Anzac Tradition*, 41–50.

11 Ibid., 107–09.

12 Walsh, "'Lest We Forget,'" 3–4.

13 Reference to football's role in Anzac was discernable during the Vietnam War. However, proliferation of this connection became increasingly rare thereafter. The 1977 Anzac Day match, which drew over 92,000 spectators, contained little reference to Anzac. See Blackburn, *War, Sport and the Anzac Tradition*, 110; Ron Carter. 1977. "Tom to blame." *Age*, April 25. 34.

14 Holbrook, *Anzac: The Unauthorised Biography*, 116–21.

15 Ibid., 214.

16 Inglis, *Sacred Places*, 572–4; McKenna, "Anzac Day: How Did It Become Australia's National Day?," 103–32.

17 Holbrook, *Anzac: The Unauthorised Biography*, 143.

18 Ibid., 116–43, 213–5.

19 Walsh, "Lest We Forget," 5.

20 Blackburn, *War, Sport and the Anzac Tradition*, 111.

21 Australian War Memorial. "Ceremonial customs." Australian War Memorial Website. Accessed September 3, 2019. https://www.awm.gov.au/commemmoration/customs-and-ceremony.

22 McKenna, "Anzac Day: How Did It Become Australia's National Day?" 123.

23 Karl Malakunas. 2000. "VFL dead remembered." *Herald Sun* (Melbourne), April 25. 81.

24 Pascoe, "The Anzac Day Match," 6–7.

25 Len Johnson. 2001. "Pies dig in, Dons over the top." *Age*, April 26. (Sport) 2.

26 James Hird. 2001. "Rising to the occasion on a day to remember." *Herald Sun*, April 25. 84.

27 Jake Niall. 2000. "A day for heroes." *Age*, April 25. (Sport) 3.

28 Chloe Saltau. 2009. "Malthouse fury over dispirited, leaderless." *Age*, April 26. (Sport) 7; Chloe Saltau. 2009. "Bombers' stirring win tempered by Hille knee injury." *Age*, April 26. (Sport) 3.

29 In 2007 alone, seven million people attended AFL home-and-away fixtures at an average of 38,000 per match, far above its domestic rival codes. Rob Hess and Matthew Nicholson, *A National Game*, 362–63.
30 Scott Gullen. 2001. "Live on the box." *Herald Sun*, April 25. 86.
31 Pascoe, "The AFL Anzac Day Match, 5; Niall, "A Day for Heroes," 3; For a discussion of the traditional omission of Indigenous-Australians from Anzac, see Inglis, *Sacred Places*, 420–7, 491, 502–03. For a discussion of the inclusion of Indigenous-Australians and other national-ethnicities into Anzac, see Bongiorno, "Anzac and the Politics of Inclusion," 81–97.
32 Mark Robinson. 2002. "Respect in victory and defeat." *Herald Sun*, April 25. 94.
33 Gilchrist, *True Colours*, 271.
34 Waugh, *Ashes Diary 2001*, 78, 80.
35 This advertisement received condemnation from ex-service personnel and media commentators for conflating professional athletes and soldiers. Andrew Horney. 1997. "Anzac battle cry puts Ruxton in the firing line." *Sydney Morning Herald*, April 22. 2.
36 Australian War Memorial. 2006. "Sport and war." Australian War Memorial Website. https://www.awm.gov.au/visit/exhibitions/sportandwar.
37 Heath Linton. 2015. "48HRS." *Age*, April 25. 57.
38 Inglis, *Sacred Places*, 572.
39 Stephanie Brantz. April 24, 2017. "Anzac Day football: Australia's perfect living tribute." ESPN Website. https://www.espn.com.au/afl/story/_/id/19228478/anzac-day-afl-nrl-football-australia-perfect-living-tribute.
40 Several journalists and historians have been prominent in questioning sports commercialisation of Anzac. For several illuminating examples of this, see Walsh, "'Lest We Forget,'" 12; Hawkins, *Consuming Anzac*.
41 *Daily Telegraph* (Sydney), April 23, 2011 cited in Blackburn, *War, Sport and the Anzac Tradition*, 114–5.
42 Sean Fagan. 2015. "Rugby answered the Empire's call in World War I." *Sydney Morning Herald*, April 24. https://www.smh.com.au/sport/rugby-union/rugby-answered-the-empires-call-in-world-war-i-20150421-1mpjys.html.
43 Cullen, *Harder than Football*, 23; *Victorian Cricket Association Annual Report for the Season 1915/16*, 7-8, Cricket Victoria Archives.
44 Victorian Sportsmen Recruiting Committee, *Enlist in the Sportsmen's 1000*, Australian War Memorial (AWM).
45 Phillips, "The Unsporting German and the Athletic Anzac," 23.
46 Blackburn, *War, Sport and the Anzac Tradition*, 41–44; See also Fuller, *Troop Morale and Popular Culture in the British and Dominion Armies*, 85–94.
47 See McKernan, "Sport, War and Society: Australia 1914–1918," 1–20; Phillips and Moore, "The Champion Boxer Les Darcy," 102–14; Phillips, "Football, Class and War"; Blair and Hess, *Australian Rules Football During the First World War*.
48 See Blair and Hess, *Australian Rules Football During the First World War*; Coe and Kennedy, *No Umpires in This Game*.
49 Adamson, "Football and War," 13–14; Hannah, State Parliament Recruiting Committee (Vic), *An Appeal from the Dardanelles*, AWM.
50 Blair and Hess, *Australian Rules Football During the First World War*, 32.
51 Ibid., 22, 31, 47, 109–11.
52 Ross, *100 Years of Australian Football*, 88–93.
53 Main, "Answering the Call," 314.
54 Walsh, "Lest We Forget," 3.
55 Ian Syson. 2016. "Soccer also made its sacrifice." *Sydney Morning Herald*, April 24. https://www.smh.com.au/sport/soccer/soccer-also-made-its-sacrifice-20150424-1msenk.html.

56 Inglis, *Sacred Places*, 551.
57 Gilchrist, *True Colours*, 271–2.
58 Mark Stevens. 2002. "'Goran fires Didak." *Herald Sun*, April 25. 93.
59 Bongiorno similarly believes ethnic-minority identification with Anzac should not be exaggerated. Bongiorno, "Anzac and the Politics of Inclusion," 95.
60 Mike Sheahan. 2002. "Sheik sadly out of place." *Herald Sun*, April 25. 94. The exclusion of foreign entities is particularly directed at former combatants, such as the Japanese and Germans. Turks, however, appear to have been warmly embraced into Anzac services. Inglis, *Sacred Places*, 516.
61 Ibid., 578.
62 Lake and Reynolds, "Moving on," 169–72.
63 Bendle, *ANZAC & Its Enemies*, 5.
64 Peter Ker and Caroline Wilson. 2003. "Stand-off looms over war ban." *Age*, March 21. (Sport) 1.
65 "No war in footie please." *Sydney Morning Herald*, March 28, 2003. https://www.smh.com.au/opinion/no-no-war-in-footie-please-20030328-gdgief.html.
66 Ibid.
67 Caroline Wilson. 2003. "AFL is treading carefully with its message over our troops." *Age*, March 28. (Sport) 3.
68 "Should AFL goal umpires wave Australian flags to support our troops?" *Herald Sun*, March 28, 2003. 89.
69 Peter Ker. 2003. "Keep anti-war statements off field: Sheedy." *Age*, March 22. (Sport) 3.
70 "No war in footie please," *Sydney Morning Herald*. https://www.smh.com.au/opinion/no-no-war-in-footie-please-20030328-gdgief.html.
71 For wider discussion of this transition, see Goot, "Public Opinion and the Democratic Deficit."
72 Angus Fontaine. 2003. "Steve Waugh – The tribute." *Inside Edge* 39, 9–10.
73 Chris Fotinopoulos. 2005. "Hallowed ground maybe, battleground… never." *Age*, April 25. 7; *Dominion Post* (Wellington), April 14, 2007 cited in Blackburn, *Sport, War and the Anzac Tradition*, 133.
74 The Cronulla riots were a series of racially and ethnically motivated attacks between groups of Anglo-Australians and Lebanese-Australians in 2005. Davidson, "Sport with Guns," 12.
75 Jon Ralph and Ben Higgins. 2016. "Alex Rance offered two man ban, host of players fined over melees by AFL MRP." *Herald Sun*, April 25. https://www.heraldsun.com.au/sport/afl/footy-form/alex-rance-offered-twomatch-ban-host-of-players-fined-over-melees-by-afl-mrp/news-story/51a53f67ba6360a015058e5bcd007577.
76 *AFL 360*, aired 27 April, 2016, Fox Footy, Television Programme.
77 Ibid., aired 25 April, 2019.
78 Newton, "Other People's War," 31.

Bibliography

Adamson, Lawrence. "Football and War" in *Wesley College Chronicle*, May, 1915.

Bean, C.E.W. *The Official History of Australia in the War of 1914–1918*, vol. II, *The Story of Anzac: From 4 May, 1915, to the Evacuation of the Gallipoli Peninsula*. Sydney: Angus & Robertson, 1924.

Bendle, Mervyn F. *ANZAC & Its Enemies: The History War on Australia's National Identity*. Sydney: Quadrant Books, 2015.

Blackburn, Kevin. *War, Sport and the Anzac Tradition*. London: Palgrave Macmillan, 2016.

Blair, Dale and Hess, Rob. *Australian Rules Football During the First World War.* Hampshire: Palgrave Macmillan, 2017.

Bongiorno, Frank. "Anzac and the Politics of Inclusion." In *Nation, Memory and Great War Commemoration: Mobilizing the Past in Europe, Australia and New Zealand*, edited by Shanti Sumartojo and Ben Wellings, 81–97. Oxford: Peter Lang, 2014.

Cashman, Richard. *Paradise of Sport: The Rise of Organised Sport in Australia.* South Melbourne: Oxford University Press, 1995.

Coe, Bruce and Kennedy, Bruce. *No Umpires in This Game: The Victorian Football League During Two World Wars.* Canberra: Instant Colour Press, 2016.

Cullen, Barbara. *Harder than Football: League Players at War.* Richmond: Slattery Media Group, 2015.

Davidson, Jim. "Sport with Guns." *Meanjin Quarterly* 67 (2008): 10–13.

Frame, Tom, (ed). *Anzac Day: Then & Now.* Sydney: NewSouth Publishing, 2016.

Fuller, John G. *Troop Morale and Popular Culture in the British and Dominion Armies, 1914–1918.* New York: Oxford University Press, 1990.

Gilchrist, Adam. *True Colours: My Life.* Sydney: Macmillan, 2008.

Goot, Murray. "Public Opinion and the Democratic Deficit: Australia and the War against Iraq." *Australian Humanities Review* 29 (May 2003). http://australianhumanitiesreview.org/2003/05/01/public-opinion-and-the-democratic-deficit-australia-and-the-war-against-iraq/

Hannah, Jim. State Parliament Recruiting Committee (Vic). 1915. *An Appeal from the Dardanelles: Will They Never Come?* ARTV07583, Poster, Australian War Memorial.

Hawkins, Jo. *Consuming Anzac: A History of Australia's Most Powerful Brand.* Crawley: University of Western Australia Publishing, 2018.

Hess, Rob and Nicholson, Matthew. *A National Game: The History of Australian Rules Football.* Camberwell: Penguin Books, 2008.

Hobsbawm, Eric. *Nations and Nationalism since 1870.* New York: Cambridge University Press, 1992.

Holbrook, Carolyn. *Anzac: The Unauthorised Biography.* Sydney: University of New South Wales Press, 2013.

Inglis, Ken. *Sacred Places: War Memorials in the Australian Landscape*, 3rd edition. Carlton: Melbourne University Press, 2008.

Lake, Marilyn and Reynolds, Henry. "Moving on." In *What's Wrong with Anzac?: The Militarisation of Australian History*, edited by Marilyn Lake and Henry Reynolds, 161–73. Sydney: University of New South Wales Press, 2010.

Lake, Marilyn and Reynolds, Henry. *What's Wrong with Anzac?: The Militarisation of Australian History.* Sydney: University of New South Wales Press, 2010.

Main, Jim. "Answering the Call." In *The Australian Game of Football*, edited by James Weston, 314–20. Docklands: Slattery media Group, 2008.

Mandle, William F. "Cricket and Australian Nationalism in the Nineteenth Century." *Journal of the Royal Australian Society* 59 (1973): 225–45.

McKenna, Mark. "Anzac Day: How Did It Become Australia's National Day?" In *What's Wrong with Anzac?: The Militarisation of Australian History*, edited by Marilyn Lake and Henry Reynolds, 103–32. Sydney: University of New South Wales Press, 2010.

McKernan, Michael. "Sport, War and Society: Australia 1914–1918." In *Sport in History*, edited by Richard Cashman and Michael McKernan, 1–20. St Lucia: University of Queensland Press, 1979.

Newton, Douglas. "Other People's War: The Great War in a World Context." In *The Honest History Book*, edited by David Stephens and Alison Brionowski, 16–31. Moorebank: NewSouth Publishing, Moorebank, 2017.

Pascoe, Robert. "The AFL Anzac Day Match." *Communication Culture and Languages Review* 1 (2007): 1–8.

Phillips, Murray. "Football, Class and War: The Rugby Codes in New South Wales, 1907–1918." In *Making Men: Rugby Union Masculine Identity*, edited by John Nauright and Timothy J.L Chandler, 158–80. London: Frank Cass, 1996.

Phillips, Murray. "The Unsporting German and the Athletic Anzac: Sport, Propaganda, and the First World War." *Sports History Review* 27 (1996): 14–29.

Phillips, Murray and Moore, Katherine. "The Champion Boxer Les Darcy: A Victim of Class Conflict and Sectarian Bitterness in Australia During the First World War." *International Journal of the History of Sport* 11 (1994): 102–14.

Pugsley, Cristopher. *The ANZAC Experience: New Zealand, Australia and Empire in the First World War.* Auckland: Reed Publishers, 2004.

Ross, John, ed. *100 Years of Australian Football.* Ringwood: Viking, 1996.

Seal, Graham. *Inventing Anzac: The Digger and National Mythology.* St Lucia: University of Queensland Press, 2004.

Victorian Sportsmen Recruiting Committee. 1917. *Enlist in the Sportsmen's 1000.* ARTV05616, Poster, Australian War Memorial.

Victorian Cricket Association Annual Report for the Season 1915/16, Cricket Victoria Archives.

Walsh, Melissa. "'Lest We Forget': The Tradition of ANZAC Day Football." *Sporting Traditions* 25 (2008): 1–15.

Waugh, Steve. *Ashes Diary 2001.* Sydney: Harper Collins Publishers.

4 'Our war'

National memory, New Zealand and Te Papa's Gallipoli

Rowan Light

Introduction

Gallipoli: The Scale of Our War opened at the National Museum of New Zealand Te Papa Tongarewa in Wellington in 2014. With its eight-million dollar price tag, *Gallipoli* was the centrepiece of the New Zealand government WW100 Centenary programme, with the aim of commemorating New Zealanders' experience during the war, to create a 'heightened awareness', and 'leave a lasting and impactful memory of this most important of events in New Zealand's history'.[1] The exhibition was a joint venture between Te Papa, led by curator Kirstie Ross, and Weta Workshop, Richard Taylor's globally renowned special effects company. This collaboration was unprecedented in two ways. Te Papa allowed, for the first time, an outside group to direct the project with full creative control. Moreover, the national museum did not, until now, 'do war', instead having prioritised natural and ethnographic histories.[2] *Gallipoli* represented both a shift in authority over remembrance at the national museum and a new focus on the 1915 Gallipoli campaign, despite the remit of WW100 to commemorate the wider 1914–18 period.[3]

The unique meeting of museum curation and the creative talents of 'Wellywood' was reflected in the exhibition's cinematic design and structure. Without a centralised national war collection at their disposal, the exhibition designers literally manufactured their own.[4] The story of the New Zealand Expeditionary Forces (NZEF) during the Gallipoli campaign was told through eight giant life-like historical figures, specially chosen for the letters, diaries, and photographs they left behind, drawn from various repositories (Figure 4.1). Visitors encountered each figure in dark, almost shrine-like rooms as they walk through the exhibition 2.4 times larger than life, the figures act as 'film stills', offering a snapshot into different personal experiences of Gallipoli at different times during the campaign and evoking different emotions; in turn, resignation, grief, boredom, rage and despair.[5] This emotional orchestration was aided by an array of visual, textual, and spatial narratives, including a specially composed soundtrack and various interactive multimedia platforms.[6] Any written narrative is told from the

Figure 4.1 Visitors reflect at the large-scale model of Percival Fenwick, 2015. Photo by Michael Hall.
Source: Museum of New Zealand Te Papa Tongarewa.

perspective of the figures themselves – the invocation of 'our enemy', 'our empire', 'our war' connect the visitor to the events, following the stories of the figures as they might characters in a film. The 'look and feel' of an epic, cinematic experience was intended to represent, literally, the scale of the war in New Zealand historical consciousness, dwarfing all else.

Gallipoli represented an unprecedented commitment to a national memory of war by the national museum, mediated through a spectacle of cinema. The collective effect of *Gallipoli*'s cinematic 'spirit' was the palpable sense that the experience of Gallipoli in 1915 (and the exhibition in 2019) produced something that transcends war: a national memory, which provides New Zealanders with a shared emotional connection. In ahistorical remembrance, the past is *felt* before it is understood.[7] In Te Papa's production, creative artistry is privileged over historical critique, reflecting, in local terms, a global phenomenon of public war memory created, as John Chambers and David Culbert argue, less from a remembered past than a manufactured one, 'substantially shaped by images in documentaries, feature films, and television programs'.[8] This has the effect of transforming social remembrance, embedded in personal relationships and local communities, into a totalising cultural memory that makes cosmic claims about the basis of society, even as it becomes more homogenous and disconnected from social relationships.[9] As Jay Winter points out, nations do not 'remember'; rather 'national memory' is a political project – incomplete and ever changing – that is cemented by the work of individuals, groups, and institutions, and the texts they produce.[10]

Rather than focusing on a historical analysis of *Gallipoli*'s depictions of the events of 1915, or foregrounding a contemporary study of museum interpretation, this chapter places the exhibition in this memory history and the longer trajectory of cinematic production about the Gallipoli campaign over the last 40 years. The need to assert 'the scale of *our* war', invoked in the full title of the exhibition, was implicitly set against other, competing, nationalist claims around Gallipoli; in particular, Australian claims over that space. Beginning with the changes in Australian national cinema in 1981, this chapter traces the counter-strategy around 'the New Zealand story', a multi-textual project that opened with Maurice Shadbolt's theatre production *Once on Chunuk Bair*. The 1980s were a crucial decade in which classic, social modes of remembrance in Australia and New Zealand were transformed by a new nationalist cinema. Although the 'New Zealand story' failed in the short term, the genealogy of spectacle and remembrance of which *Gallipoli* is the chief descendant shows its long-term success. By exploring this history of failure and success, this chapter understands remembrance in a wider 'ecosystem' of memory: that is, the deliberate and intentional 'work of memory' by groups, individuals, institutions, texts, and their audiences, that make 'national memory' possible and give it a sense of permanence. In these genealogies of remembrance, the contours of New Zealand's First World War centenary were less about the war of 1914–18 and more about the contemporary needs of communities and the dedicated political and cultural agendas of specific groups.

'I felt like I was really touching history': *Gallipoli*, 1981

The 1981 Australian film *Gallipoli*, directed by Peter Weir, is the inevitable starting point of scholarly discussions on the history of Anzac cinema. Weir's film itself was part of an explosion in television and film production around war memory in the late 1970s and early 1980s that included *Report from Gallipoli* (1977) and the highly popular miniseries *Anzacs* (1985). *Gallipoli* re-presented many of the classic tropes of 'the Anzac story', including the centrality of white, masculine characters Archy Hamilton (Mark Lee) and Frank Dunne (Mel Gibson), the linkage between war experience and mateship, and the rugged landscape of the bush, in the contemporary context of anxieties around national identity in post-imperial Australian society, represented especially by the film's didactic anti-British sentiment.[11] *Gallipoli* has since been read as a central cultural landmark of the Anzac 'revival', a period in which Anzac Day was re-scripted as a national day that celebrated Australian values distinct from any British origins.[12] As a film text, *Gallipoli* reinforced an emerging national commemoration that linked the space of Gallipoli to Australian nationhood. In this way, Weir's film became celebrated as *the* 'Australian film' – the translation of the 'great Australian story' to 'the great Australian film'.[13] This was a powerful imaginative proposition in the face of disruptive narratives of decolonisation, as exemplified at the Bicentenary of British settlement in 1988 when attempts to present an image of Australia as a modern, multicultural society at Sydney Cove collided with indigenous protests.[14] In the lead up to the 75th anniversary of Gallipoli in 1990, the memory of the landing was solidified as the national birthplace, independent of imperial ties, with Weir's *Gallipoli* as its chief text.

Gallipoli made very specific claims about history. In interviews following the film's release, Weir cited a 1975 visit to the Gallipoli peninsula as an inspiration for the script. Walking among the rugged landscape and debris of war, Weir 'felt like [he] was somehow touching history'.[15] In another interview, Weir opined that 'in our country, we had no Wilfred Owen, no Robert Graves, no Sassoon, no Great War poets who could tell us about the lost generation'.[16] Subsequently, Weir undertook extensive research into the campaign based on Charles Bean's official history and Bill Gammage's influential 1974 book *The Broken Years*, which revelled in the 'authentic' voices of ordinary soldiers.[17] Gammage himself eventually became historical consultant for the film. Weir's aim was not to tell a story about Gallipoli, but *the story*, one that, through the 'unmediated voices' of the past would provide a compelling national myth. The emphasis on ordinary voices of the Anzacs as a source of national character indicated an empirical fallacy in which determination to get the details right was equated with complete historical understanding. This work also pointed to institutional networks of national commemoration that included figures such as Bean – to whom Gammage had dedicated his thesis – and the Australian War Memorial.[18] Despite comments that the film was 'apolitical', it reflected very specific historiographical claims on the memory of the campaign.[19] The publication of *The Story of Gallipoli*, which includes a preface by Weir, the film's screenplay, and chapters from *The Broken Years*, following the release of the film, reflected the broader historical project of *Gallipoli*.[20]

This new imaginative engagement with the landscape of Gallipoli affected the public in Australia and New Zealand. Contemporary observers in 1982 drew connections between increased attendances at Anzac Day with the success of the film on both sides of the Tasman Sea. Images of Mark Lee and Mel Gibson appeared alongside New Zealand newspaper editorials, supplements, and articles commemorating Anzac Day. To coincide with the film, John Wadham, curator of the Auckland Museum's war collection, arranged a display of material associated with the Gallipoli campaign; including rifles, bayonets, and jam tin bombs as well as medals and photographs.[21] Newspapers and magazines published soldiers' personal accounts that emphasised the 'horrors of Anzac' and reproduced the film's central theme: the innocence of a nation struck down by British incompetence. Indeed, such was the popularity of the film that an *Evening Post* editorial before Anzac

Day in 1982 stated that, 'many of the younger people in the audience could have been forgiven for gaining the impression that Australia fought the Gallipoli campaign by themselves, but of course, the N Z in the middle of Anzac stands for New Zealand'.[22]

It was precisely this challenge of asserting the 'NZ' in Anzac that shaped a new generation of creative artists and scholars in search of a post-imperial New Zealand identity. A seminal figure in this vanguard was Maurice Shadbolt. A writer whose oeuvre had, until then, consisted of short stories and novels, Shadbolt embarked on the writing of a stage play titled *Once on Chunuk Bair*.[23] *Chunuk Bair* centred on the experience of the New Zealand Infantry Brigade in the disastrous August offensive.[24] Shadbolt dramatised the death of Lt-Col. William Malone (re-named as Connolly in the play) as a heroic sacrifice in the face of impossible odds on the one hand, and a callous British command on the other. The play premiered in April 1982 with publication of the script the same year (Figure 4.2). The play was generally well received by critics and public; a special episode of *Kaleidoscope*, a popular television series that promoted the work of New Zealand artists, featured a behind-the-scenes look the play and interviews with Shadbolt.[25] Describing

Figure 4.2 A photograph by Michael Tubberty from the first production of Maurice Shadbolt's play *Once on Chunuk Bair* at Auckland's Mercury Theatre in 1982, with Roy Billing in the foreground.
Source: Auckland Libraries Heritage Collections, NZMS 813 (Chunuk Bair).

the play as 'an original Anzac memorial' and a 'powerful drama', *Kaleido-scope* presenter Jeremy Payne lauded how Shadbolt aimed to show 'not only the human cost of war, but also how a sense of nationalism emerged among the New Zealanders who fought there so bravely', contrasting the 'poignant illustration of the futility of war' with 'a tribute to heroism'.[26]

Shadbolt's aim was an explicitly nationalist historiographical reappraisal of the Gallipoli campaign in response to the success of Weir's *Gallipoli*. This was myth and counter-myth. Shadbolt called the battle of Chunuk Bair – and by extension his own play – 'our answer to the Australians' magnificent debacle at Lone Pine and The Nek', the battles that provided the dramatic climax of Weir's film.[27] Chunuk Bair was 'New Zealand's cruellest, and finest, hour' and 8 August was 'the day that New Zealanders lost their innocence'. Reflecting on the writing of the play, Shadbolt stated that he found the campaign 'a very painful and tragic process of self-discovery' and yet observed that 'there was nothing in our national culture about Gallipoli'. In an interesting parallel to Weir, Shadbolt records that he was inspired to write the play after a visit to the peninsula in 1977:

> No poem, no song, no novel, no symphony – nothing in our national culture – enshrines the experience of Gallipoli; and this despite the fact that ANZAC Day remains conspicuous in our calendars. Was the experience just too traumatic? Or is it that we still lack a Homer to process tribal memory? It was in that theatre in Troy that *Once on Chunuk Bair* was conceived.[28]

Shadbolt's reminiscences provide several insights. In the first place, the playwright's sense of self-importance – as New Zealand's Homer – is evident. Shadbolt draws a direct psychological parallel between his personal search for identity and the struggle of the New Zealand nation itself. Moreover, Shadbolt repeats the fallacy of visiting Gallipoli as a place imbued with meaning, rather than those meanings being constructed offshore and brought with him. As with Weir's film creation, this entailed claiming Gallipoli as a sacred space. Anzac Cove had become an extension of 'home' owing to the sacrifice of the dead, a sentiment achieved in Shadbolt's text when the character of Connolly literally renames Chunuk Bair as 'New Zealand'.[29] Perhaps most strikingly, having found a paucity of national memory around Gallipoli in New Zealand, it becomes necessary for Shadbolt to invent this work.

Shadbolt's promotion of a 'heroic' nationalism mapped onto contemporary anxieties about New Zealand's newly independent, post-imperial position in global politics.[30] Shadbolt commented that *Once on Chunuk Bair* 'is only ostensibly about New Zealand's fatal day on Chunuk Bair on August 8, 1915. It was really about New Zealanders – and New Zealand – 70 years on.'[31] This meant shearing the Anzac story of its fundamentally imperial and racial orientation – a common feature of cultural productions of war remembrance since the end of the Second World War.[32] 'National innocence' was a key part of this discourse because it resolved any tensions that, historically, New Zealanders were active participants in colonial settlement; instead positioning them as victims – not perpetrators – of empire as much as the Anzacs were victims at Gallipoli. Moreover, despite the play being an explicit reaction to Australian claims on Gallipoli, Shadbolt claimed to be telling history 'like it was' (the implication being that Weir had not).[33] Whereas *Gallipoli* was romantic myth-making, according to Shadbolt, *Chunuk Bair* was about historical reality in its gritty and gory detail.[34] To substantiate his claims, Shadbolt drew on the diaries and letters of Malone, and oral interviews of Gallipoli veterans.[35] These were to be the unmediated 'voices of Gallipoli', who would speak again through the work of the playwright and author, eventually being published for public consumption as *Voices of Gallipoli* in 1987.[36] In turn, Shadbolt would represent the emergence of a new generation of creative artists who would act as prophets of memory detached from historical critique.

'The New Zealand story' project, 1982–84

Shadbolt's work resonated with an emerging counterstrategy of New Zealand-centred commemoration around Gallipoli in the 1980s. Over the space of several years, New Zealanders were saturated with a cluster of texts related to 'the New Zealand story', spanning films, books, and museum exhibitions, and heavily framed by Shadbolt's 'tribal memory'. These productions included the release of the television documentary, *Gallipoli: The New Zealand Story,* produced with state funding through Television New Zealand (TVNZ) and released on 22 April 1984.[37] The documentary was an important project in this counter-strategy: Maurice Shadbolt wrote the script, Doc Williams directed, and former Chief of Defence Leonard Thornton narrated it. TVNZ Director General Allan Martin, formerly of the Australian Broadcasting Corporation, drove the project and ensured its consistent funding.[38]

Another crucial figure connecting these works was historian Christopher Pugsley. As a young military historian, Pugsley had supported Shadbolt in preparing, revising, and staging *Once on Chunuk Bair*. The oral interviews were the outcome of the collaboration with Pugsley, who also acted as the military advisor to the TVNZ documentary team. His own book *Gallipoli: The New Zealand Story* was published in the same year as the documentary's release – the first critical work on the campaign to be written from 'a New Zealand viewpoint'.[39] Pugsley's scholarship initiated a new historiography of the campaign and helped springboard a parallel understanding of the myth in New Zealand.[40] Less recognised is the intersection and collaboration between Pugsley's work and these broader texts, audiences, and creative producers.

The naming of Pugsley's *Gallipoli* paired it to the documentary as part of a wider commemorative strategy and coincided with a third strand of 'the

New Zealand story': a museum exhibition of the same name. *Gallipoli: The New Zealand Story* opened at Waiouru Army Museum in 1984. The exhibition displayed the Victoria Cross awarded to Cyril Bassett for 'his extreme bravery under fire on the slopes of Chunuk Bair' – the only VC won by a New Zealander at Gallipoli.[41] A diorama of the Gallipoli peninsula and Chunuk Bair, originally produced for the TVNZ documentary, was also displayed. The 'New Zealand story' exhibition reflected all the major elements in post-*Gallipoli* Anzac commemoration, asserting 'New Zealand's special role' in the campaign and centred on Chunuk Bair.[42] This was contrasted with the Australian contribution and other imperial narratives. Indeed, the project was explicitly linked to Weir's film. Updating the Waiouru Army Museum staff on the progress of the 'New Zealand story' documentary, researcher Colleen Hodge wrote that 'our film, like the Australian feature *Gallipoli*, is proving to be a slow and expensive project. However, we've great faith in our "sources".[43] Hodges' research would provide a shared knowledge-base for book, documentary, and exhibition.

What, or who, were Hodge's sources? The researchers ran into the same problem as Shadbolt had faced earlier and Weta designers would in 2014: the lack of a centralised work of national memory. 'The New Zealand story' project, therefore, entailed building this national archive. Hodge and other researchers gathered, over eight months, a large collection of diaries, letters, and various official records relating to Gallipoli that was then deposited with the Waiouru Army Museum.[44] TVNZ, as the documentary's producer, advertised in local and national newspapers in New Zealand, and the Returned and Services Association (RSA) *Review*; as well as contacting overseas Gallipoli returned-service groups in Australia and the United Kingdom.[45] Martin, in the press release announcing the launch of the project, stated that '[o]ur aim is to produce a film which will be referred to again and again in years to come', speaking to the ambition that the project would shape public commemoration in much the same way as Weir's *Gallipoli*.[46]

'The New Zealand story' was a 'nationalising' of war memory in New Zealand in an unprecedented way. Soldiers' personal and family memory were translated and repackaged within a national institutional and textual framework. The 'national' focus specifically intended to omit Australian soldiers. Offers of help from Australian Imperial Forces (AIF) returned servicemen, or their families, living in New Zealand, were politely declined as 'falling outside of the scope of the documentary'.[47] In fact, over two-thirds of the First World War returned servicemen population living in New Zealand in the 1980s were either born in Australia or the United Kingdom.[48] Social networks of memory, as fragments of empire, did not neatly stop at national borders. J. O. C. Smith, later killed in the battle of the Somme, was probably the first New Zealand-born soldier to land at Anzac Cove, as part of the AIF dawn landing. However, he was not included in the documentary which emphasised 'New Zealand-recruited troops', such as members of the Auckland Battalion who landed later on the morning of April 25.[49]

This was a conscious reaction to Weir's 'brilliant film', as Pugsley called it, providing a critical countermemory to the Australian commemoration, even as he drew on the Australia director's research of the Gallipoli battlefield.[50] The emphasis on the experiences of New Zealand-born soldiers who served in the NZEF hardly reflected the social networks of memory active in the country up to the 1980s. Rather, the research aligned with the claims of Pugsley and Shadbolt that the Gallipoli experience forged a distinct national character. This character reflected the corporate rationales of the documentary, funded on the basis that it was producing 'New Zealand content' for TVNZ, in turn reinforcing its credentials as a project of cultural nationalism.

These challenges highlighted the institutional frameworks of remembrance that, conversely, enabled Australian productions around Gallipoli. The dedicated collection of the Australian War Memorial Museum, collected by Bean and established by the Memorial's first director, John Treloar, to promote Australia's national war experience, provided Australian artists and scholars with a curated national memory.[51] Over the 1980s, the War Memorial was revamped with considerable government expenditure as the nation's chief cultural institution that would be simultaneously museum, memorial, and archive, and research centre – all geared towards promoting an Australian memory of war. Moreover, this memory – located in the War Memorial Museum – closed off postcolonial critiques of nationhood by excluding frontier wars of settlement.[52] This absence of an institutional infrastructure in New Zealand was explained by preeminent Anzac scholar Ken Inglis as a sign of a lower temperature of nationalism among New Zealanders – a comment that underscored the novelty of the nationalist project being undertaken by the creators of 'the New Zealand story'.[53]

Certainly, the lack of a similar institutional presence was acutely felt in making the 'New Zealand story' documentary. Researchers, instead, relied on returned servicemen and their families to provide references for other interviews that had already been recorded and to send materials for copying to TVNZ. A series of programmes produced and aired in the early 1970s on 1ZB radio called *The Diggers Sessions*, which included interviews with Rod Talbot recounting a full history of the campaign, was an important resource.[54] Similarly, no film crew was attached to the New Zealand Expeditionary Forces, as was the case for the AIF. The 1980s reconstruction of a 'New Zealand' narrative came to rely heavily on footage of Australian and other imperial soldiers. Pugsley and other researchers travelled to the Australian War Memorial and Imperial War Museum in London to search for relevant footage.[55] The interviews and collection of materials – diaries, letters, and manuscripts, much of which had been 'in private hands and undocumented' – were all later deposited in the Army Museum and nationalised through the focus of the documentary, passing from personal-social memory to a national commemoration.[56] In this sense, the 'New Zealand story' at once circulated in the transnational networks of imperial and

Tasman archival networks, while simultaneously, as a national project of memory, it attempted to close off those circulations.

The ambition and limitations of 'the New Zealand Story' project was best expressed in Pugsley's proposal to institutionalise this emerging national myth of Chunuk Bair as a national day. Following the success of his book, Pugsley called for the government to change Anzac Day from April 25 to Chunuk Bair Day on August 8, to mark the battle.[57] This was the day that 'we "beheld the Narrows from the hill" – a key phrasing that linked New Zealanders at the end of the twentieth century to 1915 through a 'tribal' memory. Like Shadbolt, Pugsley argued that the 'New Zealand perspective' at Gallipoli was a more *authentic* one than the Australian experience; '[u]nlike the New Zealander, the Australians went to war to live out a myth they already believed.'[58] Conversely, modern New Zealand society was irrevocably shaped by this experience of war, with Pugsley suggesting that 'we are the sum of what they did, what they found and what they lost'. 'It was', Pugsley concluded in a phrase that evoked Shadbolt's own creative rationale and this wider nationalist project, 'the loss of innocence'.[59]

'The New Zealand story' was a multi-media project, loosely connecting museum, public history, theatre, and cinema in a new spectacle of memory. The revisionist scholarship, reinvestigation of military history, and publication of soldiers' experiences in the war did not, however, provide a strong enough infrastructure to consolidate a consistent national remembrance. The apotheosis of 'the New Zealand story' might have been the film adaptation of Shadbolt's play as *Chunuk Bair* in 1992; the final countermove to Weir's 'Australian film'. Instead, the film failed, lacking funding from the New Zealand Film Commission and suffering from the poor execution by first-time director Dale Bradley, who struggled to transpose Shadbolt's theatre text to the cinematic screen.[60]

The failure of *Chunuk Bair* as a film signalled a wider state and public disengagement from 'the New Zealand story' in the 1990s. The turn of the decade marked the 75th anniversary of the Gallipoli landing. The Australian government dedicated considerable resources to the commemoration in the form of the Gallipoli 75 Taskforce. In a highly publicised pilgrimage that provided a new wave of media imagery of the Gallipoli landscape, Bob Hawke became the first Prime Minister to attend the dawn service at Anzac Cove. Hawke imbued the moment with national significance. In his dawn service speech, Hawke stated that, because 'these hills rang with [the Anzacs'] voices and ran with their blood, this place Gallipoli is, in one sense, a part of Australia'.[61] This powerful, imaginative claim on the landscape was the consummation of Weir's vision of the Anzacs, represented by Archie and Frank as sacrificial lambs being swept along in a tragic adventure beyond their control. The New Zealand government, on the other hand, showed little appetite for a national commemoration, and instead opted for traditional networks of commemoration, represented in the RSA and the Governor General who acted as Hawke's counterpart in Turkey. The RSA produced its own documentary for the anniversary. Although it adapted much of Pugsley's work, the documentary, with its title *Gallipoli: the muddle that moulded a nation*, was decidedly less emphatic about New Zealand's 'birthplace', as had been Shadbolt's insistence eight years before.[62]

1990 evidenced not only different social networks of commemoration outside of the state but distinct stories of national founding in New Zealand. The 150th anniversary of the signing of the Treaty of Waitangi – also in 1990 – commanded the focus of government and public attention. 'Waitangi 1990' represented a very different work of national memory, encapsulated in the redevelopment of the National Museum in Wellington over the 1980s and 1990s.[63] Re-established in 1992, Te Papa was tasked with creating a national identity that centred biculturalism and the Treaty partnership between Māori and Pākehā. At the opening of the new museum site in 1998, Gallipoli was nowhere to be seen in the exhibition galleries. Instead, the flagship exhibition, *Treaty of Waitangi: Signs of a Nation / Te Tiriti o Waitangi: Ngā tohu kotahitanga* focused on Waitangi as a very different 'birthplace' of the nation and the integration of a different set of 'voices' of the past and present in a living history. *Ngā tohu* operated, conceptually and architecturally, according to Conal McCarthy, 'as the hinge of the nation, cleaving the space [of the exhibition] into tangata whenua and tangata tiriti sections, uniting (or dividing) us, depending on your perspective.'[64] The Australian myth of Gallipoli was consolidated through the 1990s through a close relationship between institutional networks of war memory and political advocates, and a paucity of postcolonial alternatives, with the institution of the Australian War Memorial housing the 'national spirit' – 'the spirit of the Anzacs', in the words of Charles Bean and as echoed in Michael McKernan's institutional history.[65] New Zealanders pursued a very distinct commemorative path at this time.

'Our war': the return of the 'New Zealand story'?

This broader historical perspective shows success and failures, continuities and discontinuities, in different genealogies of memory work in Australia and New Zealand. This history is incomplete because memory work cannot be collapsed into one group; as this chapter shows, it is the interaction between texts, institutions, and groups that creates the uneven impression of national remembrance. Moreover, these interactions are shaped by various historiographical, institutional, and constitutional currents. Over the 2000s, the Australian and New Zealand public saw new state projects around Anzac commemoration under the Australian John Howard Liberal and New Zealand Helen Clark Labour governments.[66] This saw a return to an earlier theme – a renewed trans-Tasman interaction, albeit one that was more cooperative than the antagonism of the 1980s.[67] New memorials were established, respectively, in Canberra and Wellington to commemorate the joint military experience of the two nations. Similarly, both governments established national memorials in London's Hyde Park. 2005 marked the 90th anniversary with both Howard and Clark in attendance. Part of an agenda of 'cultural recovery' – as Clark termed it – this commemoration entailed healing the nation of social and economic disruption after the end of empire through a new celebratory narrative of nationhood.[68] Significantly, this new emphasis on war memory did not fixate on Gallipoli but was part of a wider remembrance of war that ranged from the battles of the Western Front to the experience of New Zealand soldiers during the Vietnam War. Broadly, war remembrance was energised by trans-Tasman linkages and the global significance of this commemoration, reconstructing post-imperial networks between Britain, Australia, and New Zealand through a diplomacy of memory that was increasingly important to articulating national identity.

By 2014, the New Zealand government saw the centenary of the First World War as an important opportunity to engage the public in discussions around national identity, in stark contrast to the relative quiet of 1990. Taking cues from its Australian federal counterpart, the New Zealand Centenary Programme was the largest commemoration in the country's history.[69] Funding from Creative New Zealand and New Zealand on Air for the creation of hundreds of war-themed plays, exhibitions, television programmes and events around the country was close to $15 million.[70] Local governments funded hundreds of thousands of dollars' worth of cultural projects, while another $17 million was allocated by the Lottery Grants Board. The largest government project for the centenary was Wellington's $120-million renovation of the Pukeahu National War Memorial Park, along with $330,000 spent digitising the Auckland Cenotaph database. While the official centenary ran for four years, most of these projects reached the public in 2014 and 2015 – a very condensed time frame to see hundreds of war-related cultural works.

Whereas other centenary projects and exhibitions told the broader story of the war – such as Auckland Museum's *Pou Kanohi New Zealand at War* – Te Papa chose, in a new and unprecedented way, to exclusively dedicate its $8-million exhibition to Gallipoli as the apex of the Great War and the forging of national identity.[71] That this centenary project came to be heavily focused on the cultural memory of Gallipoli as an epic, if tragic, cinematic spectacle was very much due to the work of 'the New Zealand story'. This limited counterstrategy that took shape in the 1980s and faded from significance during the 1990s and 2000s, laid the groundwork for a very specific national re-working of commemoration in New Zealand.

Te Papa's *Gallipoli* was, in concept and practice, a twenty-first-century 'New Zealand story', bringing together its multi-textual, theatrical, and cinematic elements in a fusion of historiography and dramaturgy. Richard Taylor and Weta artists drew on Weir's *Gallipoli* as part of the exhibition's concept design, with the tragic slaughter of young men forming the central emotional narrative. The digital artwork for the exhibition offers a pastiche

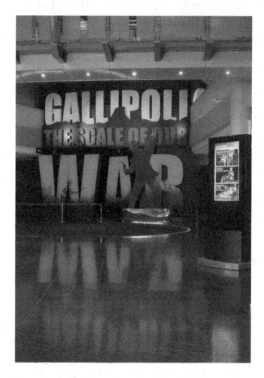

Figure 4.3 The *Gallipoli: the scale of our war* exhibition logo. Note the figure in the foreground wearing – anachronistically – the lemon squeezer hat. The NZEF officer would have worn the regulation cap; the designers, instead, privileged the 'iconic' look intended to reinforce the nationalistic portrayal of the battle.

Source: Museum of New Zealand Te Papa Tongarewa.

of 1980s imagery.[72] A heroic figure of a New Zealand officer formed part of the exhibition logo (Figure 4.3). With the figure wearing the classic 'lemon squeezer' hat, rather than the historically correct officer cap, the design eschews period accuracy for national iconography, evoking a genealogy that links back to *Once on Chunuk Bair*. Indeed, Chunuk Bair formed the dramatic climax of the exhibition: this was 'our place', as it had been invoked by the men in Shadbolt's play. The 'voice' of William Malone was, once again, a crucial component in this myth-making. Malone's Quinn's Post bunker was recreated, with his diaries narrated by a voice actor for audiences. This was Malone as Shadbolt's composite character of Connolly, selectively trimmed of his religious and imperial loyalties.

Chris Pugsley returned as the Exhibition Historical Director. Pugsley adapted *The New Zealand Story* and its interpretations of a war experience that forged New Zealand's nationhood after empire as part of the exhibition's narrative, and reproduced his work on Gallipoli dioramas in the striking digital models of the peninsula and Chunuk Bair. His influence was particularly evident in the depiction of Māori soldiers. Despite Te Papa's commitment to biculturalism – the equal place of tangata whenua and tangata tiriti that shaped the very architecture of the museum itself – Pugsley 'cut down to size' the number of Māori 'giants', to reflect the statistical presence of Māori soldiers during the 1915 campaign.[73] This empirical triumph reflected an ideological feint: a historical varnish, applied to this work of memory, obscured the nationalist agenda in which Gallipoli was to be a foundational place of nationhood, rather than a theatre that reiterated the Treaty partnership. It was the consummation of Pugsley's work: the argument, advanced in 1984, that although 'we did not even consciously go to war as New Zealanders', the experience of Gallipoli 'established a reputation and a sense of identity that is important to... who we are' – a repudiation of Bean's (Australian) assertion that New Zealanders were 'colourless' and without nationalism.[74] Rather than being one among many contested historical interpretations, 'our war' was an absolute claim on national memory. 'This exhibition', Pugsley proclaimed, 'will determine how New Zealanders remember the Gallipoli campaign for the twenty-first century' – fashioned along historiographical lines as put forward in his scholarly work.[75]

Gallipoli reflected professional relationships and institutional networks of mentoring and training: Shadbolt, Pugsley, and Taylor represented a generation of Pākehā men, coming of age in the 1970s and 1980s, searching for an ostensible national identity.[76] In this circulation of people and texts, locations such as Wellington must be understood as a space of creative production.[77] In a *Metro* interview, discussing the launch of his film *April 25*, in essence the animated adaptation of the Te Papa exhibition, Matthew Metcalfe stressed that he needed 'at least a couple of my characters to be at Chunuk Bair' because '[i]n terms of New Zealand [culture], it was the most important battle: we actually mark 8 August [when the troops arrived at Chunuk Bair] as a really important date here, rather than the day of the landing.'[78] This peculiar claim only makes sense in a very narrow thread of creative work in which Chunuk Bair is represented as a fundamental moment of national birth. Indeed, Metcalfe's work, heavily influenced by Pugsley's historiography, reiterated a fundamental fallacy that runs through the 'New Zealand story' and its reconfiguration in Te Papa's *Gallipoli* – the confusion between landscape, remembrance, and its essential artifice, shaped not by tribal zeitgeist, but the intentional hands of intellectuals and creative producers.

Conclusion

In April 2019, the WW100 steering committee published its final report on the outcome of the unprecedented investment by the New Zealand government in the centenary of the First World War.[79] The essential purpose of the final report was to track changes in New Zealanders' attitudes towards the First World War. The report focused heavily on the survey results that indicated the near complete exposure of the New Zealand public to the centenary remembrance – 93% of New Zealanders over the age of 15 were touched by the centenary, with 82% believing the First World War was relevant in shaping our national identity. New Zealanders, it seemed, overwhelmingly remember the First World War in terms of nationhood. The specific regimes of this remembrance were especially interesting. In a question that asked respondents what first came to their mind when they heard the words 'First World War', the most common responses in 2018 were 'Death', 'Gallipoli', and 'Anzac'. These clichés – conflating Anzac, Gallipoli, and the First World War – were redolent of the 'the New Zealand story' and the new nationalist historiographies of the war in the 1980s. In trans-Tasman and global circulations of war memory, the Anzacs' experience of Gallipoli was interpreted as the tragic 'death' of a national innocence.

These emotional terms, within a circumscribed historiography of the war as a tragic loss of innocence, evinced the discrete cinematic text of Te Papa's *Gallipoli* and the way that the exhibition has significantly changed how New Zealanders relate to Gallipoli in a national remembrance. The triumph of the exhibition's national, emotional, and mythological 'scales' underscores what is at stake in public remembrance and its history in New Zealand. Only in understanding the role of the 'New Zealand story' project can historians account for this unprecedented situation, where the national museum presents as New Zealand's *national memory* this central narrative of Gallipoli, mediated through epic cinema.

Although filmmakers and authors such as Weir and Shadbolt sought to authorise their national narratives through the 'voices of the past', their work was, in fact, very much a product of its time, and the needs of particular communities; in this case, the search for meaning and identity after empire. Both *Gallipoli* and *Chunuk Bair* relied on the notion of the raw, unmediated voices of memory to imbue the dramatic productions with historical verisimilitude, therefore validating their interpretation of the campaign and its commemoration. Rather than revealing a 'national character' and tribal memory provided through the unique experience of Australia or New Zealand soldiers, the new cultural remembrance obscured social networks of memory – defined by imperial relationships – through the cultural nationalist dramaturgy of cinema and theatre. National cinema provided the means to share new cultural stories of Gallipoli, through mass media, allowing audiences to imagine the past as their own through an epic spectacle. This national memory was not spontaneous but reflected the work of committed intellectuals, institutions, and governments. To understand the tone and texture of an exhibition such as Te Papa's *Gallipoli*, this work undertaken by intellectuals, as well as the relationship between Australian and New Zealand cultural fields, must also be understood.

The success of *Gallipoli* comes at a significant time for Te Papa. As lead curator Kirstie Ross observes, the exhibition will be the last major exhibition before the renewal of the museum's first generation of exhibitions since the 1998 re-opening.[80] *Gallipoli* reflects a 20-year process in which the 'New Zealand story' work went from marginal to central in the national museum, to align with broader state priorities and public engagement. Moreover, the exhibition's success means it will exert considerable influence on future exhibition design and structure – especially around the collaboration between museum and creative industry. This evolution of the national museum and the broader changes in New Zealand remembrance after empire are still debatable. In focusing on Gallipoli as a forge of national memory, it becomes increasingly difficult for the national museum to address the commemoration of the New Zealand Wars of the nineteenth century. Can these wars of settlement be 'our wars', if the epicentre of national identity is fixed on the slopes of Chunuk Bair, rather than the battlefields of Waikato or Taranaki?[81] The process of 'historical remembrance' in which memory and history interact in creating meanings from the past requires scholars to understand this memory work, its organic development, and artificial operations. The national historiography of 'New Zealand's Gallipoli' has more to do with this dynamic of commemorative strategy and counterstrategy, myth and its revision in trans-Tasman circulations, revealing a genealogy or dialogue of texts, in which the aim of historical understanding is only one among many.

Acknowledgements

I would like to thank the editors for their time and insights in preparing this chapter for publication. A special thanks to Kirstie Ross who generously gave of her time at the beginning of the project. Ngā mihi nui.

Notes

1 "Te Papa and Weta Workshop open ground-breaking Gallipoli exhibition", *Te Papa*, April 2015: https://www.tepapa.govt.nz/about/press-and-media/press-releases/2015-news-and-media-releases/te-papa-and-weta-workshop-open (accessed October 2, 2019).
2 McCarthy, *Te Papa*, 12.
3 For a lengthier discussion of this shift in authority, see Haig, "Once More, with Feeling", 49.
4 Technically, the war relics collection, distributed around museums in New Zealand, by the Defence Department from 1919 to 1922, was a 'national war collection'. For the broader discussion around imperial war relic collecting, see Wellington, *Exhibiting War*, 1–12.
5 "Te Papa and Weta Workshop".
6 Winter, *War Beyond Words*, 3–5.
7 McKenna, "Keeping in Step", 152.
8 Chambers and Culbert, "Introduction", 6.
9 Assmann and Assmann, "Collective Memory and Cultural Identity", 125–33.

10 Winter, "Film and the Matrix of Memory", 863–64.
11 Reynard, *Celluloid Anzacs*, 185; Curran and Ward, *The Unknown Nation*.
12 McLeod, "Fall and Rise of Anzac Day", 159.
13 Reynard, 188.
14 McKenna, "Anzac Day", 110.
15 "Peter Weir on Gallipoli", *Literature/Film Quarterly*, 1981: http://www.peter weircave.com/articles/articlej.html (accessed October 4, 2019).
16 "Interview with Peter Weir", *Cineaste*, 1982.
17 CEW Bean, *Official History of Australia*; Gammage, *The Broken Years*.
18 Gammage, "Acknowledgements", in *The Broken Years*.
19 Lohrey, "Gallipoli", 29.
20 Gammage, Weir, and Williamson, *The Story of Gallipoli*.
21 *Auckland Institute and Museum News*, March 1982.
22 *Evening Post*, 22 April 1982.
23 Gadd, "A Bibliography of Maurice Shadbolt", 75–96.
24 For an overview of the August offensive, see Ekins, *Gallipoli* and Crawley, "The Myths of August".
25 *Evening Post*, 23 April 1982.
26 *Kaleidoscope,* 1982, TVNZ, Auckland.
27 Shadbolt, *Once on Chunuk Bair*, iv.
28 Shadbolt's introduction to the play's opening night programme, quoted in Mann, "Maurice Shadbolt the Dramatist", 131.
29 Shadbolt, *Once on Chunuk Bair*, 83.
30 Wilson, "*Once on Chunuk Bair* and the Anzac Myth", 40.
31 Mann, "The first production of *Once on Chunuk Bair*", 15.
32 Das, "Introduction", 4. See also, Haggith and Smith, "Sons of Our Empire", 35–53.
33 Jeremy Payne, *Kaleidoscope*, 1982, TVNZ, Auckland.
34 This flattering contrast has been endorsed by Jock Phillips, James Bennett, and Christopher Pugsley: see Jock Phillips, *To the* memory, Bennett, "Maurice Shadbolt, William Malone and Chunuk Bair", and Pugsley, *The Anzacs at Gallipoli*.
35 Shadbolt had access to the diaries and letters of Malone over the 1980s, before the Malone family papers were deposited with the National Library in 2008.
36 Shadbolt, *Voices of Gallipoli.*
37 *Gallipoli: The New Zealand Story,* TVNZ, 1984.
38 Pugsley, "Military Advisor's Perspective", *NZ on Screen,* April 2009: https://www.nzonscreen.com/title/gallipoli-the-new-zealand-story-1984/background (accessed October 2, 2019).
39 Pugsley, *Gallipoli: The New Zealand* Story, 1.
40 Also see, Pugsley, *The Anzac Experience.*
41 Promotional material, Eph-D-MUSEUM-1984-01, 1984/1985, National Army Museum (NZNAM), Waiouru.
42 *Evening Post*, 24 April 1984.
43 Hodge to Wilson, 30 March 1983, Eph-D-MUSEUM-1984-01, 1984/1985, NZNAM, Waiouru.
44 See 'The New Zealand Story', Eph-D-MUSEUM-1984-01, 1984/1985, NZNAM, Waiouru.
45 Stretton to Banner, 26 August 1982, Eph-D-MUSEUM-1984-01, 1984/1985, NZNAM, Waiouru.
46 *New Zealand Herald*, 14 April 1982; (Press Release) TVNZ, 22 March 1982. Also see: *Timaru Herald*, 30 March 1982.
47 'The New Zealand Story', Eph-D-MUSEUM-1984-01, 1984/1985, NZNAM, Waiouru.

48 This estimation is based on research from the World War 1: Oral History Archive, conducted by Nicholas Boyack and Jane Tolerton in 1987. Boyack and Tolerton interviewed 84 NZEF veterans and published the oral history as *In the shadow of war: New Zealand soldiers talk about World War One and their lives* in 1990.

49 Robinson to TVNZ, 13 February, 1983; C. Hodge to I. J. Robinson, 23 February, 1983, Eph-D-MUSEUM-1984-01, 1984/1985, NZNAM, Waiouru.

50 'Gallipoli - research notes', p. 4, Eph-D-MUSEUM-1984-01, 1984/1985, NZNAM, Waiouru.

51 Inglis, "The Unknown Australian Soldier," 15. A similar observation was made by Jock Phillips as he contemplated the relationship between state institutions, history, and national identity: Phillips, "Our History, Our Selves," 107–23, 114.

52 The problems of the Australian War Memorial omitting Australian colonial violence remains a contested issue in Australia. See, Paul Daley, "Why Does the Australian War Memorial Ignore the Frontier War?", *The Guardian*, 12 September 2013: https://www.theguardian.com/world/2013/sep/12/australian-war-memorial-ignores-frontier-war (accessed October 24, 2019).

53 Inglis, *Sacred Places*, 63, 250.

54 Talbot to TVNZ, 14 April, 1982; Hodge to Talbot, 6 May 1982; Eph-D-MUSEUM-1984-01, 1984/1985, NZNAM, Waiouru.

55 'The New Zealand Story', Eph-D-MUSEUM-1984-01, 1984/1985, NZNAM.

56 Martin to Fleming, 29 November 1982, Eph-D-MUSEUM-1984-01, 1984/1985, NZNAM, Waiouru.

57 This was first intimated by Pugsley in *The New Zealand Story*, then reiterated in subsequent works, with the author advocating for legislative change over the 1990s: see *The New Zealand* Story, 356, the introduction to *The Anzac Experience*, and 'Papers relating to Chunuk Bair Day', MS-Papers-11408-30, 1990–2012, National Library of New Zealand.

58 Pugsley, *Gallipoli: The New Zealand Story*, 355.

59 Ibid., 356. The 'loss of innocence' became an enduring theme of Pugsley's work. In 1992, he collaborated in the curating of the exhibition 'A Loss of Innocence' through the National Archive Collection, Wellington, which exhibited paintings, photographs, and documentary other material from various archive collections. See "A Loss of Innocence", *Bulletin*, No.78, May/June 1992, 2.

60 *Chunuk Bair*, Daybreak Pictures, 1992; Bennett, 56.

61 "Speech by the Prime Minister Dawn Service, Gallipoli 25 April 1990", 25 April 1990: https://pmtranscripts.pmc.gov.au/release/transcript-8013 (accessed October 2, 2019).

62 *Gallipoli: The Muddle that Moulded a Nation*, Quilla Production House, 1986.

63 McCarthy, 31–32.

64 Ibid, 70.

65 McKernan, *Here Is Their Spirit*.

66 McKenna, "Keeping in Step," 165–165.

67 This cooperation was contrary to Pugsley's argument that the experience of Gallipoli generated a heightened sense of nationalism between the two parts of the ANZAC forces. Pugsley, *The New Zealand Story*, 13.

68 Hucker, "A Determination to Remember", 106.

69 WW100, "New Zealand's First World War Centenary Programme – The programme overview July 2014": https://ww100.govt.nz/sites/default/files/files/WW100%20-%20Information%20Sheet%2001%20-%20Jul%2014%20-%20V1_1.pdf (accessed October 24, 2019).

70 "Govt Spends $20m on WWI Arts and Culture", *Stuff*, 19 April 2015: https://www.stuff.co.nz/national/last-post-first-light/67781872/govt-spends-20m-on-wwi-arts-and-culture (accessed October 24, 2019).

71 "Pou Kanohi New Zealand at War': https://www.aucklandmuseum.com/war-memorial/galleries/pou-kanohi-new-zealand-at-war (accessed October 24, 2019).
72 See, for example, the depiction of Anzac Cove at night, an image that aligns with Weir's famous "Crossing the River Styx" scene in the 1981 film, on the Te Papa website here: https://www.tepapa.govt.nz/visit/exhibitions/gallipoli-scale-our-war (accessed October 25, 2019).
73 Cairns, "The Wait and the Fight".
74 My emphasis. Pugsley, *The New Zealand Story*, 11, 12, 27.
75 "Te Papa and Weta Workshop open ground-breaking Gallipoli exhibition", *Te Papa*.
76 For a commentary on this distinct generational history, see Phillida Bunkle's review, "A Marriage and Self-Serving Boomer Men", *Newsroom,* 11 September 2019: https://www.newsroom.co.nz/2019/09/11/783867/scenes-from-a-marriage-a-personal-feminist-essay-by-an-ex-wife# (accessed October 24, 2019).
77 Bonelli, "This is Wellington", 44.
78 *Metro*, March 1, 2016.
79 *WW100 Final Report*, April 2019: https://ww100.govt.nz/final-report (accessed October 2, 2019).
80 Ross, "Conceiving and Calibrating *Gallipoli: The Scale of Our War*", 30.
81 See Danny Keenan's prescient commentary, "We Came of Age on Battlefields of New Zealand", *New Zealand Herald*, 24 April 2006: https://www.nzherald.co.nz/nz/news/article.cfm?c_id=1&objectid=10378631 (accessed October 25, 2019).

Bibliography

Assmann, Jan, and Aleida Assmann. "Collective Memory and Cultural Identity." *New German Critique*. 65. 1995. 125–33.

Bean, C.E.W. *Official History of Australia in the War of 1914–1918, Volume I – The Story of Anzac: The First Phase*. Sydney: Angus and Robertson, 1921.

Bean, C.E.W. *Official History of Australia in the War of 1914–1918, Volume II – The Story of Anzac: from 4 May 1915 to the Evacuation*. Sydney: Angus and Robertson, 1924.

Bennett, James. "Man Alone and Men Together: Maurice Shadbolt, William Malone and Chunuk Bair." *The Journal of New Zealand Studies*. 13. 2013. 46–61.

Bonelli, Diego. "This is Wellington: The Representation of Wellington in New Zealand Tourism Film from 1912 to 2017." PhD Thesis. Victoria University of Wellington, 2018.

Boyak, Nicholas, and Jane Tolerton. *In the Shadow of War: New Zealand Soldiers Talk about World War One and Their Lives*. Auckland: Penguin, 1990.

Cairns, Puawai. "The Wait and the Fight – Telling Māori WW1 Histories and the Search for Alternative Platforms." https://www.academia.edu/24306500/The_Wait_and_the_Fight_Telling_Maori_WWI_Histories_and_the_search_for_alternative_platforms. Accessed October 24, 2019.

Chambers, John Whiteclay and David Culbert. *World War II, Film, and History*. Oxford: Oxford University Press, 1996.

Crawley, Rhys. "The Myths of August at Gallipoli." In Craig Stockings, ed. *Zombie Myths of Australian Military History*. Sydney: New South Books, 2010, 50–69.

Curran, James, and Stuart Ward. *The Unknown Nation: Australia after Empire*. Melbourne: Melbourne University Press, 2016.

Daley, Paul. "Why Does the Australian War Memorial Ignore the Frontier War?" *The Guardian*. September 12, 2013. https://www.theguardian.com/world/2013/sep/ 12/australian-war-memorial-ignores-frontier-war. Accessed October 24, 2019.

Das, Santanu. *Race, Empire and First World War Writing*. Cambridge: Cambridge University Press, 2011.

Ekins, Ashley. *Gallipoli: A Ridge Too Far*. Canberra: Australian War Memorial Press, 2013.

Gadd, Murray. "A Bibliography of Maurice Shadbolt: 1956–1980." *Journal of New Zealand Literature*. 2. 1984. 75–96.

Gammage, Bill. *The Broken Years: Australian Soldiers in the Great War*. Sydney: Penguin Books, 1975.

Gammage, Bill, Peter Weir, and David Williamson. *The Story of Gallipoli*. New York: Penguin Books, 1981.

Haggith, Toby, and Richard Smith. "Sons of Our Empire: Shifting Ideas of "Race" and the Cinematic Representation of Imperial Troops in World War I." In Lee Grieveson and Colin MacCabe, ed. *Empire and Film*. London: Palgrave Macmillan, 2011. 35–53.

Haig, Nicholas. "Once More, with Feeling: An Enquiry into The Museum of New Zealand Te Papa Tongarewa's Exhibition *Gallipoli: The Scale of Our War*." MA Thesis, Massey University, 2016.

Hucker, Graeme. "A Determination to Remember: Helen Clark and New Zealand's Military Heritage." *Journal of Arts Management, Law, and Society*. 40, 2. 2010. 105–18.

Inglis, Ken. *Sacred Places: War Memorials in the Australian Landscape*. Melbourne: Melbourne University Press, 1998.

Inglis, Ken. "The Unknown Australian Soldier." *Journal of Australian Studies*. 23, 60. 1999: 8–17.

Lohrey, Amanda. "Australian Mythologies – Gallipoli: Male Innocence as a Marketable Commodity." *Island Magazine*. 1982. 29–34.

Mann, Philip. "Maurice Shadbolt the Dramatist: On the Dramaturgy of Once on Chunuk Bair." In Ralph Crane, ed. *Ending the Silences: Critical Essays on the Works of Maurice Shadbolt*. Auckland: Hodder Moa Beckett, 1995. 130–46.

Mann, Philip. "The First Production of *Once on Chunuk Bair*." *Illusions*. 11. 1989.

McCarthy, Conal. *Te Papa: Reinventing the National Museum, 1998–2018*. Wellintgon: Te Papa Press, 2019.

McKenna, Mark. "Anzac Day: How Did It Become Australia's National Day?" In Henry Reynolds and Marilyn Lake, eds. *What's Wrong with Anzac?*. Sydney: New South Books, 2010. 110–34.

McKenna, Mark. "Keeping in Step: The Anzac 'Resurgence' and 'Military Heritage' in Australia and New Zealand." In Shanti Sumartojo and Ben Wellings, eds. *Nation, Memory and Great War Commemoration: Mobilizing the Past in Europe, Australia and New Zealand*. Oxford: Peter Lang, 2014. 151–67.

McKernan, Michael. *Here Is Their Spirit: A History of the Australian War Memorial 1917–1990*. St. Lucia: University of Queensland Press, 1991.

McLeod, Jenny. "Fall and Rise of Anzac Day: 1965 and 1990 Compared." *War & Society*. 20, 1. 2002. 149–68.

Phillips, Jock. "Our History, Our Selves: The Historian and National Identity." *New Zealand Journal of History*. 30, 2. 2001. 107–23.

Phillips, Jock. *To the Memory: New Zealand's War Memorials.* Nelson: Potton & Burton, 2016.

Pugsley, Christopher. *The Anzac Experience: New Zealand, Australia, and Empire in the First World War.* Auckland: Oratia Press, 2004.

Pugsley, Christopher. *The Anzacs at Gallipoli: A Story for Anzac Day.* Auckland: Reed, 1999.

Pugsley, Christopher. *Gallipoli: The New Zealand Story.* Auckland: Oratia Media, 1984.

Reynard, Daniel. *Celluloid Anzacs: The Great War through Australian Cinema.* Melbourne: Australian Scholarly Publishing, 2007.

Ross, Kirstie. "Conceiving and Calibrating *Gallipoli: The Scale of Our War.*" *Museums Australia Magazine.* 24, 1. 2015. 22–31.

Shadbolt, Maurice. *Once on Chunuk Bair.* Auckland: Hodder and Stoughton, 1982.

Wellington, Jennifer. *Exhibiting War the Great War, Museums, and Memory in Britain, Canada, and Australia.* Cambridge: Cambridge University Press, 2017.

Wilson, Janet. "Colonize. Pioneer. Bash and Slash': Once on Chunuk Bair and the Anzac Myth." *Journal of New Zealand Literature.* 34, 1. 2016. 27–53.

Winter, Jay. "Film and the Matrix of Memory." *The American Historical Review.* 106, 3. 2001. 857–64.

Winter, Jay. *War Beyond Words Languages of Remembrance from the Great War to the Present.* Cambridge: Cambridge University Press, 2017.

WW100. "New Zealand's First World War Centenary Programme – The Programme Overview July 2014." https://ww100.govt.nz/sites/default/files/files/WW100%20-%20Information%20Sheet%2001%20-%20Jul%2014%20-%20V1_1.pdf. Accessed October 24, 2019.

Part II
The centenary in practice

5   Voicing war

Canadian soldiers' oral culture during and after the First World War

Tim Cook

The First World War was an attritional struggle that pitted armies of millions against each other. Along the Western Front, the primary battlefield of the Canadian forces, the citizen-soldiers from the Northern Dominion struggled as did all others in spaces of violence. Death came at any moment to the soldiers who spent much of the war in the front-line trenches lurking in what appeared to be open graves. The large-scale offensives, as rare as they were, led to even greater mass carnage in short periods of time.

Over 100 years later, we continue to wonder how the soldiers endured in such conditions. Why did they continue to fight? To survive the strain soldiers turned to many coping mechanisms, from rewards of rum, cigarettes, periodic leave, and medals, to the paternalistic support of officers, through to punishment within the rigid system of army discipline.[1] And yet the social cohesion in small units, bands of men coming together to rely on each other to see it through the storm, was also crucial. Isolated from civilisation and a tribe onto themselves, the soldiers' society has held together by a unique culture.[2] This culture drew upon civilian culture in Canada and Britain, and occasionally from interactions with the French behind the lines, but it was shaped and repurposed by the soldiers in the trenches. A study of this culture is revealing 100 years later of the ways that these men coped and survived. With their voices silenced with time, their vibrant culture remains a way for us to engage with their legacy.

Soldiers' culture

Culture has had no shortage of scholars attempting to define it, but adopting a broad anthropological definition that includes beliefs, practices, customs, and values that define groups of people, societies, and nations, perhaps gives us the breadth to explore this soldiers' culture.[3] Culture is created in communities and is shared to strengthen bonds and relationships, and it consists of high-brow artistic endeavours and the everyday experiences of individuals to provide social meaning and insight into a group. While there are many studies of war and culture, often scholars have been drawn to the elites, the novelists or artists who fashioned moving visual works or stirring

word pictures.[4] With the 620,000 Canadians who served during the war having an average grade-six level of education, the vast majority would never
paint in the official war art program or write poignant prose or poetry like
the university-educated officers.[5] But they too created and contributed to a
culture that helped to sustain the soldiers' society.

The citizen-soldiers forged their own culture in sites of destruction, and
it included writing and performing songs, composing doggerel and simple
rhyming couplets, collecting souvenirs, producing newspapers, and mount-
ing plays. There was an identifiable death culture, sports culture, hospital
culture, and material culture. This chapter examines three aspects of the
Canadian soldiers' voice culture: slang, swearing, and song. Voice culture
was an aspect of the larger soldiers' culture and the war was not conducted
in silence. The mass of men at the front, underground and often engaging
in manual labour or sentry work, carried on with all manner of talk as they
chatted quietly, argued boisterously, mumbled incoherently, pontificated on
the latest rumour, and shared news from home. This voice culture underpinned almost all aspects of the larger soldiers' culture and it also reveals
issues of masculinity and identity (Figure 5.1).

Figure 5.1 Canadian soldiers out of the line, enjoying a mug of tea. There was a
rich oral culture throughout the war, but the experience behind the firing line was different than that of the trenches. Away from the shells and
snipers, soldiers were able to relax, tell stories, talk about life after the
war. Courtesy of Library Archives of Canada, PA-003125.

The normalising nature of talk is worthy of note, if only to reinforce the idea that the war on the Western Front was not one constant battle. Instead, much of the soldiers' time in the trenches was plagued by boredom and there were many breaks for leisure activities, from writing letters to reading novels. But soldiers' conversations in their many forms was the most common method of engaging in interpersonal relations with fellow soldiers. This chapter also explores whether that soldiers' culture, which was deeply tied to and influenced by the spaces of violence along the Western Front, made its way back to Canada. Did the soldiers' voice culture of slang, swearing, and song that acted as a shield along the Western Front find itself repurposed by the veterans who returned to Canada?

Talking

Even amid the carnage of shelling and snipers, in the mud and muck, soldiers talked. They shared fears and hopes, and they speculated on all manner of issues related to the war and life at home. Lieutenant Stanley Rutledge remarked of the constant chatter and conversations up and down the line, on the firing step and in the dugouts, where men huddled for safety and companionship. In those dark holes in the ground, 'One can hear more rumours, more complaints, more jests than in any other part of the line.' With all the chatty gossip, Rutledge likened it to an 'afternoon quilting party.'[6] There were avid conversations on how the war might end and what was wrong with the Brass-Hats (senior officers). New men huddled around the old soldiers who had survived longer than others, to learn their secrets. There were animated conversations and even debates. George Timmins noted that his chums in the 116th Battalion often sat around and held mock peace conferences, where 'we draw up terms & settle the war offhand, to our own satisfaction.' The terms, he said slyly, required Germany to pay a 'huge indemnity,' hand over occupied territory, and reimburse 'Canada's sons for their trouble.'[7] Another Canuck, Sergeant Thomas Clark Lapp, revealed in a letter home, 'No debating society ever had more earnest speakers than I have heard in my experience of some five months in France (Figure 5.2).'[8]

As part of the soldier's oral culture, they embraced their own slang and idioms to better express their experiences and bind together the group against the outsider.[9] 'Trench slang is a language all its own,' wrote a Canadian infantryman in the 7th Battalion's regimental paper, *The Listening Post*.[10] When the citizen-soldiers of the Canadian Expeditionary Force (CEF) enlisted, trained, went overseas, and ultimately served on the Western Front, they encountered a rolling barrage of new slang that underpinned the soldiers' society.[11]

> The vocabulary as it existed was the same in all parts of the line, one section generously sharing with another any new words or phrase it had been fortunate enough to acquire, by passing it along from unit to unit,

Figure 5.2 The Leaning Virgin of Albert on the Somme sparked many rumours. Soldiers passing through the ruined city to the Somme battlefield were told that when the Virgin Mother and baby fell the war would end. It was one of countless rumours shared by the soldiers during the war to make sense of the war. Author's collection.

recounted French Canadian E.L. Chicanot.[12] Word of mouth, bawdy song, trench newspapers, and theatre shows also helped to keep the words alive. With the Canadians fighting in France and Belgium, they encountered French and Belgian words, which were cheerfully corrupted and expressed with great meaning with the soldiers' culture. Coningsby Dawson, a professional writer turned soldier, was taken with how the British and Dominion soldiers anglicised French words to craft a new soldiers' slang. 'The great word of the Tommies here is, 'No bloody bon' – a mixture of French and English,' recounted Dawson, 'which means that a thing is no good.'[13] Most soldiers' newspapers – published by the soldiers for the soldiers and with about 30 papers circulating among the Canadian forces – periodically published the definitions of slang words and phrases with humorous meanings, in the hope of educating raw recruits. In the case of *The Listening Post* edition of 10 August 1917, the target of mirth was the Americans, who were welcomed by the Canadians to the Western Front – even if they were three years late. 'Study this list thoroughly,' the paper advised, and when you arrive in the trenches you will be able to greet the old soldier in his own language, whilst the shrapnel burst around and the machine-gun beats its devil's tattoo in your ears—that is, of course, if the old soldier hasn't disappeared into the deepest dug-out on the first whisper of the approaching storm. There are some things we cannot teach you by mail![14]

Of course, recent Canadian recruits arriving at the front also had to absorb this slang to find their place in the otherwise closed society. As stretcher-bearer F.W. Noyes remarked, new soldiers 'had to learn a whole new language – a weird vernacular of war-slang, pidgin-French, barrack-room jargon and front-line wisecracks – all rolled together.'[15]

Swearing

Every bit of kit and weapon had its own slang term and acronym, along with nicknames for other allies and the enemy. The Hun, Kraut, Fritz, and Jerry were just some of the printable words for German soldiers. Almost every descriptor for the Germans was enlivened by vulgarities. Many Canadians were initially shocked at the prevalence of swearing, although they soon found the words rolling from the tongue in the hyper-masculine environment. The *Kilt*, the trench newspaper of the 72nd Battalion, chided its readers that they 'used to lie in bed to nurse a headache,' but now they had been transformed into 'men.'[16] This manly atmosphere encouraged – even demanded – swearing, which reinforced the difference of the trench world from the civilian realm of non-combatants.[17]

There was no shortage of swear words for the soldiers but the most common seemed to be bugger, cunt, and fuck. Fuck was used in the form of a noun, verb, adjective, and adverb, and possibly in other ways as well. In one rough if revealing letter, Brooke Claxton, a wartime gunner and future Minister of National Defence, deftly illustrated how the word was employed as an intensifier and an amplifier. Writing in the last year of the war, Claxton noted the difference, in his mind, between Canadian and British troops:

> We get into a hole & our feeling is 'Come on, boys, this—thing is a hole. We've got to get into action as soon as possible so let's get it out and get to bed' & everyone jumps and & pulls & heaves and uses the brain. The Imperial says 'fuck the fucking thing. I'm going to fucking well stay in the bloody hole.[18]

The words bloody, balls, dick, shit, and bugger were also used in weird and wonderfully ungrammatical ways, with cunt being equally popular with soldiers who even employed it as an adjective by adding 'ing.'

Swearing was useful in the hard world of the trenches and some soldiers described it as a type of verbal armour against the strain of service and combat. E.L.M. Burns, a Lieutenant in the war and a Lieutenant-General in the Second World War, believed the propensity to swear came from the impotence felt by men confined to the trenches. 'The forces beyond the power of the soldier drove men to volleys of curses in the hope of warding off the angst and perhaps "blowing off steam."' Some men also swore as a form of 'magic spells and incantations.... If words of a sufficient power are pronounced in a certain unfavourable situation, something has been done to ameliorate that situation' (Figure 5.3).[19]

After the war, Newfoundlander W.C. Hawker captured some of the idioms of speech among the Empire's troops, noting,

> All spoke the same language, and gave evidence of being sprung from a common stock, all had the same grand basic traditions that are known as British, yet each had its own peculiar mode of expression, its turn dialect and speech, which perhaps more than anything else, marked its individuality.[20]

The language of war, as well as manly swearing, brought the different armies together, but, as Hawker observed, each component of the Empire's 'common stock' distinguished itself through its members' accepted slang, which

Figure 5.3 Canadian gunners chalk slang and sayings on shells to be fired against the enemy. Courtesy of Library Archives of Canada, PA-000622.

in turn reinforced its distinct identity. Canadians incorporated some of the slang from Canada and the United States into their daily trench talk, and often exaggerated it when around British soldiers as a badge of distinctiveness. George McFarland, second in command of the 4th Canadian Mounted Rifles in the last two years of the war, described one Western Canadian on a First Army musketry course who deliberately exaggerated his jargon:

> We Canadians were a sort of curiosity, especially Ormond, who was a breezy Westerner with an amazing vocabulary of slang. At the onset he was talking a language which was like Greek to most of the chaps, and he just set himself out to use all the slang he could rake up, much to the amusement of all the rest of us.[21]

Canadian soldiers seemed to think they were using a lot of unique slang, but much of it appeared similar to the other British or Dominion soldiers, although accent and inflection helped to distinguish, as did some phrases that were more North American, such as 'jake' – as in meaning 'fine.' The soldiers' slang helped to bring together the disparate groups that formed the CEF, with French Canadians, new Canadians, and even Indigenous Canadians using slang and swearing in a pigeon English to communicate with comrades.

Swearing too could help to distinguish the many groups that formed the British Empire's forces. Tom Johnson of the 102nd Battalion felt that swearing revealed elements of the Dominion's character. He wrote in one letter home:

> Let me contrast the difference between the Canadian and the Englishman with one example: The Canadian swears more. His language is richer and more original in curses and obscenity. The Englishman swears too, but it is hackneyed and lacking in ideas. He swears with a sort of apology in his voice, whereas the Canadian is conscious that he is inventing phrases which are his own, so he has pride in his own language. Perhaps this is a superficial distinction, but in warfare it is one which seems essential to success. This originality tends to make him a more dangerous opponent.[22]

It seems unlikely that swearing made a soldier more dangerous, but perhaps the credence of that is worth considering in more detail. More profitable, perhaps, is how swearing and slang helped to both distinguish the various forces within the British Expeditionary Force and brought them together in common language.

Singing

Much of the slang and swearing was presented, shared, and reinforced in the soldiers' songs, which were a rousing part of the isolated trench culture.[23] Such songs were warbled during the conflict to give strength, to unify men,

ANY OLD NIGHT 'CHUB' LE BARON WAS AROUND

Figure 5.4 A cartoon capturing an informal moment in the trenches, with one soldier playing the violin and the others singing along. Author's collection.

and to uplift morale. Songs sustained and shaped the closed soldiers' society. Men in uniform sang heartily and lustily in training camps in Canada, on the troop ships, in England, marching behind the lines, and in the trenches. Officers and men even sang together. In mid-1916, Canadian trench newspaper *The Forty-Niner* described a recent 'sing-song,' the third in a series, which had been a great success: "All the officers of the staff were present and shedding their 'august majesty,' which is so necessary on active service."[24] Soldiers were bound through blood and belonging, but songs welded them even tighter within the closed society (Figure 5.4).

The soldiers sang cheerful pop songs, wistful romantic refrains, swaggering masculine ditties of drink or girls but also hymns and folk songs. Ralf Sheldon-Williams, a pre-war farmer at Cowichan Station, British Columbia, as well as a poet and illustrator who served as a sergeant in the 10th Canadian Machine Gun Company, noted that he and his comrades welcomed the lowbrow:

> Chopin, Grieg, Mendelssohn? Where are your laurels when the fighting man finds solace in 'Keep the Home Fires Burning,' 'Pack all your Troubles' and 'Roses are Blooming in Picardy'? The writers of these hackneyed, stale effusions, anonymous so far as we were concerned,

could move us and lift us more surely with their homely notes than all your classic masters.[25]

The low-brow or popular culture resonated strongly across the rank and file, and the latest musical-hall songs were brought back from soldiers on leave, sometimes in the form of song sheet music and other times with men jauntily singing them.

But soldiers also took pride in parodying popular songs of the day, twisting them to make them their own. The Canadian trench newspaper, *The Brazier,* told its readers in November 1916 that 'Parodies on popular songs are always in demand.'[26] With an established melody or beat, soldiers added their own lyrics to reflect their closed culture. This sentiment was expressed in many ways but the soldiers' song 'Never Mind' captured the powerful idea of the need to carry out despite the strain.

> If the sergeant drinks your rum, never mind
> And your face may lose its smile, never mind
> He's entitled to a tot but not the bleeding lot
> If the sergeant drinks your rum, never mind
> When old Jerry shells your trench, never mind
> And your face may lose its smile, never mind
> Though the sandbags bust and fly you have only once to die,
> If old Jerry shells the trench, never mind[27]

And it went on and on. Soldiers added verse after verse, of increasingly awful situations for the soldiers to encounter – and to shrug off – to 'never mind.' Songs like this were a means of communicating the need to cope. This is a shrugging off of the trials of the war, a powerful motif in the soldiers' culture, with a grin and bear it attitude running through poems, cartoons, prose, and all manner of cultural products.

While much of the Canadian soldiers' culture was similar to that of British Empire troops, with shared songs, jokes, trench newspapers, as well as empire-wide heroes like Harry Lauder, Bruce Bairnsfather, and Charlie Chaplin, there was still much that was unique to the Canadian culture. Soldiers' correspondence reveals that folk songs from Canada were part of the repertoire. In particular, songs from French Canada, be it Quebec, parts of Ontario, New Brunswick, or other isolated communities were sung by French Canadians to carve out a distinct identity from English soldiers. Pre-war songs or specific wartime songs that referenced Canada or Canadian places, spaces, or characteristics also helped 'Jonny Canuck' – as one popular wartime song was called – to distance himself from the British Tommy. The references voiced on stage, in plays, and in poems were to Canada or Canadian history, heritage, geographical places, celebrities, sports and all manner of identifiable content. French-Canadian, Indigenous, and even new Canadians, be they of Slavic origin or Icelandic, all contributed to this culture, and one can see the diversity of the Canadian Corps as reflected in its culture. As soldier Andrew Napier observed in September 1915 of the many comrades in his unit: it was 'very cosmopolitan, [and filled with] Canucks, British, French, + some Indians'– all of whom sat around 'playing cards + singing all the latest choruses.'[28] Katsuji Nakashima, a Japanese Canadian serving in the Canadian Corps, one of at least 222 identified by scholars, wrote of the night before the assault on Vimy Ridge in April 1917, recalling, 'Everyone had the strained look of men waiting to go into battle. At nine in the evening we joined the *hakujin* in singing songs, the words of which we did not understand.'[29] Language barriers could be breached by songs and oral culture because they could be sung without full command of their language of composition. The songs of the war were thus a means by which some of the differences between the soldiers – of language, ethnicity, region, and class – could be more easily overcome, and they assisted in forging new bonds within the soldiers' tribe.

Veterans' culture

The soldiers' voice culture was formed and sustained in sites of violence and death. It brought the soldiers together, it expressed issues of identity and masculinity, and it was a shield. But what happened to the culture of these citizen-soldiers once they returned to Canada, and again became citizens, albeit now as veterans? Harold Simpson, a gunner from Prince Edward Island, reflected on what awaited him after the fighting stopped:

> A fellow has been through a battle and his soul is sick with the horror of it all, for no matter how hardened one may be the sight of shattered broken men is a cruel one….The memory follows him, haunts him. Even in his dreams he sees again those cruel, gaping wounds, hears those heart-rending cries of pain and his whole being revolts. It is unbearable. He must forget for a time.[30]

Soldiers like Simpson were conflicted over the war. Many wished to leave it behind and find a new life free from the filth and execution of the trenches. And yet few were ever free from the war. It imprinted itself on bodies, minds, and spirits. A surprising number of soldiers found solace in the memories of their service, refusing to cast aside the war that ran as a deep scar across their lived history.

While this is not to minimise those tens of thousands of veterans who suffered from war-time wounds on meagre pensions and the countless more who could not escape the traumatic battles that haunted their minds, there were parts of the war that were redeeming, primarily the comradeship formed in uniform and a deep sense of satisfaction at having served in a time of great need.[31] All survivors knew they had lived through an historic event. Sergeant R.G. Kentner, who served with the

46th Battalion, used his wartime journals and diaries to pen his memoirs during the 1920s.

> The experiences I have had are stamped indelibly upon my memory and nothing can possibly erase them. I can remember what happened the first night I spent in the Line as clearly as I can what I was doing two hours ago. It is the Gravest Chapter in the Book of My Life, the most important and most valuable.[32]

Over the years there was a powerful nostalgia that drove many veterans to band together.

Soldiers' voice culture was intricately linked to that wartime comradeship and it is not surprising that this culture was carried forward into the post-war years. While much of the soldiers' culture was exclusionary and not meant to be shared with civilians – some of the wartime slang and vernacular entered the English language. Phrases like 'lousy' and 'crummy,' applying to the lice-infected soldiers, are still used, although applied more generally to show disapproval or shabbiness. Having a 'chat' remains part of the English language, although it no longer refers to picking lice from one's clothes. 'Souvenir,' of French origin, replaced 'keepsake,' which was a more common English word for objects of remembrance. 'Shell shock,' the phrase banned by the military authorities during the war for fear of encouraging malingerers who would use mental wounds to escape the front, retains a similar meaning today as it did in the war. 'Firing Line,' 'Behind the Lines,' and 'Over the Top' are all still in use, as is the phrase, 'back to the trenches' or some variation of that, to denote re-engaging with a difficult task. This soldiers' language and slang has infused the memory of the war and has been incorporated into how we talk about the war even after all the participants are gone.

During the war, Padre George Wells was one concerned clergyman who agonised over the soldiers' dirty language, which had become, in his belief, 'steadily worse as the war raged.'[33] He used his influence to drive for a 'language purge.' It had little impact in curbing the soldiers' swearing, but when the war ended there was a more determined push by the army to clean up the vulgarities.[34] Years after the war, *The Legionary* magazine – voice piece of the Canadian Legion in Canada – joked that the attempt to clean up the soldiers' language was 'like prohibition in the United States ... a 'noble experiment.' It had about the same result.'[35]

However, Canadian society would not stand for foul-mouthed veterans, and as ex-service men returned to their communities most learned to swallow the vulgarities. At the same time, much of the outright swearing was removed from post-war novels and memoirs, although occasionally it was revealed. *The Legionary* noted in an April 1938 issue about how Hollywood was planning to make a new war movie, *The Road Back*, a sequel of sorts to *All Quiet on the Western Front*. The Legion endorsed it but chaffed a little because there was no profanity in the script. The director had announced that 'men in great anger do not swear; their hate or emotion is invariably expressed more succinctly in biting sarcasm.' In a remarkable rebuke, *The Legionary* noted 'Men in great anger do not swear as much as in small anger, it is true, but the troops swore pretty continuously in all degrees of anger.' For matters of general swearing,

> troops did plenty, and any suggestion that they did not is false.... The troops swore more freely (and harmlessly) when in high spirits than in low. In fact, it was the periods of bouts with a sense of hopelessness at the folly of it all which reduced profanity to its lowest ebb.[36]

If the slang filtered into the English language but the swearing was reduced to acceptable levels of vitriol, the soldiers' songs had even greater influence and longevity. These songs were the sound track to the war. Soldiers had sung them with relish and gusto during the war and it is not surprising that these songs – from the sentimental to the lewd, from the pop hits to the rollicking limericks, and everything in between – were important cultural icons after the guns fell silent. Hearing songs could provide a tremendous rush of emotions. Gunner Ernest Black, who survived several years at the front, wrote of their impact:

> Someone would start *There's a Long Trail*. I wish you could have heard us sing that. Unconsciously we put months or years of yearning into that song. It seemed to be an outlet for things that needed expression but could not be said. I could sing it then but I cannot sing it now... After 40 years the emotions that song expressed for me behind the lines in France rise up again and choke me.[37]

The songs also reverberated in the veterans' halls that began to be erected across Canada in the late 1920s as sanctuaries for the veterans. These new exclusive sites allowed veterans to rejuvenate wartime culture. Here, and at other reunions, veterans traded freely on their old stories, rehashed old jokes, and lubricated their throats for hours of singing. While the scars of war could not be hummed away with a tune, the songs were a way for veterans to stay connected with one another, to engage with the past, and to relive wartime comradery.[38]

Listening for soldiers' culture

Few veterans wished to fully forget their war experience, which was complex and even contradictory, with loss and horror mixed with laughter and comradery. Yet the memory of the First World War remained contested and a veterans' disillusionment emerged in the difficult post-war years. After debilitating and crushing economic Depression, along with the rise of war-hungry dictators like Adolf Hitler, and even the Second World War against the evil Nazi regime, the First World War faded into obscurity.

The comradeship of the trenches was further replaced in popular memory by hardship, loss and death, especially around the 50th anniversary when the war was rediscovered in Britain and the Dominions. At that point, the deluge of films, books, plays, and documentaries focused on the horror and futility of the war, condemning the generals and wondering how the soldiers survived. It was not wrong to question the war's casualties or inflicted suffering, but nor was it usually a balanced presentation.[39]

The soldiers' culture was increasingly muted. One of the reasons for this was the exclusionary nature of the veterans' culture. Like the comradery that sustained the soldiers in the trenches, this culture was not meant to be shared. Returned veteran Ben Wagner recounted that those at home 'tried to understand, but you gradually got to the point where you only talked about the war with [other veterans].'[40] Bill McNeil remembered the First World War veterans

> came home blind, crippled, sick, mentally ill, or alcoholic. Many old soldiers would never talk about the horrors of war. If they talked at all, it was about the great times they had had 'over there' – about the wine, the women, and the song. Down at the Legion hall they were always singing, and it made us youngsters, listening through an open window wonder, who the hell was this 'Madamoiselle from Armyteers,' anyway? She must have really been something to have all those old men down at the Legion crying their eyes out over her.[41]

Even as the First World War was being denigrated or forgotten by much of society decades later, in the veterans' society there remained much happiness and nostalgia for the war years and their complex meaning to those that served.

The rich scholarship on the shifting nature of the war's constructed meaning over the previous three decades has created a deeply nuanced understanding of the war over time, but almost all of the popular cultural products surrounding the war – be they novels, plays, and films – have the soldier-as-victim narrative as the dominant theme. This is the war depicted almost exclusively as a tragedy: no jokes; no laughter; all horror, all the time. Those not killed in battle are left as ruined men with shattered minds. And yet for many veterans they had different memories of the war. There was amusement, joy, adventure, and the powerful impact of comrades to be relied upon for survival. Most who served were proud of their service, even if it had been hard and at times traumatising. They did not talk about being tricked into serving King and country. Decades after the armistice, First World War soldier Charles Carrington recounted his discomfort over how the war's meaning had moved firmly into the realm of ridicule and contempt:

> I never meet an old 'sweat,' as we liked to describe ourselves, who accepts or enjoys the figure in which we are now presented.... Just smile and make an old soldier's wry joke when you see yourself on the

television screen, agonized and woebegone, trudging from disaster to disaster, knee-deep in moral as well as physical mud, hesitant about your purpose, submissive to a harsh, irrelevant discipline, mistrustful of your commanders. Is it any use to assert that I was not like that, and my dead friends were not like that, and the old cronies that I meet at reunions are not like that?[42]

This is not to suggest that war was good and that soldiers embraced the memories of standing in the mud, preparing to kill other men, and watching their mates killed. But there were few who denied that it was a momentous event in their lives, and it was not just one unending horror show. One method of unpacking the complexities of the war is through the enduring nature of soldiers' wartime oral culture and how it continued to reverberate within the veterans' culture. And yet as the veterans passed away, their voices were silenced.

The commemorative period for the centennial saw many acts of remembrance, education, and action, but it was never easy for contemporaries to locate the soldiers' resiliency within the mud and mayhem of the battles of the imagined past. This investigation of the soldiers' voice culture not only reveals how slang, swearing, and songs united the Canadian soldiers and sustained trench communities but is a means to better understand the veterans' experience now that they are gone. While some aspects of this oral culture are forever lost to time, much can be salvaged by investigations into the soldiers' produced records, be it letters, diaries, trench newspapers, or other ephemera. The soldiers' society reveals that the combatants were not passive victims but active participants in shaping their war experience. And this culture returned to Canada with the veterans, allowing them to continuing forging new bonds of comradery in the post-war years, giving voice to their shared war experiences. More than a 100 years later, if we reframe the war experience from suffering to struggle, and pivot from victims to active participants, or at least provide a space for this agency in future studies and cultural products, we will have a better sense of how these citizen soldiers coped and endured in the First World War, and how their language legacies live on long after voices have been silenced.

Notes

1 See Sheffield, *Leadership in the Trenches*; Iacobelli, *Death or Deliverance*; Smith, *Between Mutiny and Obedience*; Hodgkinson, "*Glum Heroes.*"
2 For work on soldiers' culture, see Audoin-Rouzeau, *Men at War 1914–1918*; Fuller, *Troop Morale and Popular Culture*; Saunders, *Trench Art*; Nelson, *German Soldier Newspapers*; Cook, *The Secret History of Soldiers*.
3 There are thousands upon thousands of books written on culture. The most useful entry is Burke, *What Is Cultural History?*.
4 See, for example, Fussell, *The First World War and Modern Memory*; Laura Brandon, *Art or Memorial?*; Eksteins, *Rites of Spring*.

5 For education, see Cook, "From Destruction to Construction," 109–43. This would be the equivalent of year seven in New Zealand or the school level for a ten or eleven year old.

6 Rutledge, *Pen Pictures from the Trenches*, 59–60.

7 Bennett, ed., *Kiss the Kids for Dad*, 35.

8 Canadian Letters and Images Project (CLIP), T.C. Lapp, 20 September 1918.

9 Walker, *Words and the First World War*.

10 *The Listening Post* 27, August 10, 1917, 10.

11 See Edwards, *Language, Society and Identity*; Eastman, *Aspects of Language and Culture*; Rottman, *FUBAR: Soldier Slang*, 10.

12 Chicanot, E.L., "French—a la Guerre," *The Legionary*, August 2, 1930, 16.

13 Dawson, *Khaki Courage*, 56.

14 *The Listening Post* 27, August 10, 1917, 10.

15 Noyes, *Stretcher-Bearers... At the Double!*, 128.

16 Library Archives of Canada (LAC), RG 9, v. 5079, *Kilt*, November 27, 1916, 2.

17 For a discussion of swearing in societies, see Hughes, *An Encyclopedia of Swearing*; O'Connor, *Cuss Control*; Montagu, *The Anatomy of Swearing*.

18 Bercuson, *True Patriot*, 40.

19 LAC, MG 31 G6, ELM Burns papers, v. 9, file Articles, papers—U, Untitled Document on soldiers' slang in the First World War, n.d.

20 Hawker, W.C. "Some Characteristics and Traditions of the Royal Newfoundland Regiment," *The Veteran* 7.1, April 1928, 48–49.

21 Canadian War Museum (CWM), Military History Research Centre (MHRC), 58A 2 7.7, George Franklin McFarland Major, memoirs, 21–23 May 1918.

22 Miller, ed., *Letters Bridging Time*, 22.

23 See Sweeney, *Singing Our Way to Victory*; Brophy and Partridge, *Songs and Slang of the British Soldier*.

24 CWM, MHRC, *The Forty-Niner* 1.3, 4.

25 Sheldon-Williams, *The Canadian Front in France and Flanders*, 190.

26 CWM, *The Brazier* 6, November 15, 1916, 2.

27 See "Trench Songs," Virtual Seminars for Teaching Literature, University of Oxford, http://projects.oucs.ox.ac.uk/jtap/.

28 CLIP, Andrew John Napier, 26 September 1915.

29 Ito, *We Went to War*, 46.

30 CWM, MHRC, Hagen (ed.) *World War I Letters*, 169.

31 Much of the Canadian and international scholarship focuses on traumatised Canadians. Humphries, *A Weary Road*; and for the foundational text on veterans, see Morton and Wright, *Winning the Second Battle*.

32 Kentner, *Some Recollections of the Battles of World War*, 1.

33 Wells, *The Fighting Bishop*, 202–04.

34 Crerar, *Padres in No Man's Land*, 130.

35 The Orderly Sergeant, "Five Nines and Whiz Bangs," *The Legionary*, Christmas Number, December 1933, 18.

36 "Soldiers and Swear Words," *The Legionary*, April 1938, 32.

37 Black cited in Wood, *Vimy!*, 48.

38 For songs and nostalgia, see Barrett et al., "Music-Evoked Nostalgia," *Emotion* 10.3, 2010, 390–403. For veterans' halls, see Jonathan Vance in *Death So Noble* and Cook, *The Secret History of Soldiers*.

39 See Todman, *The Great War: Myth and Memory* and Bond, *The Unquiet Western Front*.

40 Read, ed., *The First World War and Canadian Society*, 207.

41 McNeil, *Voices of a War Remembered*, 5.

42 Carrington, "Some Soldiers," 157.

Bibliography

Audoin-Rouzeau, Stéphane. *Men at War 1914–1918: National Sentiment and Trench Journalism in France during the First World War.* Translated by Helen McPhail. Providence: Berg, 1992.

Barrett, Frederick S., et al. "Music-Evoked Nostalgia: Affect, Memory, and Personality," *Emotion* 10, no. 3 (2010): 390–403.

Bennett, Y.A., ed. *Kiss the Kids for Dad, Don't Forget to Write: The Wartime Letters of George Timmins, 1916–18.* Vancouver: University of British Columbia Press, 2009.

Bercuson, David Jay. *True Patriot: The Life of Brooke Claxton, 1898–1960.* Toronto: University of Toronto Press, 1993.

Bond, Brian. *The Unquiet Western Front: Britain's Role in Literature and History.* New York: Cambridge University Press, 2002.

Brandon, Laura. *Art or Memorial?: The Forgotten History of Canada's War Art.* Calgary: University of Calgary, 2006.

Burke, Peter. *What Is Cultural History?* Cambridge: Polity Press, 2004.

Canadian Letters and Images project, Cobourg World Letter (accessed September 17, 2019) https://www.canadianletters.ca/collections/all/collection/20576

Canadian Letters and Images project, Andrew John Napier (accessed September 17, 2019) https://www.canadianletters.ca/collections/all/collection/20566

Carrington, Charles. "Some Soldiers," in George Panichas (ed.) *Promise of Greatness: The War of 1914-1918.* London: Littlehampton, 1968: 155–66.

Cook, Tim. "From Destruction to Construction: The Khaki University of Canada, 1917–1919," *Journal of Canadian Studies* 37, no.1 (Spring 2002): 109–43.

Cook, Tim. *The Secret History of Soldiers: How Canadians Survived the Great War.* Toronto: Allen Lane, 2018.

Crerar, Duff. *Padres in No Man's Land: Canadian Chaplains and the Great War.* Montreal: McGill-Queen's University Press, 1995.

Dawson, Coningsby. *Khaki Courage: Letters in War-Time.* London: Bodley Head, 1917.

Eastman, Carol. *Aspects of Language and Culture.* Sam Francisco: Chandler and Sharp, 1975.

Edwards, John. *Language, Society and Identity.* Oxford: Oxford University Press, 1985.

Eksteins, Modris. *Rites of Spring: The Great War and the Birth of the Modern Age.* Toronto: Lester & Orpen Dennys, 1994.

Fuller, J.G. *Troop Morale and Popular Culture in the British and Dominion Armies, 1914–1918.* Oxford: Clarendon Press, 1990.

Fussell, Paul. *The Great War and Modern Memory.* Oxford: Oxford University Press, 1975.

Hodgkinson, Peter E. *"Glum Heroes": Hardship, Fear and Death—Resilience and Coping in the British Army on the Western Front 1914–1918.* Solihull: Helion & Company Limited, 2016.

Hughes, Geoffrey. *An Encyclopedia of Swearing: The Social History of Oaths, Profanity, Foul Language, And Ethnic Slurs in the English-speaking World.* Armonk: M.E. Sharpe, 2006.

Humphries, Mark. *A Weary Road: Shell Shock in the Canadian Expeditionary Force, 1914–1918.* Toronto: University of Toronto Press, 2018.

Iacobelli, Teresa. *Death or Deliverance: Canadian Courts Martial in the Great War.* Vancouver: University of British Columbia Press, 2013.

Ito, Roy. *We Went to War: The Story of the Japanese Canadians who Served During the First and Second World Wars.* Stittsville: Canada's Wings, 1984.

Kentner, Robert George. *Some Recollections of the Battles of World War I.* Fredonia: Irene Kentner Lawson, 1995.

McNeil, Bill. *Voices of a War Remembered: An Oral History of Canadians in World War Two.* Toronto: Doubleday Canada, 1991.

Miller, Ollie, ed. *Letters Bridging Time: Tom Johnson's Letters.* Self-published, 2007.

Montagu, Ashley. *The Anatomy of Swearing.* Philadelphia: University of Pennsylvania Press, 2001.

Morton, Desmond and Glenn Wright. *Winning the Second Battle: Canadian Veterans and the Return to Civilian Life, 1915–1930.* Toronto: University of Toronto Press, 1987.

Nelson, Robert L. *German Soldier Newspapers of the First World War.* Cambridge: Cambridge University Press, 2011.

Noyes, Frederick. *Stretcher-Bearers... At the Double!: History of the Fifth Canadian Field Ambulance which Served Overseas during the Great War of 1914–1918.* Toronto: Hunter-Rose, 1937.

O'Connor, James. *Cuss Control.* New York: Three Rivers Press, 2000.

Read, Daphne, ed. *The Great War and Canadian Society: An Oral History.* Toronto: New Hogtown Press, 1978.

Rottman, Gordon L. *FUBAR: Soldier Slang of World War II.* London: Osprey Publishing, 2007.

Rutledge, Stanley. *Pen Pictures from the Trenches.* Toronto: HarperCollins, 1992.

Saunders, Nicholas J. *Trench Art: A Brief History and Guide, 1914–1939.* Barnsley: Leo Cooper, 2001.

Sheffield, G.D. *Leadership in the Trenches: Officer–Man Relations, Morale and Discipline in the British Army in the Era of the First World War.* Basingstoke: Palgrave Macmillan, 2000.

Sheldon-Williams, Ralf. *The Canadian Front in France and Flanders.* London: A. and C. Black, 1920.

Smith, Leonard V. *Between Mutiny and Obedience: The Case of the French Fifth Infantry Division During World War I.* Princeton: Princeton University Press, 1994.

Sweeney, Regina M. *Singing Our Way to Victory: French Cultural Politics and Music During the Great War.* Hanover: Wesleyan University Press, 2001.

Todman, Dan. *The Great War: Myth and Memory.* Hambledon: Continuum, 2005.

Vance, Jonathan. *Death So Noble: Memory, Meaning, and the First World War.* Vancouver: University of British Columbia Press, 1997.

Walker, Julian. *Words and the First World War: Language, Memory, Vocabulary.* London: Bloomsbury Academic, 2017.

Wells, George Anderson. *The Fighting Bishop.* Toronto: Cardwell House, 1971.

Wood, Herbert F. *Vimy!* Toronto: Macmillan of Canada, 1967.

6 New Zealand's war in the air

A centenary exhibition in review

Louisa Hormann

Introduction

For public historians worldwide, the greatest challenge posed by the First
World War centenary was also its great opportunity: 'bringing fresh perspectives to a conflict that is already familiar to audiences through not only
their family history and memorabilia, but also a shared culture of remembrance, and the arts and media.'[1] So wrote historian Kate Hunter and curator Kirstie Ross in their 2014 book, *Holding onto Home: New Zealand
Stories and Objects of the First World War*. In Aotearoa New Zealand, this
historiographical and curatorial challenge resulted in wide-ranging centenary projects that engaged with the anniversary in different ways. From
big-budget, national flagship projects like *Gallipoli: The Scale of Our War*,
which used new design technologies and modes of display to represent familiar Anzac stories at the national museum, to regionally based exhibitions and publications which focused instead on the forgotten and untold
stories of New Zealand's wartime experience.

The *War in the Air: New Zealanders in Military Aviation 1914–1918* centenary exhibition at the Air Force Museum of New Zealand in Christchurch
attempted to fill one such historiographical and commemorative gap in
New Zealand's national memory. In addition to the 100,000 men who served
in the New Zealand Expeditionary Force (NZEF) during the war, some 850
New Zealanders also participated in the air war, serving in the British Army's Royal Flying Corps (RFC), the Royal Naval Air Service (RNAS), the
Australian Flying Corps, the Women's Royal Air Force (WRAF) and from
April 1918, the Royal Air Force (RAF).[2] It is perhaps unsurprising that over
the past century, the predominance of the NZEF's role in the war has developed into a cultural fixation on the contribution and wartime experience of
the army, at the expense of other significant wartime narratives – namely,
the important naval and aviation contributions made by New Zealanders in
this conflict.

As a result, New Zealand airmen occupy a detached position within the
nation's memory of the war. However, many bright, colourful characters,
popular clichés and fallacies relating to the air war, continue to enthral the

generations since the conflict. From the appealing but simplified "Black-adder Goes Forth" television series to the undying intrigue of "The Red Baron" and cult of the flying ace, memory of the air war exists today, but it is mainly remembered in popularised form, and not as part of the New Zealand First World War story. The Air Force Museum thus found itself, like Hunter and Ross describe, challenged to tell a new and unfamiliar New Zealand war narrative within a pre-established public remembrance culture, largely informed by popular culture and an NZEF-centric national Anzac tradition. So what a challenge: how to engage and inform the museum visitor, familiar with the First World War but unfamiliar with this particular part of the New Zealand story?

I joined the Air Force Museum of New Zealand as an emerging museum professional in January 2017. I was myself, at that point, ignorant of New Zealand's particular role in the air war above the trenches. In my first permanent museum role, and only two months in, I cast myself into the deep end, researching and writing for the Museum's major centenary exhibition, *War in the Air*. This was a completely new experience for me, as I had never worked on an exhibition from concept development right through to installation before. As a lead writer in the Exhibition Team, I was privy to curatorial decisions informing the exhibition's development. But I was also a relative newcomer to working in the museum sector (as opposed to studying it), and it is from this unique position that I cast a critical eye over *War in the Air*.

As a reflective chapter, which considers the staging of an exhibition through personal experience, my discussion explores the opportunities and unique challenges of communicating New Zealand's First World War military aviation history through the museum exhibition medium. Beginning first with an introduction to the Air Force Museum, the significance of the air war and its prominence in the centenary programme, the following sections overview the established historiography of New Zealand's aviation role in the First World War, and how this influenced the exhibition's development, display, and representation of key themes. Using the *War in the Air* centenary exhibition as a case study, it examines how this exhibition sought to challenge established understandings of the First World War, especially the air war, and highlights implications for future commemorative projects.

Wigram, earthquakes and the centenary

As the national museum for the Royal New Zealand Air Force (RNZAF) and New Zealand military aviation, the *War in the Air* was always a story the Museum needed to tell – it is, after all, its national responsibility and mandate to tell that story. Its mission statement, 'To preserve and present the history of New Zealand military aviation for commemoration, inspiration, learning and enjoyment', reflects the Museum's overarching function

as the national RNZAF memorial.[3] Located on the site of the former air
base at Wigram, the site became the birthplace of New Zealand military
aviation when Christchurch businessman and politician Sir Henry Wigram
established the Canterbury Aviation Company (CAC) at Sockburn (later re-
named Wigram) in 1916. Two decades later, the RNZAF was established on
1 April 1937. 2017, therefore, marked two significant anniversaries in New
Zealand military aviation history: 100 years since the first pilots graduated
from the CAC flying school in 1917 and the 80th anniversary of New Zealand's Air Force.

Plans to mark the upcoming centenary began in 2010, with collections
staff setting aside stories and objects that could usefully be included in a
potential exhibition. Retrospective cataloguing of the Air Force Museum's
First World War collections and digitising these formed the basis for this
activity, as part of the Museum's centenary efforts focused on obtaining
funding to digitise all its First World War collections, 'not only for the exhibition, but as part of the centenary programme.'[4] In 2013, the Air Force
Museum Trust Board adopted four key concepts to support meeting its strategic objectives, one which included making First and Second World War
commemorations a priority.[5] As part of this, more than 1,600 objects were
processed for the Museum, with future plans to make them publically accessible.[6] Although initial planning for *War in the Air* began in 2012, the
Museum ultimately had a relatively short timeframe for the development of
an exhibition project of this scale: March 2017–November 2017.

The Canterbury earthquakes of 2010 and 2011 disrupted institutional
plans to mark the centenary in Christchurch and across the Canterbury region. So, while the Air Force Museum's digitisation project went ahead, the
War in the Air exhibition was put on hold for the first half of the centenary.
At the time, all the Museum's efforts went into supporting several other
community projects, like the Canterbury Cultural Collections Recovery
Centre (CCCRC), the *Canterbury Stories: Remembering the First World War*
collaborative exhibition (also held at the Air Force Museum) and associated
Canterbury 100 events, focussing on Canterbury's First World War experience more generally. *Canterbury Stories,* in particular, was created to relieve
the pressure on other local institutions to display centenary exhibitions in
the years following the earthquakes.

While not originally planned for display so late in the centenary cycle, the
War in the Air exhibition opened in the Museum's Cochrane Gallery in November 2017, following the deinstallation of *Canterbury Stories.* Intending
to tell the story of New Zealand's airmen using the Museum's collections,
and with special emphasis on locally trained CAC airmen, the exhibition
aligned with 2017, 'as the centenary of the graduation of the first pilots from
the Canterbury Aviation Company … that is a unique story to this site at
Wigram; that's part of our [Air Force Museum and RNZAF] history.'[7] New
Zealanders joined the air war before 1917, training near Auckland through
the New Zealand Flying School at Kohimarama or in England, but in terms

of Wigram's history and the significance of the Museum site, 2017 became the overarching centenary date for *War in the Air*.

Narratives of war

The exhibition's primary focus was the important role New Zealanders played in the air war, and the contribution of aviation technologies to the changing nature of warfare heralded by the First World War. This emphasis was developed in response to the particular lack of this subject in the national centenary programme. Despite the significance of the air war, and that New Zealanders actually served in it, history appeared to repeat itself during the 2014–18 period, with the prevailing emphasis of major centenary projects focused on the NZEF and 'soldiering' experience. The national preoccupation with the New Zealand soldier experience of the war is reflected in the established historiography of the conflict, and the striking absence of an official historical record of New Zealand's aviation role in the First World War.

Unlike the concerted efforts made by the New Zealand Government from 1949 to 1986 to record in 48 volumes the *Official History of New Zealand in the Second World War 1939–45*, no such wide-ranging official history was prepared at the end of the First World War. Only four official volumes on the war were published in New Zealand between 1919 and 1923. These volumes were written by senior army officers and only detailed the NZEF campaigns; they did not include any aspect of the New Zealand home front, New Zealanders in the naval or air war, or those serving with other dominion and imperial forces. The only official account of the air war was the seven-volume set, *The War in the Air* by Walter Raleigh and H.A. Jones, completed in 1937; being the British official history of the RAF in the war meant it did not focus on stories of New Zealanders.

Adam Claasen's 2017 book, *Fearless: The extraordinary untold story of New Zealand's Great War airmen*, was, therefore, a welcome and long-overdue addition to the historiography. Produced as part of the official 'WW100 First World War Centenary History series', a collaboration between Massey University, the Ministry for Culture and Heritage (MCH), the New Zealand Defence Force and the Royal New Zealand Returned and Services' Association, *Fearless* is the first dedicated monograph on the subject of New Zealanders serving in the first air war. Published in October 2017, one month before the *War in the Air* exhibition opened, the development of Claasen's book coincided with the Museum's own centenary research and digitisation programme. While there was no formal relationship between Claasen and the exhibition, and he was not involved in its development, both parties shared their research findings throughout the centenary, as they encountered many of the same research challenges – chiefly, the lack of a contemporary official history detailing New Zealand's aviation role in the conflict.

Given the New Zealand Government's lack of enthusiasm for military aviation, considered by most contemporaries to be a 'useless and expensive fad', it is unsurprising that New Zealand's role in the war in the air was not celebrated at the time, at least not through official channels.[8] As Claasen noted, the New Zealand military publicly declared its assessment on military aviation as 'a "waiting policy"' in 1914, and by the outbreak of war, the only opportunities to serve as a pilot or observer lay outside of the New Zealand military system.[9] In New Zealand especially, the fiscal reasons against establishing an air section were repeated during the pre-war years and into the post-war decades.

Despite pre-war public interest in aviation and the wartime media craze over the flying aces (including the New Zealand aces), the New Zealand Government refrained from establishing its own permanent, independent air arm in the first decade immediately following the war. At the behest of the New Zealand Government, Lieutenant Colonel Arthur Vere Bettington was sent to advise the government on this subject in 1919. Bettington urged New Zealand to seize the moment, recommending the use of skilled veterans to train the next generation of airmen.[10] But as Simon Moody suggests, 'the time was not right for such a major undertaking in post-war climate of austerity and uncertainty', and New Zealand did not form an independent air force until 1937.[11]

The historical divide between the NZEF soldiers and their fellow airmen is also clearly present in the archival records. Widespread pay disparity is evidenced in the base records files of New Zealand airmen; one of the most common issues recorded in airman files relate to pay, allowances and war pensions in service of the RFC/RNAS/RAF compared to their NZEF counterparts. Such bureaucratic divisions also extended to the treatment of their families. The only reference to a New Zealand airman in *Holding on to Home* describes Arthur Sherriff's 'wrangle with the Defence Department to get a next-of-kin railway pass to meet his son Royes at the Auckland wharf because Royes had served with the Royal Flying Corps, not the NZEF.'[12]

Lieutenant Sherriff, who never recovered from crashing his BE.2c aircraft in March 1916, was invalided out of service and returned to school teaching in New Zealand.[13] His portrait featured in *Centenary Faces*, a photographic display designed as an extension to the main *War in the Air* exhibit. Here, he could be remembered precisely *because* he served with the RFC – a centennial contrast with his overlooked treatment by the Defence Department. Sherriff's story exemplifies the situation of New Zealanders serving in the imperial forces. They, like the historical narrative they were part of, came to exist outside of the national focus on New Zealand's landbound experience of the war. But the centenary offered an opportunity to highlight these forgotten wartime stories, put them into historical context and bring them to new audiences (Figure 6.1).

Figure 6.1 Studio portrait of Lieutenant Royes Page Sherriff, wearing his Royal Flying Corps uniform. Collection of the Air Force Museum of New Zealand, 2002/307.3.

Exhibition development

Several factors, including the established historiography on the subject, determined the scope and interpretive focus of the *War in the Air* exhibition. As Claasen noted, there are 'few secondary sources and published primary materials available' on New Zealand airmen in the First World War, and most sources are archival, scattered across private collections, libraries and museum archives.[14] Even our own Air Force Museum archive collection, the largest dedicated First World War aviation collection of its kind in Aotearoa is small compared with the rest of the Museum's collection, which is overwhelmingly related to the Second World War; the collection reflecting the much greater prominence of New Zealand's air power commitment in this later conflict.

The original concept for *War in the Air* showcased the stories of just 4–5 individual airmen. This approach reflected findings from the Colmar Brunton pre-centenary national survey, which determined two key themes for effective public engagement with the centenary: 'Gallipoli and a personal connection.'[15] According to the survey, 'the types of exhibits that are of most interest to people (photographic exhibitions, survival stories and diaries) facilitate a more personal connection and appreciation of what it was like for those who fought or served in it.'[16] *War in the Air* intended to use the personal accounts of individual airmen to illustrate the role of New Zealanders in the air war, and appeal to a broad visitor audience. But it was soon realised such a narrow focus would be insufficient to communicate the level of information needed to place New Zealand's wartime aviation story in historical context.

Results from the survey also suggested public audiences attending centenary events would have little background knowledge of the war. Although 47% of survey participants believed they had a basic understanding of the war in general, only 24% indicated they knew a 'reasonable amount' about the war, with only 6% describing themselves as having a 'reasonably advanced level of understanding'.[17] Centenary exhibitions needed to include sufficient background information to the general topic to help visitors engage with the exhibition. Like the Imperial War Museum (IWM) centenary efforts, the Air Force Museum endeavoured to strike 'a balance between delivering a clear message on the one hand and on simultaneously engaging and challenging visitors on the other.'[18] The IWM approach was based on Australian research which confirmed many visitors 'still long for a tangible, factual and validated scholarly narrative', whilst simultaneously desiring 'more subjective information that expresses a range of differing opinions on a given topic'.[19]

Although *War in the Air* specifically focussed on aviation, the historical significance of air power in this war can only be understood in relation to the unprecedented nature and scale of industrialised warfare. As the introductory interpretation explained, over the course of the war, 'the aeroplane went from playing a very minor role in military operations to an essential element of modern, technological warfare.'[20] It was imperative to provide visitors with some general context to the war, so that they understood how the air war related to the rest of the conflict: its origins, pre-war aviation and air power development, and balancing these points with New Zealand's own contributions to the Allied aviation effort. These main points were addressed in an introductory panel on the external corridor wall of the gallery, using timelines and map displays. This enabled visitors to learn about the general context of the war and pre-war aviation before entering the main exhibition gallery space (Figure 6.2).

The *War in the Air* exhibition occupied a central gallery space. Its structure was thematic, based on sections roughly chronicling the development of air power in the First World War, and New Zealand's role in it – and designed to feature New Zealand airmen throughout each section. Later additions to *War in the Air* opened in December 2017; these helped to re-personalise the exhibition and highlight the human stories behind the conflict.[21] These displays, including rotating medal group displays and the *Centenary Faces* photography exhibit, were made accessible from the adjacent Caldwell Gallery, named in honour of one of New Zealand's most famous First World War airmen, Keith Caldwell. Accompanied by a suspended full-scale replica Sopwith Pup biplane on permanent display, visitors could explore in greater detail the background of individual New Zealanders who took part in the war in the air. The airman portraits displayed in *Centenary Faces* literally "put a face to the names" of a diverse selection of New Zealand's First World War airmen, including former schoolteachers, farmers, mechanics, lawyers, and insurance clerks – even a beekeeper! The personal element was

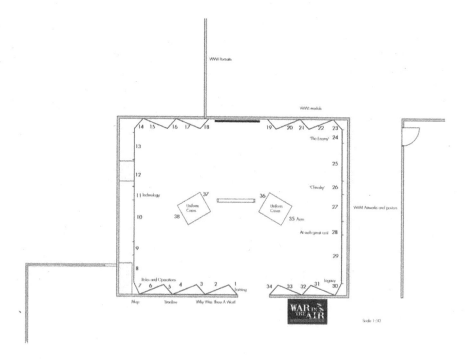

Figure 6.2 Final floor plan for the *War in the Air* exhibition. Design courtesy of the Air Force Museum of New Zealand.

further reinforced by panel text explaining how airmen departing for overseas service arranged for their portraits to be taken for their families and loved ones; photographs were therefore practical, portable, and made perfect mementos.

While these additional displays helped to highlight individual experience of the war, thus personalising the historical narrative, changing to a thematic structure meant many interesting stories about individual airmen were eventually left out of the main exhibit. Due to parameters and despite best intentions, the exhibition as a whole became less of a personal, 'Kiwi-centric interpretation' as a result.[22] Exhibition development is an iterative process, and making such changes during development is common practice in museum work. But exhibitions are also 'a medium of systematic yet mediated communication', and within this context, 'museums construct and transmit meaning for visitors … through interpretation of material evidence.'[23] Commemoration is therefore constructed, and the constructed nature of the exhibition medium can indicate much by what – or who – is left out.

New Zealand identity – or who to include – in *War in the Air* was a significant contextual point to establish during development. New Zealand gained dominion status in 1907 and did not become an independent nation until after the Second World War, so those considered (rather parochially) to have been "Kiwis" at this time were in fact officially designated British citizens. Furthermore, 1914 New Zealand had 'a diverse population of just over one million, of whom nearly a quarter – 228,779 – were born elsewhere'.[24] As such, the *War in the Air* exhibition, like Claasen's *Fearless*, featured individuals either born in Aotearoa, those who served in the New Zealand armed forces, or those who lived here before the war.[25]

War in the Air was subtitled "New Zealanders in Military Aviation 1914–18", and yet the concept of "what is a New Zealander?" was not explicitly explained in the displays.[26] This was perhaps a missed opportunity: to unpack the nation-building phenomenon around the First World War and truly ask why non-NZEF narratives of New Zealanders in the war have taken a whole century to come to light. The war in the air was fought by New Zealanders serving, not in a New Zealand air force but in a fledgling *British* air force (RFC and RNAS, and the later RAF). New Zealand's air war story, therefore, sits outside the popular New Zealand narrative of the First World War forging, or at the least playing a formative role, in the development of New Zealand's national identity.

Nationalist reinterpretations of history, stemming in large part from the influential works of journalist Maurice Shadbolt and others, strengthened the state-building narrative.[27] But unlike the NZEF, which as a uniquely New Zealand military force, was a perfect fit for this popular interpretation of the war, New Zealand airmen served with British, not New Zealand forces. Likewise, Glyn Harper's recent work on *For King and Other Countries: The New Zealanders Who Fought in Other Services in the First World War* shows that New Zealanders who fought for the British Empire with other services and under other flags were not previously included in official statistics.[28]

Perhaps this is also why the aviation story has been forgotten, left out of general public commemorations of the First World War, because the New Zealand war in the air story does not fit the traditional historic mould of the First World War nation-building narrative. Ultimately, New Zealand identity was not a central focus of the *War in the Air* exhibition, and again, the challenge of balancing the specific and general in exhibitions influenced decisions around addressing this issue. However, by presenting this unfamiliar story to centenary audiences, exhibition visitors might indeed question why they had not known more of this history before.

Display and representation

War in the Air made a conscious effort to challenge existing depictions of the war in the air through its democratisation of the airman – that is, its inclusion of both air and ground roles and operations undertaken by Allied air services during the war. In an effort to steer the wider Exhibition Team away from being 'drawn towards myths and clichés that have grown about the subject and try to encourage challenging those myths', the writers made a determined effort to feature personnel across *all* roles, including other ranks – ground crew as well as aircrew.[29] As Peter Hart argues in the RAF Museum's *First World War in the Air* exhibition publication, 'the phenomenon of the ace scout pilot has dominated all perceptions of the First World War in the air', but at the cost of 'glamoris[ing] a few, whilst marginalising the achievements of the vast majority of aviators.'[30] Communicating history through such a public medium, we saw an opportunity to challenge this assumption by describing the changing roles of aircraft, and the variety of skills and trades required to keep up with changing technology and operational tactics.

This approach is consistent with what has been termed the 'new military history', or military social history, 'emphasizing the common soldier, the experience of war, and the place of the armed forces in society.'[31] Gaining prominence since the 1980s, a new kind of military museum also emerged, drawing on military social history as the framework for telling new stories usually left out of the traditional military museum display.[32] Having opened in 1987, most of the Air Force Museum displays reflect this major shift in exhibition in military museums 'from simply displaying artefacts to using them to tell stories.'[33]

The stories and objects selected for display in *War in the Air* were chosen with the above concerns in mind, but logistical issues like gallery conditions and limited archival and object sources ultimately shaped the way artefacts were used. A total of 44 objects were displayed in the main exhibition gallery. In the case of audio-visual content, a digital copy of early RFC and RAF footage from the IWM was used; in other instances, objects on private loan and the occasional use of a British person's quote to illustrate a subject, due to there being no relevant New Zealand testimony available, were used. The difficulty was trying to make the collection fit the subject of the exhibition; *War in the Air* was not exhibiting based on the strength of the museum collection, but rather, the exhibition was motivated instead by the commemoration trend. This highlights a key constraint when exhibiting in a commemorative environment.

Furthermore, we were dealing with an unfortunate but common reality in museum work: poor records across the collection, and objects with no provenance. As one member of the Exhibition Team explained, 'when you're creating an exhibition where the emphasis is very much on personal stories and personal experiences, it's frustrating when you don't have stories around objects....'[34] However, in the case of photographic images, this issue was significantly mitigated by the First World War Digitisation Project. By the time we got to the exhibition development stage, most collections had been processed, giving greater access to, and overview of, the collection. For example, image research was made a lot easier by the fact that many photographs selected had already been scanned and processed ready for use. A notable benefit of aviation-related image research is that, unlike the anonymity of the trenches, photographs of fighters in the air war are often identifiable, thanks to the historical use of unique aircraft numbers and our subsequent ability to link identified aircraft to their pilots and crews.

Even so, at times we had to be creative in our approach to display as the exhibition's themes had already been decided. For example, our Keeper of Photographs struggled to find appropriate large format images in our collection to represent memorialisation and commemoration, and ended up using a photograph of German airmen carrying a coffin at one of their own military funerals.[35] While not directly representing New Zealanders' experience, the image creates a visual and conceptual link between two of the exhibition's more provocative sections, Enemies and Legacy, and serves to remind the visitor of the fatal consequences of war, as experienced by airmen on both sides of the conflict.

Throughout the exhibition development process, we were highly conscious of our responsibility to work against what Jay Winter has called the 'stylized fascination with combat [fetishisation of weapons]' by offering audiences 'alternative ways of approaching the terror of the battlefield.'[36] With exhibitions of this nature and working with military collections in general, how we represent stories and objects that are often concerned with death and killing is an ethically fraught undertaking. Winter suggests one method of challenging audiences is 'to ensure that for every weapon on display there is an image or an object pointing to the injury or mayhem that weapon causes to the human body.'[37] While not quite so exacting in our approach, we did ensure the displays recognised not only those killed in aerial warfare but also the issues surrounding those airmen maimed and injured – whether in body, mind or spirit – and how this experience impacted their post-war lives. This was achieved through careful use of text panels and imagery. Introducing new concepts such as morale and PTSI (Posttraumatic Stress Injury) to our displays was an important part of this exhibition, as much for complicating popular representations of the First World War airman as reminding the visitor of the more bodily impacts of aerial warfare (Figure 6.3).

One of the most challenging themes to communicate in the exhibition was Technology and Innovation, which included weapons. Objects in this section included a single Bentley BR2 model engine, some unusual weaponry (flechettes and a Ranken explosive dart), examples of communication equipment (Sterling spark transmitter, message streamer, a flying helmet with Gosport communication tube fittings), enemy technology (Zeppelin fragments, German gyro compass), and aircraft fragments (BE2 tail skid, aircraft fabric remnant, Fokker triplane fragments rumoured to belong to the Red Baron's own aircraft). Our focus was on telling the story of the war in the air as told through the stories of New Zealanders, and while most of these objects bear a connection to a New Zealand airman, there were not many objects available to tell the technology story from the perspective of personal experience. Furthermore, on this occasion we lacked time, resources, physical space,

Figure 6.3 War in the Air exhibition display. Note the panel featuring an unknown injured serviceman on the right. Image courtesy of the Air Force Museum of New Zealand.

and specialist knowledge in this area. These factors are all evident in the display's lack of interactives, from which this section in particular would have benefitted greatly. As the exhibition designer noted, technology in any exhibition context is a topic most effectively communicated without minimal text, but in this case, it was also the section hardest to illustrate, due to a lack of visual references and resources.[38]

In the absence of interactive display technologies, infographic illustrations were used to demonstrate the more practical concepts of aerial warfare in the First World War. These graphics used visual elements to present information to the viewer, so that the information could be seen rather than read. This technique worked well for visualising combat manoeuvres developed by fighter pilots during the war, providing simple but effective diagrams of famous techniques such as 'The Spin', 'The Renversement' and 'The Immelmann Turn'. But for explaining technical concepts like how early engines and the revolutionary interrupter gear or synchronisation gear operated, static diagrams were less effective (Figure 6.4).

In the case of victory scores of flying aces, where the statistics are varied and open for interpretation, the writers had to balance this infographic design approach with problematic and often conflicting historical sources. Here was an example of exemplified aesthetic versus content, a common curatorial concern that Piet de Gryse refers to as the 'fragile balance between

Figure 6.4 The Technology section of *War in the Air*, featuring weapons and infographic panel. Image courtesy of the Air Force Museum of New Zealand.

aesthetics and historically accurate representations'.[39] To communicate
this to the visitor, we decided to be transparent about the research process,
adding disclaimers and historical context to infographic elements where required. For example, the introductory text for the infographic on the war's
top scoring aces explains the different ways victories were classified during
the war (*shot down, destroyed* or *driven down out of control*), that unconfirmed
claims for victories were treated differently by the participating air forces,
and so for these reasons, 'speculation about some claims persists today.'[40]

The final problematic theme was Legacy, with the Writing Team finding
difficulties with its conceptual framework and suggesting a re-think of this
section. I personally felt the original proposed topics of Snoopy's Christmas and Blackadder to be incongruous with the commemorative element
and tone established in the exhibition, and with what few related objects we
had to display. Even now, it grates me a little that an edition of the popular *Biggles* adventure series by airman veteran Captain W.E. Johns was set
together with Second Lieutenant Ninian Hyslop's memorial scroll and Second Lieutenant Stuart Richardson's bronze memorial plaque (or so-called
"dead man's penny") in the same display case. Both latter objects were issued by the British Government to the deceased next-of-kin.[41] That said, the
arrangement did illustrate the incongruity of the conflict itself and served
to remind the visitor that for many, the experience of the First World War in
the air was as equally brutal as it was popularised (Figure 6.5).

Figure 6.5 Biggles of the Camel Squadron book, Memorial plaque (S. H. Richardson), and Memorial scroll (N. S. Hyslop) as displayed in exhibition. Collection of the Air Force Museum of New Zealand [1987/154.206; 1995/258.6; 2011/2154.4].

Conclusion

The final section of *War in the Air*, titled "Legacy: Centenary Reflections", concluded with the observation that while New Zealand's First World War aviation story had 'perhaps faded from national memory, other truths – and some myths – remain at the forefront of public consciousness and collective memory of the Great War', and that the centenary itself offered 'an opportunity to remember all who contributed to early military aviation in New Zealand.'[42] This statement summarises the paradox of curating this exhibition and highlights the opportunity and challenge posed by this particular centenary project: exhibiting a new and unfamiliar historical event to audiences engaged in an existing public remembrance culture, drawing from a museum collection lacking in related object source material.

Using the *War in the Air* as a case study, this chapter examined how this exhibition confronted established understandings of the war, specifically of New Zealand's role in the air war. In doing so, it illustrates the challenges of curating history exhibitions in a commemorative environment, especially when exhibiting not based on the strength of the museum collection but motivated by the centenary itself. The main lesson learned from this experience was the value of foresight and planning, and the importance of digitised collections, especially when lacking physical objects. Digitisation is only one example, but it is key to enabling curators and designers to create impactful displays, despite a lack of three-dimensional objects. Other alternatives, some of which were used in this exhibition, include loaned objects, audio-visual collections, photographic images and documentary archives, used to their full potential, either as original artefacts or digitised reproductions.

Reflecting on these curatorial challenges, the centenary presented an opportunity to consider the practice and impact of museum collecting and exhibitions. This chapter discussed how gaps in the established historiography influenced the *War in the Air* exhibition's development, display, and representation of key themes. As the centenary commemorations have shown, how these objects and stories are displayed and interpreted can either confirm or challenge our understanding of the past; reinforcing existing historical narratives, and sometimes offering new insights into a nation's wartime experience. The *War in the Air* exhibition was our attempt to share a part of New Zealand's wartime experience previously excluded from the national historical narrative and to challenge existing perceptions of the air war.

Acknowledgements

I would like to thank my museum colleagues for sharing their time and insights for this chapter, especially Simon Moody, Matthew O'Sullivan, Michelle Sim and Sam McKinnon.

Notes

1 Hunter and Ross, *Holding on to Home*, vii.
2 Claasen, *Fearless*, 8.
3 AFMNZ, "Annual Report 2016", 2.
4 Interview with M. Sim and S. McKinnon.
5 AFMNZ, "Annual Report 2016", 7.
6 Ibid., 15.
7 Sim and McKinnon.
8 AFMNZ, "War in the Air" exhibition. Sir William Nicholson, British Army Chief of Staff, 1908–12 on the military potential of aircraft before the First World War, as quoted in the *War in the Air* exhibition.
9 Claasen, p. 53.
10 Moody, "Reflecting on the Bettington Report of 1919 - a Centennial Legacy", in *Journal of the Royal New Zealand Air Force (Part B)*, 61.
11 Ibid., 63.
12 Hunter and Ross, 258.
13 AFMNZ, "War in the Air" exhibition.
14 Claasen, 7–8.
15 Colmar Brunton, "Benchmark Survey", 6.
16 Ibid.
17 Ibid., 5.
18 Wallis and Taylor, "The Art of War Display", in *Commemorative Spaces of the First World War: Historical Geographies at the Centenary*, 108.

19 Cameron, "Conscientiousness and Shifting Knowledge Paradigms", in *Museum Management and Curatorship*, 229.
20 AFMNZ, "War in the Air" exhibition.
21 Questionnaire response by Simon Moody, 2018.
22 Ibid.
23 Wallis and Taylor, 103.
24 Claasen, 8.
25 Ibid.
26 Questionnaire response by Simon Moody, 2018.
27 Both Australian and New Zealand critiques of this interpretation abound; most notably in the journalism field, but New Zealand academics have also entered the debate. See Charles Ferrall, "Maurice Shadbolt's Gallipoli Myth" and works by Jock Phillips and Christopher Pugsley in *How We Remember: New Zealanders and the First World War* edited by Charles Ferrall and Harry Ricketts, Victoria University Press, Wellington, 2014.
28 See Harper.
29 Questionnaire response by Simon Moody, 2018.
30 Hart, "The 'Aces': Knights of the Air?" in *First World War in the Air*, 83.
31 Hacker and Vining, "Military Museums and Social History", in *Does War Belong in Museums?*, 58.
32 Ibid., 42.
33 Ibid., 41–42.
34 Sim and McKinnon.
35 Questionnaire response by Matthew O'Sullivan, 2018.
36 Winter, "Museums and the Representation of War", in *Does War Belong in Museums?*, 37.
37 Ibid.
38 Sim and McKinnon, interview.
39 de Gryse, "Introduction," in *Does War Belong in Museums?*, 16.
40 AFMNZ, "War in the Air" exhibition.
41 Hunter and Ross, 225.
42 AFMNZ, "War in the Air" exhibition.

Bibliography

Air Force Museum of New Zealand (AFMNZ). "Annual Report 2016." Christchurch: Air Force Museum of New Zealand, 2016.
Air Force Museum of New Zealand (AFMNZ). "War in the Air: New Zealanders in Military Aviation 1914–1918." Christchurch: Air Force Museum of New Zealand, November 2017.
Colmar Brunton. "Benchmark Survey of the New Zealand Public's Knowledge and Understanding of the First World War and Its Attitudes to Centenary Commemorations." New Zealand: First World War Centenary Programme Office, Auckland War Memorial Museum and Museum of New Zealand Te Papa Tongarewa, 2013. https://ww100.govt.nz/benchmark-survey
Cameron, Fiona. "Conscientiousness and Shifting Knowledge Paradigms: The Roles of History and Science Museums in Contemporary Societies." *Museum Management and Curatorship* 20, no. 3 (2005): 213–33.
Claasen, Adam. *Fearless: The Extraordinary Untold Story of New Zealand's Great War Airmen*. WW100 First World War Centenary History Series. Auckland: Massey University Press, 2017.

de Gryse, Piet. "Introduction." In *Does War Belong in Museums? The Representation of Violence in Exhibitions*, edited by Wolfgang Muchitsch, 13–20. Bielefeld: Transcript Verlag, 2013.

Ferrall, Charles, and Harry Ricketts, eds. *How We Remember: New Zealanders and the First World War*. Wellington: Victoria University Press, 2014.

Hacker, Barton C., and Margaret Vining. "Military Museums and Social History." In *Does War Belong in Museums? The Representation of Violence in Exhibitions*, edited by Wolfgang Muchitsch, 41–62. Bielefeld: Transcript Verlag, 2013.

Harper, Glyn. *For King and Other Countries: The New Zealanders Who Fought in Other Services in the First World War*. Auckland: Massey University Press, 2019.

Hart, Peter. "The 'Aces': Knights of the Air?." In *First World War in the Air*, edited by Ross Mahoney, 83–87. Edgware, UK: Royal Air Force Museum, 2015.

Hunter, Kate, and Kirstie Ross. *Holding on to Home: New Zealand Stories and Objects of the First World War*. Wellington: Te Papa Press, 2014.

Moody, Simon. "Reflecting on the Bettington Report of 1919- a Centennial Legacy." *Journal of the Royal New Zealand Air Force (Part B)* 5, no. 1 (2019): 55–66.

Sim, Michelle, and Sam McKinnon. "Interview with M. Sim and S. Mckinnon." By Louisa Hormann. *War in the Air Exhibition Review*, no. 02/02. Voice 001.m4a. Unpublished recording (3 May 2018, Christchurch).

Wallis, James, and James Taylor. "The Art of War Display: The Imperial War Museum's First World War Galleries, 2014." In *Commemorative Spaces of the First World War: Historical Geographies at the Centenary*, edited by James Wallis, and David C. Harvey. Routledge Research in Historical Geography, 101–14. Abingdon, Oxfordshire: Routledge, 2018.

Winter, Jay. "Museums and the Representation of War." In *Does War Belong in Museums? The Representation of Violence in Exhibitions*, edited by Wolfgang Muchitsch, 21–40. Bielefeld: Transcript Verlag, 2013.

7 Uncovering the hidden stories of the voices against war in a New Zealand province

Margaret Lovell-Smith

Commemorations of First World War in Aotearoa New Zealand largely focussed on the military aspect of the war and the individuals involved in war-time service, with only a few references made to those who actively promoted peaceful settlement of international disputes, or refused to serve. The cumulative general impression given by the many books, articles, displays and events was of a country united in the war effort. Overall, the effect of the commemorations, as noted by Troughton and Fountain, was to 'reinforce the centrality of warfare in shaping global geopolitics and national identities' while another effect was 'to further normalise and entrench the institution of war'.[1]

'Voices Against War', initiated in 2016 by Christchurch's Disarmament and Security Centre, was a commemorative, regional, public education project which aimed to present an alternative perspective to the prevailing narrative. Christchurch, the main city in the province of Canterbury in the South Island of New Zealand, was the home of the National Peace Council and acknowledged by other centres as having the strongest organisational base and being a leader in the contemporary anti-war movement. By telling the personal stories of men, women and organisations who took a stand for peace before and during First World War, the project aimed to redress a lack of knowledge and understanding specifically about those who dissented, and, more broadly, Canterbury's anti-war history.

Conscientious objectors (COs) have commonly been regarded with contempt and derision as cowards, weaklings and shirkers.[2] 'Voices Against War' researchers found COs to be courageous individuals with the strength to resist verbal attacks as well as the physical privations of prison life. Their beliefs, whether Christian, socialist, or based on humanist beliefs in equality and the common humanity of the worlds' citizens – in fact many COs held a combination of such beliefs – speak of a strong morality and an adherence to principles of equality, freedom of speech and freedom of conscience. Those who resisted military training and conscription, intentionally broke the law, knowing that it would in most cases lead to a prison sentence.

Post-war, most COs kept a low profile and their stories remained largely unknown. One hundred years after First World War, public perception of the war and the peace movement had changed. The memory of the social stigma against being a CO had faded and relatives were keen to place on record something of the life story, beliefs and motivations of their family member. Family members not only helped voice the story of COs but also provided personal photographs of conscientious objectors or those involved in the anti-militarist movement, which helped bring their stories to life.

The main source of funding for the project was the World War I Commemoration Heritage Lottery Fund, with smaller amounts received from Quaker Peace and Service Aotearoa/New Zealand and the Peace and Disarmament Education Trust, PADET. Working in partnership with the University of Canterbury's (UC) School of Humanities and Creative Arts, it was agreed that the first step would be a website (designed and developed by the UC Arts Digital Lab) which the University agreed to fund and maintain. In addition, the project provided opportunities for UC students to gain community work experience as summer scholars and as student interns. The content of the website http://voicesagainstwar.nz launched in May 2016 has been edited by Associate Professor Jane Buckingham and continues to be added to.

In addition to its website, 'Voices Against War' communicated with the public through a display initially prepared for Christchurch's 2016 Heritage Week programme, and which later went to eight of the Christchurch City Libraries, several community venues and to the University of Otago's 'Rethinking Pacifism' conference in 2017. In December 2016, 'Voices Against War' organised a commemorative re-enactment to mark the centenary of the first trials for sedition during First World War, and since 2016 lectures and presentations have been given to numerous community groups, at seminars and at the 2017 'Dissent and World War I' conference in Wellington. Blogs and articles have been written for local media and websites. One of the project's summer scholars, Dan Bartlett, has remained involved and with the author is co-writing a book about Canterbury's anti-militarists and conscientious objectors both before and during the war.

In reflecting on 'Voices Against War' as a commemorative activity, this chapter will not only record where the 'hidden voices' were found but also give prominence to the beliefs that motivated the objectors and their supporters, so that this article itself becomes an opportunity to make their voices better known. Biographical essays about all the men and women quoted in this chapter can be read on the website http://voicesagainstwar.nz.

Previous coverage

The fact that hundreds of young men were imprisoned in New Zealand before and during First World War has been mentioned in general histories, and given more detailed treatment by historians of the peace movement like Elsie Locke, or Paul Baker writing about conscription.[3] Journal articles and theses by historians including R. L. Weitzel, Ryan Bodman and P.S. O'Connor provided more in-depth treatment of the subject.[4] Several former COs have since received biographical treatment in the Dictionary of New Zealand Biography (DNZB) where other aspects of their lives have been worthy of record. A few peace workers, including Charles Mackie, have also been included in the DNZB. But the views, beliefs and experiences of the COs themselves has barely been touched upon.

There are a few significant exceptions: Archibald Baxter's shocking and moving 1939 memoir, *We Will Not Cease,* about his experiences as one of 14 New Zealanders sent to Europe in an attempt to turn COs into fighters is still in print and has provided important insight into Baxter's beliefs and the worst aspects of the CO experience. David Grant's retelling of the Baxter and Mark Briggs story contextualised and added to Baxter's memoir.[5] But the magnitude of the suffering and horror described by Baxter has perhaps contributed to the lack of knowledge about the more mundane experiences of the COs who knew that their time in a New Zealand prison in no way matched the experiences of Baxter and 'the fourteen' who were sent to Europe. This realisation may have discouraged other COs from placing their memories on record.

Another exception to the general rule that the COs' experience has been 'hidden' is Harry Holland's *Armageddon or Calvary* published soon after the war in an attempt to publicise the shocking results of the New Zealand Government's conscription policy.[6] A socialist who had himself been imprisoned in 1913 for sedition, and editor of the staunchly anti-militarist Federation of Labour newspaper, the *Maoriland Worker*, Holland was well placed to record the experiences of New Zealand's imprisoned objectors. Central to the book are several chapters about the 14 men sent to Europe (including brief mention of David Robert Gray from Canterbury, who as a religious CO was deported in error), while other chapters cover the enquiry that arose from the appalling brutality experienced at the Wanganui Detention Barracks. The statement made by James Worrall, a former leader in Christchurch's Passive Resisters' Union (PRU), about brutality he experienced at Featherston Military Camp is also included, but in general the individual voices of COs are not represented.[7]

There is other published work which is less well known. Winston Rhodes wrote a biography of his friend Kennaway Henderson devoting several pages to Henderson's experiences as a CO, the most complete published study of a Canterbury CO to date.[8] Published more than 20 years after Henderson's death it relied heavily on the recollections of Henderson's friends, however, rather than Henderson's own words or recollections.[9] One of the few anti-militarists to have written about her own experiences is Sarah Page, who in 1936 wrote two articles, 'Wartime Reminiscences' and 'Paths to Permanent Peace' for the magazine *Working Woman*.[10] Her son Robin Page, who became a CO while a student at Canterbury College, was the subject of a rare study by historian Jim Gardner, published in 2003 but once again what Robin himself thought was not included. It is fair to say that probably very few people have either read or heard of these articles or of Henderson's biography.[11]

Given the lack of secondary sources 'Voices Against War' relied heavily on newly available digitised reports and archival records including the correspondence of the National Peace Council. The New Zealand National Library's 'Papers Past' project provided ready access to newspaper reports of objectors' military board hearings and court martials. Reports which quoted the objector, giving insight into his beliefs and motivation, provided many of the 'voices' of the individual COs. Tim Shoebridge's lists of imprisoned conscientious objectors and convictions for sedition, published in 2016 on the NZ History website, were another great resource, enabling ready identification of the 66 Canterbury men who became prisoners of conscience during the war.[12] The Charles Mackie papers in Canterbury Museum, which include the correspondence of Mackie as secretary of the National Peace Council, were another important source of information. As well as correspondence and reports the collection also provided cartoons, flyers, tickets and other ephemera, some of which have been posted on the 'Voices Against War' website as graphic 'items'.[13] Another significant find was a page of 60 signatures in the Richard Thompson papers in the Macmillan Brown Research Library at the University of Canterbury. Headed 'Paparua Prison – In Memory of Those Who Suffered for Conscience Sake 1916–19' the page is evidence that someone at the time, possibly one of the prisoners themselves, wanted there to be an historical record of at least some of New Zealand's 'prisoners of conscience' and made a point of collecting their signatures (Figure 7.1).[14]

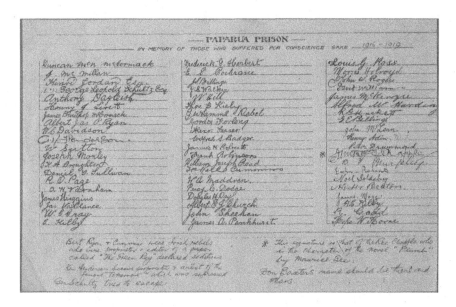

Figure 7.1 Paparua Prison – In Memory of Those Who Suffered for Conscience Sake 1916–1919.

Credit: MB287, Richard Thompson papers, item 51,734, Macmillan Brown Library, Christchurch.

Pre-war agitation

While the 'voices against war' featured in this article are mainly those of COs imprisoned during the war, the project was equally committed to telling the stories of the peace movement established before the war and those peace workers who were not directly affected by conscription.

The catalyst for the movement was the introduction of compulsory military training for all teenage boys which prompted Baptist layman Charles Mackie and others to found the National Peace and Anti-Militarist League in Christchurch in 1911. The following year the League evolved into two separate organisations: a local membership-based Anti-Militarist League (AML) and a delegate-based National Peace Council (NPC) with Mackie as the long-serving and conscientious unpaid secretary.[15] Both groups continued to work closely together.

Assisting Mackie in this work were several key individuals associated with other groups in the community. Harry Atkinson, who with his wife Rose became an active member of the anti-militarist movement, had founded the Socialist Church in Christchurch in 1896 and was involved with several other middle-class radical groups. He also had strong links with the trade union movement.[16] The newly established peace movement also had the support of the Canterbury Women's Institute (CWI), a feminist organisation which began work in 1892 on a wide range of issues including votes for women (achieved the following year) and the removal of all women's disabilities.[17] Among the members of the NPC and AML were socialists, trade unionists, Christians, young labourers and tradesmen, middle class couples, teachers, mothers of some of the objectors and members of the CWI.

The formation of a PRU in Christchurch in 1912, whose membership was limited to the young men liable for compulsory military training, further added to the strength of the movement.[18] While the NPC and AML worked in traditional ways with street corner speaking, writing letters and submissions, taking delegations to politicians, calling meetings, and educating the public by printing, importing and distributing literature, the PRU carried out a campaign of civil disobedience. Hundreds of young men were arrested, fined and many were imprisoned for their refusal to pay fines imposed after they had failed to attend compulsory drill sessions or for other offences against the Defence Act 1909 (and its amendments) (Figure 7.2).

This highly effective and visible peace movement, which successfully organised large meetings and demonstrations, appeared to come to a halt when New Zealand joined Britain in the European war in August 1914. War regulations prevented the movement from distributing anti-militarist literature and holding public meetings. The NPC's correspondence came under military censorship. With the introduction of conscription in 1916, war regulations were tightened further, to prevent any criticism of the war effort. But despite this the NPC continued to work quietly in the background and supported those who spoke out or objected to military service. From December 1917 until beyond the end of the war, 353 New Zealand men were

Figure 7.2 More than a 1,000 people are estimated to have attended this meeting in Victoria Square on 9 March 1912 held to protest against the imprisonment of nine members of the Passive Resisters' Union.
Credit: The Director, Zealandia Milling Co Ltd. Canterbury Museum, Ref 421.

imprisoned: either for making seditious statements which went against war regulations, or for refusing to serve in the military.[19] In the North Island, imprisoned objectors included Māori who came from iwi which had expressed their determination not to support the British, because of the Crown's confiscation of their land. But because the South Island iwi Ngāi Tahu were not conscripted, it appears there were no Māori among Canterbury's imprisoned conscientious objectors (COs).[20]

The 'voices'

The reasons that Canterbury men gave for refusing to serve during World War I can be broadly categorised as being either 'religious' or 'political' and within these categories were many strongly individualistic statements made at court martials or in letters. But even before conscription was introduced several Canterbury men were arrested early in 1917 and imprisoned for expressing seditious intentions, when they spoke against conscription. Freedom of conscience and general pacifist principles were also brought into the argument by these first Canterbury men to be imprisoned during the war.

Leading trade unionist and socialist, Fred Cooke, referred to Britain's hard-won tradition of freedom of conscience at his trial: 'So long as I am at liberty, while the Conscription Act prevails, I shall make speeches. Therefore I have to submit myself to the Court. But I as a Britisher protest against it … I cannot obey that law.'[21] Cooke, at the age of 50, had little fear of being conscripted but his strong conviction that conscription was wrong saw him serve a one-year sentence in prison.

Another socialist trade unionist, Peter Ramsay who had arrived in New Zealand from Britain in 1912, saw his stand as part of a class struggle but, unusually, also mentioned his long-standing membership of the peace movement: 'I have been a member of the peace movement since I was 14 and a half and I am not going to give up the principles for which I have fought for so many years for the class to which I do not belong.'[22] He was sentenced to 11 months in prison.

Reg Williams, who had been a leading figure in the pre-war PRU, argued at his trial that he had a right to speak against conscription and introduced a note of internationalism when he said: 'I am an Internationalist, opposed to war, and I shall oppose it as long as I have a tongue in my head.'[23] Williams, who had served numerous prison sentences pre-war, received a 12 months sentence for sedition as well as serving time in prison as a CO later in the war.

After the introduction of conscription in 1916, socialist pacifists and internationalists were among the COs imprisoned for refusing to serve in the military. George Samms, for example, saw the issue in terms of a class struggle. He told his court martial he stood for socialism, 'and all that Socialism stood for against militarism … He believed in the spirit of internationalism against the spirit of nationalism. Therefore he must refuse to become a soldier'.[24] But he was also a pacifist, explaining that after serving as a teenager for the British in the South African War he had sworn he would never 'shoulder a rifle again to shoot one of his own class… Wars were fought for the greed of one class … To try and kill men … was not only criminal but insane (Figure 7.3).'[25]

Figure 7.3 Conscientious objectors at Paparua Prison. Robin Page is sitting centre front. Frank Robinson is seated third from left next to George Samms and brothers James and John Roberts.

Credit: Patricia Smith.

Henry William Reynolds, boot-maker and pacifist, served sentences for both sedition and as a CO. On trial in 1916 for displaying seditious literature in his shop window, Reynolds presented mainly moral, humanitarian and internationalist arguments. His aim, he said, was to:

> bring people to realise the stupid, cruel and hellish uncivilised action by declaring war on each other.... My sole desire is to promote PEACE amongst my fellows, whether German, French, or any nationality. I look upon war as murder and the work of imbeciles, and I hope the days are not far away when nations will blush with shame to think that they took the sword against their brothers.[26]

The following year when Reynolds was brought before a court martial, he demonstrated his complete indifference to military authority by reading a copy of the Federation of Labour newspaper, the *Maoriland Worker,* during the hearing. On being advised to pay more attention to the proceedings, he replied that he didn't want a hearing, he ignored the Military Service Act and did not want to plead.[27]

Brothers John and James Roberts, court-martialled in March and June 1918, respectively, expressed moral and socialist arguments and referred to the importance of freedom of conscience but also commented on the impact that their punishment would have on their families. John Roberts, who was active in the labour movement, told the court that he believed killing to be murder, and as a Socialist he believed that all wars were waged for economic ends:

> It was futile to put conscientious objectors into gaol or to punish or torture them otherwise, as that could not kill their consciences... He was a married man, and the penalty would press heavily upon his family and himself, but he would submit to any penalty rather than violate the dictates of his conscience.[28]

His brother James, who appeared in court with a child standing at his knee, argued that 'any old thing' could be made legal by Parliament but that did not make it right. If British militarism really was different from Prussian militarism men should not be dragged off to fight, or thrown into prison: 'The court had married men before it that day. If the members had a spark of manhood left they would spare the wives and children the sorrow of having their husbands and fathers wrenched from them'.[29]

Religious objectors

About half of Canterbury's COs objected on religious grounds, with almost two thirds of that number coming from two small fundamentalist sects; the

Christchurch-based Richmond Mission and the Testimony of Jesus. Several other COs were not affiliated to any church. Broadly speaking New Zealand's largest churches supported the war.[30] Given that fundamentalist Christians tried to live as Jesus had taught in the New Testament, where among other teachings he urged his followers to 'Love your enemies and pray for those who persecute you', it's not surprising that fundamentalist Christians were often also pacifists.[31]

The largest group of religious objectors from Canterbury came from the loosely associated Testimony of Jesus which had been brought to New Zealand by evangelists from a schism of the Faith Mission in Northern Ireland in 1905.[32] By 1917, there were between 700 and 800 members in New Zealand. The sect had no written constitution but followed New Testament teachings and believed that the bearing of arms was forbidden by Christ. The sect's evangelists, who were required to have given away all their possessions to the poor, were dependent on voluntary contributions.[33]

Among the imprisoned Canterbury members of the Testimony of Jesus was an evangelist James (Jim) Vallance, a farmer from Coopers Creek. A member of a small evangelistic church which had sent him as a missionary to South Australia in 1908, he continued in this work for 30 years.[34] He refused non-combatant work because of his religious scruples, telling his military board hearing that he was an un-ordained minister who received no salary but lived on what Christians gave him and occasionally worked on farms in return for his keep.[35] A fellow evangelist Bertie Morgan who gave evidence to support him, said they 'tried to preach the Gospel as Christ had done'.[36] Both men served an initial 28 days plus 13 months of a two-year prison sentence.

Nine members of the Richmond Mission, whose members believed in living true to a literal reading of the New Testament, were imprisoned as COs while another two agreed to do non-combatant work. Typical of the attitude of the press to religious COs was an editorial response to a letter written by Richmond Mission member, Douglas Day. COs, said the *Sun*, deserved no sympathy and were unfit to live in a free country:

> Brave and gallant fellows are giving their lives by the thousand to protect snuffling "conscientious objectors" from the fate of the inhabitants of northern France and Belgium, and any man who would rather be enslaved by the Huns than lift his little finger in resistance to them is unfit to be a citizen of a free country.[37]

It was possible to make a successful appeal against military service on religious grounds, but in order to do so appellants had to belong to a church which had pacifism as a central tenet. Only three small churches met the criteria: the Society of Friends, or Quakers, the Christadelphians and the Seventh Day Adventists. Even men from these churches often served a prison term because of their unwillingness to engage with the military, and like all COs, were generally treated with scorn and contempt as 'shirkers'.

Noel Goldsbury, a Quaker, who could have made a successful appeal on religious grounds, instead refused to co-operate with the military authorities, was court martialled and imprisoned at Paparua Prison, 18 kilometres from the centre of Christchurch. Public controversy arose when he requested leave of absence from work:

> As I have been imprisoned by the military authorities for obeying what I conceive to be the Divine Will revealed by the teachings of Jesus Christ, I beg to apply for leave of absence until my release has been obtained.[38]

His employer, the Board of the Technical College, initially granted the leave which caused an outcry: most of the College's funding organisations threatened to withdraw their contributions. Under the onslaught of a newspaper furore Goldsbury resigned his position and the College Board rescinded its decision to grant him leave.

Of most value in providing insight into the thoughts, beliefs and the feelings of an imprisoned religious objector are the letters and diaries of Frank Money. A member of the Oxford Terrace Baptist Church in Christchurch, Money's objections were based on a close study of the New Testament: 'I find it impossible to take part in a struggle which has for its object the killing of men. God alone is the giver of life.' Acknowledging that his stand was against the law, he was nonetheless 'fully persuaded' his action was 'right in the sight of Almighty God.'[39] Once in prison, church bells ringing on Sunday prompted him to record that he now saw churches merely as social centres. 'I believe the true Christian of today is to be found outside her walls'.[40]

Several of Canterbury's religious objectors did not belong to any church. Robin Page, a 20-year-old graduate about to embark on a master's degree in science was banned from attending lectures at Canterbury College, where he was the only defaulter.[41] A scrapbook of photos, letters, and clippings compiled by his family includes the statement Page made at his Court Martial noting his objections came from his reading of the New Testament.

> As a Christian, I believe War to be wrong and think that our aim in life is Love, and not Hate and Fear. I cannot find anything in the New Testament which, to my mind, in any way supports War, and I do find much that is against it.[42]

Because he regarded war as 'simply organised murder' he was not prepared to do any non-combatant work for the military machine.[43]

Artist and cartoonist, Kennaway Henderson (previously mentioned), asked that the statement he had sent to the Minister of Defence, Sir James Allen, be read to his first court martial in March 1918. While the Church had supported militarism since Constantine, Henderson said his own religious convictions were based on the teachings of Christ and 'all of our greatest thinkers'.[44] He criticised the church for turning its back on the teachings of Christ regarding war and argued that 'a man need not belong to a church to be a conscientious objector; all that was necessary was that he should be a true follower of Jesus Christ'. [45]

The reasons why Charles Warden objected to military service were found in the archives of the Lyttelton Harbour Board, which had sacked him because of his views.[46] In a letter to his former employer Warden criticised the Military Service Act as being 'un-Christian and unconstitutional'. Conscription, he argued, would not help maintain 'the liberty loved by all Britishers' which had been 'wrested at great cost from both Kings and Parliaments'.[47] An original thinker with socialist leanings, Warden voiced Christian concepts in the letter as he put forward a vision for a better world:

> When men recognise that Love is stronger than War, and try to do to others as they would that others do to them, then perhaps the greed of gain and the lust of power which make war possible, will die out; the cruelty and misery will cease; and the Kingdom of Heaven may be recognised on Earth.[48]

Women speak out

While they might not have agreed with every argument put forward by every CO, members of the Canterbury Women's Institute and National Peace Council were, like Warden, working towards a better world. While their age, occupation or gender made them ineligible for conscription they supported the COs, both morally and practically as best they could. Some women took a more public role.

Sarah Page and Ada Wells, for example, leaders in the CWI, wrote and spoke against the war and militarism despite the war regulations. In May 1916, when the Government was considering bringing in conscription, Page, on behalf of the CWI, denounced war and made a plea for international arbitration:

> Increasingly large armies are ineffective to bring about peace ... war never ends war. It is ended by conference. We ... implore you to ... urge upon the Home Government the necessity of initiating such a conference ... Our contention is that war is all atrocity. It is the supreme national and international crime. It is the insanity of the age which regards brute force as the deciding power.[49]

Speaking as a Labour candidate to a public meeting in Linwood prior to the 1917 local body elections, Ada Wells, already well known as a strong advocate for women and children, spoke out for peace and freedom and against imperialism:

> She was out for the cause of peace .... She had been termed unpatriotic, and if to believe in the brotherhood of man was to be unpatriotic – well, then, she was unpatriotic. They were at the parting of the ways. Were they going to sell their glorious British freedom for Imperialism? Their forefathers had shed their blood for freedom of conscience and freedom of speech. Imperialism had taken away those gifts.[50]

Her bid was successful and she became the first woman elected to the Christchurch City Council.

The formation of a branch of the Women's International League (WIL) in 1916, which met regularly over the next few years (later renamed the Women's International League for Peace and Freedom or WILPF) show that there was another group of women publicly taking an anti-militarist stance.[51] Perhaps emboldened by the fact no woman speaking in defiance of the war regulations had been arrested for sedition, a large number of women began joining members of the NPC at hearings of the military service boards and court martials when they were held in Christchurch. At the court martial of COs Charles Warden and Arthur Borrows, for example, the court room was predominantly filled with women who were clearly not over-awed by the occasion. Before the hearing began a woman made 'loud-voiced' calls for more chairs for the 'poor old women' who didn't have seats. Another woman who stood and argued that people could not legally be kept out of the court room was threatened with removal. When other women laughed at this threat, they were all threatened with removal. At the close of the court hearing it was reported that a large number of women marched out of the barracks singing 'Keep the Red Flag Flying'.[52]

By 1917, it became clear that Second Division men would be conscripted and leagues formed throughout the country to seek better conditions for these married men. In Christchurch, the Second Division League took an anti-conscription stance. In 1918, when married men with one child were balloted, more than 1,600 men and women attended a large meeting on 28 April. The following day, when the first of the Second Division men had been asked to mobilise at the King Edward Barracks, a huge crowd of 5,000 – mostly women, children and babies according to one report – gathered at the Barracks with the aim of dissuading the men from going, and preventing the army from taking them.[53] They succeeded in preventing half of the men from being processed that day.[54]

Ending the silence

Children and grandchildren of First World War veterans often reported that their father or grandfather had 'never talked about the war'. When interviewing more than 80 First World War veterans seven decades on, when only a couple of 100 veterans were still living, historian Jane Tolerton found they were ready to talk.[55] But some of the reasons they put forward for not talking before this time, could equally be applied to the COs, many of whom were released from prison in 1919 at about the same time as the veterans returned home. The war was long over by this time and everyone was keen to put it behind them. Most families in the country had lost a family member or had someone injured and found it upsetting to dwell on it. There were 'layers of grief' in families, wrote Tolerton, which had been heightened by the influenza epidemic when at least 9,000 New Zealanders died in November and December 1918.[56] Above all, veterans were busy establishing themselves in what was a tough economic time. This was also the priority for the newly released COs.

Added to these factors were the guilt and humiliation that COs felt in response to public attacks made on them in newspaper reports, snide comments made by others in the community or through the presentation of white feathers to those considered cowards.[57] The social stigma against COs was strong. A desire to 'hide', leave the city and retreat to the countryside was typical of several of the COs whose stories are on the 'Voices Against War' website, including Kennaway Henderson, Charles Warden and Reg Williams.

The commemoration of the centenary of First World War was an opportunity to tell some of the war-time personal stories that have hitherto been neglected. How successful was the 'Voices Against War' project in making COs' and anti-militarists' stories better known? Many who attended our presentations said this was a part of our history they had known nothing about. Similar appreciative comments were received about the display. A report on visits to the 'Voices Against Website' show that over the 12-month period from 1 September 2017 to 31 August 2018 the site had 1,607 visitors and almost 6,000-page views. These figures together with the hundreds reached through the display and presentations give us confidence that Canterbury's First World War voices against war are now being heard and that the stories recorded on the website, along with the planned book, will provide a permanent record for future generations. 'Voices Against War' uncovered and recovered stories that had previously not been known and in doing so acknowledged a small but significant segment of the population who had dissented from prevailing attitudes (Figures 7.4–7.11).

Figures 7.4–7.11 Left to right from the top: Charles Mackie c. 1907, Secretary of the National Peace Council 1912–43; Rose and Harry Atkinson, 1901. Second row: Sarah and Samuel Page; CO Noel Goldsbury c. 1913; Ada Wells c. 1918. Third row: CO Robin Page; CO Charles Warden; CO Frank Money with his wife Ruth and son John.

Credits: Charles Mackie, H H Clifford Collection, Canterbury Museum 1980.175.51548; Harry and Rose Atkinson, William Ranstead Collection, Alexander Turnbull Library, MS-Papers-0071-18-1; Sarah and Samuel Page, Page family; Noel Goldsbury, H H Clifford Collection, Canterbury Museum, 1980.175.22715; Ada Wells, H.H. Clifford collection, Canterbury Museum, 1980.175.89232; Robin Page, Page family; Charles Warden, Charlie Warden collection, Canterbury Museum, 1989.28.1; Frank Money, Extended Money family.

Notes

1 Troughton and Fountain, 'Pursuing Peace in Godzone', 23.
2 Baker, *King and Country Call*, 21, 23, 173.
3 Locke, *Peace People*; Baker, *King and Country Call*.
4 Weitzel, 'Pacifists and Anti-Militarists', 128–47; Bodman, '"Don't Be a Conscript"'; O'Connor, 'The Awkward Ones,'" 118–36.
5 Baxter, *We Will Not Cease*; Grant, *Field Punishment No. 1*.
6 Holland, *Armageddon or Calvary*.
7 Biographical essays about Gray and Worrall can be found on the website http://voicesagainstwar.nz.
8 Rhodes, *Kennaway Henderson*.
9 Kennaway Henderson also receives mention in *Armageddon or Calvary* in a section discussing the unfair and apparently random sentences COs received for the same offence. Holland, *Armageddon or Calvary*, 108.
10 Page, 'Wartime Reminiscences', 6; and 'Paths to Permanent Peace', 9.
11 Gardner, 'Tradition and Conscience', 7.
12 Shoebridge, 'Imprisoned Conscientious Objectors 1916–1918', and 'Convictions for Sedition 1915–18'.
13 Charles Mackie Papers, 2017.38. Canterbury Museum, Christchurch.
14 MB287-51734. Miscellanea. Folder, n.d., Richard Thompson papers. Macmillan Brown Library, Christchurch.
15 Lovell-Smith, 'Charles Mackie'.
16 Lovell-Smith, 'Rose Atkinson'; Roth, 'Harry Albert Atkinson', 18–20.
17 Lovell-Smith, 'Canterbury Women's Institute', 75–76.
18 Bartlett, 'The Passive Resisters Union'.
19 Shoebridge, 'Imprisoned Conscientious Objectors 1916–18', and 'Convictions for Sedition 1915– 1918'.
20 The 'Voices Against War' project did not cover early peace-making by Māori leaders who non-violently resisted settler occupation of their land: notably Te Whiti-o-Rongomai at Parihaka in 1881, and Te Maiharoa in the South Island, who led a heke or migration of several hundred people from Temuka to Omarama to reoccupy land which had been taken from them. They were forcibly evicted in 1879. Somerville, 'Te Maiharoa, Hipa'. Keenan, 'Te Whiti-o-Rongomai III, Erueti'.
21 'Mr. Fred. R. Cooke', *Maoriland Worker*, 3 January 1917, 5.
22 'Seditious Tendency', *Maoriland Worker*, 7 February 1917, 5.
23 'Mr. Reg. Williams', *Maoriland Worker*, 31 January 1917, 4.
24 'Local and General', *Sun*, 27 June 1918, 9.
25 'Court-Martial', *Star*, 1 July 1918, 5.
26 'The Price of Glory', *NZ Truth*, 29 January 1916, 7.
27 'Court-Martialled', *Sun*, 2 June 1917, 2.
28 'Court Martial', *Lyttelton Times*, 8 March 1918, 8.
29 'Local and General', *Sun*, 27 June 1918, 9.
30 Lineham, 'The Rising Price of Rendering...', 191–2.
31 Marshall, 'Remembering Jesus on Anzac Day', 223–4.
32 Lineham, 'Sects and War in New Zealand', 173.
33 'Military Service Board', *Dominion*, 26 July 1917, 9.
34 Jack, Hilary, 'Early Days in Oxford'. Private collection.
35 'Conscientious Objector', *Auckland Star*, 15 May 1918, 4; 'Unordained "minister"', *New Zealand Herald*, 16 May 1918, 4.
36 'Unordained "minister"', *New Zealand Herald*, 16 May 1918, 4.
37 'Richmond Mission', *Sun*, 14 June 1918, 4.
38 Letter to the editor, *Sun*, 7 October 1918, 4.
39 Frank Money to the Defence Department, 20 January 1917. Photocopy in Money family private collection.
40 'F. Money. My Diary 1917', 24 June 1917. Photocopy in Money family private collection.

41 Gardner, 'Tradition and Conscience', 7.
42 'Robert Owen Page's defence', Robin Page Scrapbook, Page family collection.
43 Ibid.
44 Andrew Kennaway Henderson to Sir James Allen, 22 January 1918, Material relating to Kennaway Henderson, Lincoln Efford Papers, MS-Papers-0445-49, Alexander Turnbull Library, Wellington.
45 'Court Martial', *Lyttelton Times*, 8 March 1918, 8.
46 'To All Whom It May Concern', 27 January 1917, Lyttelton Harbour Board Letter Book, 1916–18. Archives New Zealand/Te Rua Mahara o Kawanatanga Christchurch Regional Office [Archives Reference: XBAA CH518 Box 1090, XBAH-A003-24, R25018918].
47 C Warden to the Secretary of the Lyttelton Harbour Board, 17 January 1917. Lyttelton Harbour Board Correspondence European War 1914–18. Archives New Zealand/Te Rua Mahara o Kawanatanga Christchurch Regional Office [Archives Reference: XBAA CH518 Box 793, XBAH-A002-1008, R25017755].
48 Warden to the Lyttelton Harbour Board, 17 January 1917.
49 'Reply to the Prime Minister', *Maoriland Worker*, 17 May 1916, 3.
50 'Labour Candidates', *Lyttelton Times*, 17 April 1917, 6.
51 Lovell-Smith, 'The Women's International League'.
52 'Court-martialled', *Sun*, 22 January 1918, 5; 'Local and General', *Evening Post*, 24 January 1918, 6.
53 'Mobilisation Scenes', *NZ Truth*, 4 May 1918, 4.
54 Baker, *King and Country Call*, 142, 147–9; 'Riots in Christchurch', *North Otago Times*, 1 May 1918, 7.
55 Tolerton, *An Awfully Big Adventure*, 13–14.
56 Tolerton, *An Awfully Big Adventure*, 13.
57 Baker, *King and Country Call*, 21, 23.

Bibliography

Auckland Star newspaper.

Baker, Paul. *King and Country Call: New Zealanders, Conscription and the Great War.* Auckland: Auckland University Press, 1988.

Bartlett, Dan. "The Passive Resisters Union." Accessed 9 September 2019. http://voicesagainstwar.nz/exhibits/show/pre-war-anti-militarism-and-th/the-passive-resisters-union.

Baxter, Archibald. *We Will Not Cease.* Auckland: Cape Catley, 2003.

Bodman, Ryan. "'Don't Be a Conscript, Be a Man!:' A History of the Passive Resisters' Union, 1912–1914." Postgraduate Diploma in Arts in History diss., University of Auckland, 2010.

Charles Mackie Papers, 2017.38, Canterbury Museum.

Dominion newspaper.

Evening Post newspaper.

Gardner, Jim. "Tradition and Conscience: Canterbury College and R.O. Page, Conscientious Objector, 1918–1919." *History Now*, 9, no. 2, (May 2003): 6–9.

Grant, David. *Field Punishment No. 1.* Wellington: Steele Roberts, 2008.

Holland, Henry Edmond. *Armageddon or Calvary: The Conscientious Objectors of New Zealand and the "Process of their Conversion."* Wellington: Maoriland Worker Printing and Publishing Co. Ltd, 1919.

Jack, Hilary. "Early Days in Oxford." Private collection.

Keenan, Danny. "Te Whiti-o-Rongomai III, Erueti." *Dictionary of New Zealand Biography*, first published in 1993, updated November, 2012. *Te Ara – the Encyclopedia of New Zealand*. https://teara.govt.nz/en/biographies/2t34/te-whiti-o-rongomai-iii-erueti.

Lineham, Peter. "Sects and War in New Zealand." In *Saints and Stirrers: Christianity, Conflict and Peacemaking in New Zealand 1814–1945*, edited by Geoffrey Troughton, 163–82. Wellington: Victoria University Press, 2017.

Lineham, Peter. "The Rising Price of Rendering to Caesar: The Churches in World War One." In *New Zealand Society at War, 1914–1918*, edited by Steven Loveridge, 190–205. Wellington: Victoria University Press, 2016.

Locke, Elsie. *Peace People: A History of Peace Activities in New Zealand*. Christchurch: Hazard Press, 1992.

Lovell-Smith, Margaret. "Canterbury Women's Institute." In *Women Together*, edited by Anne Else, 75–76. Wellington: Historical Branch Department of Internal Affairs and Daphne Brassell Associates, 1993. Accessed 9 September 2019. https://nzhistory.govt.nz/women-together/canterbury-women%E2%80%99s-institute.

Lovell-Smith, Margaret. "Charles Mackie and the National Peace Council (NPC)." Accessed 15 October 2019. http://voicesagainstwar.nz/exhibits/show/pre-war-anti-militarism-and-th/charles-mackie-and-the-nationa.

Lovell-Smith, Margaret. "Rose Atkinson: A Long-standing Commitment to Peace." Accessed 9 September 2019. http://voicesagainstwar.nz/exhibits/show/women-peacemakers/rose-atkinson--a-long-standing.

Lovell-Smith, Margaret. "The Women's International League for Peace and Freedom (WILP): The Oldest Women's Peace Organisation in the World Meets in Christchurch." Accessed 9 September 2019. http://voicesagainstwar.nz/exhibits/show/the-legacy-of-the-world-war-i-/the-women-s-international-leag.

Lyttelton Harbour Board Correspondence European War 1914–1918. Archives New Zealand.

Lyttelton Harbour Board Letter Book, 1916–1918. Archives New Zealand.

Lyttelton Times newspaper.

Maoriland Worker newspaper.

Marshall, Chris. "Remembering Jesus on Anzac Day: Just War or Just Another War?" In *Pursuing Peace in Godzone: Christianity and the Peace Tradition in New Zealand*, edited by Geoffrey Troughton and Philip Fountain, 213–27. Wellington: Victoria University Press, 2018.

Money family private collection.

MS-Papers-0445–49, Alexander Turnbull Library, Wellington.

New Zealand Herald newspaper.

North Otago Times newspaper.

NZ Truth newspaper.

O'Connor, P. S. "The Awkward Ones: Dealing with Conscience, 1916–1918." *The New Zealand Journal of History*, 8, no. 2, October (1974): 118–136.

Page, Sarah. "Wartime Reminiscences." *Working Woman*, March 1936: 6–7.

Page, Sarah. "Paths to Permanent Peace." *Working Woman*, October 1936: 8–9.

Rhodes, H. Winston. *Kennaway Henderson: Artist, Editor and Radical*. Christchurch: Publications Committee University of Canterbury, 1988.

Richard Thompson papers (MB287, Ref51734). Macmillan Brown Library, Christchurch.

Richardson, Dan. "John and James Roberts: Socialist Brothers Against Conscription." Accessed 18 October 2019. http://voicesagainstwar.nz/exhibits/show/the-response-of-the-labour-mov/john-and-james-roberts---socia.

Robin Page Scrapbook, Page family collection.

Roth, Herbert. "In Memoriam: Harry Albert Atkinson." *Here and Now*, June 1956: 18–20.

Shoebridge, Tim. "Convictions for Sedition 1915–1918." https://nzhistory.govt.nz/war/sedition-conviction-list.

Shoebridge, Tim. "List of Imprisoned Conscientious Objectors 1916–1918." https://nzhistory.govt.nz/war/the-military-objectors-list.

Somerville, Ross. "Te Maiharoa, Hipa." In *Dictionary of New Zealand Biography*, first published in 1990. *Te Ara – the Encyclopedia of New Zealand*. https://teara.govt.nz/en/biographies/1t48/te-maiharoa-hipa.

Star newspaper.

Sun newspaper.

Tolerton, Jane. *An Awfully Big Adventure*. Auckland: Penguin Books, 2013.

Troughton, Geoffrey and Fountain, Philip. "Pursuing Peace in Godzone." In *Pursuing Peace in Godzone: Christianity and the Peace Tradition in New Zealand*, edited by Geoffrey Troughton and Philip Fountain, 17–29. Wellington: Victoria University Press, 2018.

Weitzel, R L. "Pacifists and Anti-Militarists in New Zealand, 1909–1914." *The New Zealand Journal of History*, 7, no. 2, (1973): 128–147.

8 Reclaiming *Salute to Valour*

The official Canadian film of the pilgrimage to the Vimy monument

Sarah Cook

In April 1917, all four Canadian divisions, fighting together for the first time, captured a seemingly impregnable German position held since the start of the war in the Battle of Vimy Ridge. The four divisions consisting of Canadians from across the country achieved the victory at a terrible cost with more than 10,000 casualties.[1] At the time, the British Empire celebrated Vimy as the first major Canadian victory of the war; almost 20 years later Canada's national memorial was unveiled on the same ridge, constructed over a 15-year period by its architect Walter Allward.[2] It is a monument of mixed meanings, a place of sorrow and of pride. Erected to honour all of Canada's war dead, the names engraved on the monument represent only the fallen Canadian soldiers with no known graves on French soil, although there are 20 carved figures representing service, sacrifice, loss and mourning, and two pylons that stand for Canada and France.[3] Since the monument's unveiling in 1936, the battle and the memorial have become not only a focal point for commemoration of Canada's First World War experience but have reached iconic status for many Canadians as powerful symbols of sacrifice, indicative of Canada's coming of age during the war.[4]

On 26 July 1936, 6,200 Canadian veterans and other Canadians crossed the Atlantic in a pilgrimage to the battlefields and to visit historic places in Britain and Scotland.[5] The religious connotations were deliberate and the Canadian contingent of pilgrims' primary focus was the unveiling of the Vimy monument. Before the advent of television, the main conduit for sharing this experience was through radio and film. *Salute to Valour* was the official government film of the pilgrimage and the monument's unveiling. This film, surprisingly, has never been the subject of a sustained study, partially because the film was lost. A 1967 fire in the National Film Board of Canada's (NFB) storage facility, that housed much of the Government of Canada's film archive, destroyed it, and much of Canada's early film history.[6] While it is difficult to discuss a film when it has been lost, this chapter explores the making of *Salute to Valour,* its context of creation, reception by audiences, and its history as a record of remembrance. It concludes with a discussion of lost audiovisual records and archives and how this affects commemoration and the memory of an event.

The Canadian Legion, the central organisation for veterans that planned the pilgrimage, first suggested a film of the event in February 1936.[7] The Legion had organised and prepared for the massive trip since 1934 and it hoped to promote the organisation, attract new members, and create a legacy film that honoured the fallen. The Department of National Defence (DND) was also interested in creating a film of the unveiling to be used for commemorative purposes as well as an official record and it agreed to work with the Legion to fund the picture. Instead of turning to a commercial company, the Canadian Government Motion Picture Bureau (CGMPB), a small agency responsible for creating motion pictures for government departments, undertook the role. The Legion took responsibility for distribution, but they subcontracted with Columbia Pictures of Canada to ensure a robust circulation in theatres.[8] There was a precedent here with the partners, as these were the same that worked on the highly successful government film, *Lest We Forget*. Produced in 1934, it was Canada's official film of the First World War and used archival film footage recorded behind the front lines and on the battlefield. This film also acted as a commemorative object, capturing the war experience for Canadians who served, their next of kin, and, it was hoped, future generations. Captain Frank Badgley, Director of the CGMPB, was the main cameraman and Captain W.W. "Jock" Murray was responsible for the script for the Vimy pilgrimage; both had worked together on *Lest We Forget*.[9] However, unlike *Lest We Forget*, CGMPB would not be relying on a supply of archival film footage from which the official historians of DND could select the best parts to support the film's script and overall message. Instead, they planned to film the live event, despite the difficulties of this approach. Rather than depending solely on footage shot by CGMPB, Badgley used a cooperative approach with newsreel companies or local cameramen and paid them for their footage and services as well.[10]

The pilgrimage and unveiling was a great success, with massive newspaper and live radio coverage. The world watched as King Edward VIII, whose presence raised the profile of the event from a Canadian to an Empire-wide spectacle, unveiled the memorial on 26 July 1936. Not surprisingly, with an estimated 50,000 French civilians and thousands of Canadians, there were problems with filming the live event. An aeroplane circled above the memorial during the unveiling, and, according to Deputy Minister of DND, Léo LaFlèche, 'the noise made by the aeroplane was of course recorded with the result that some of the sound track was spoiled.'[11] Captain Badgley also ran out of film just before Minister of Justice Ernest Lapointe spoke at the unveiling.[12] More successfully, radio commentator H. Rooney Pelletier broadcasted live to Britain and Canada from a small opening at the top left side of the monument. There was some concern that Pelletier would ruin Badgley's shots, but as one reporter noted, 'in none of the hundreds of snapshots taken of the Memorial during the ceremony is Mr. Pelletier's head in evidence, though he missed nothing of what was going on nearly 200 feet below.'[13]

The Legion hoped to extend this positive act of public commemoration to a wider audience across Canada and planned to release the film in time for Remembrance Day 1936. Alex Ross, a wartime brigadier and President of the Legion, excitedly compared this film to *Lest We Forget*, noting, 'that a picture, prepared along similar lines but centring on the Ceremony of the Unveiling and the events relating to the Legion Pilgrimage, would have an even warmer reception.'[14] *Lest We Forget* not only documented the experiences of the war, it had also led to financial profits for the Legion. The Legion expected that the new film on Vimy would further raise its profile and garner substantial revenues to benefit ex-servicemen. LaFlèche agreed in principle to the Legion's goal of the new film, but he warned that it might not be as successful as *Lest We Forget*, as it 'depends upon the nature of these pictorial records and whether there can be compiled therefrom a feature film of the character you suggest.'[15]

The CGMPB struggled with the film footage and the post-production work took longer than expected. There were several issues, but, primarily, Badgley did not feel he had enough footage to produce a full-length picture. He studied, edited, and spliced the film together, but he was missing key shots. He turned to the commercial newsreel footage, but it took time, and even with new footage, there was not enough for a feature film. LaFlèche, Badgely, Murray, representatives of Columbia Pictures of Canada, and the Legion met in October 1936 but were unhappy with the first cut, and decided to again view all the footage in the hope of teasing out a coherent and evocative story. They also discussed the possibilities of producing two films – one intended for immediate release and one to act as the historical record for later release, both distributed by the Legion.[16] Having missed the Remembrance Day deadline, there was a new complication in late 1936.[17]

On 11 December 1936, King Edward VIII announced his abdication of the throne. This created a predicament among the filmmakers because the King played a very prominent role in the Vimy ceremony and was a central figure in the film footage. The Legion's President wrote of the King's popularity at the unveiling,

> I shall never forget the moment when I was privileged to conduct His Majesty to the parapet of the monument... As the King suddenly came into view one was conscious of something like a gasp from the 10,000 Canadians assembled in front of the memorial, and then, as one man the whole parade burst into cheers which for sincerity I have never heard equalled.[18]

The attention on the King and the wild joy of the veterans at his appearance was apparent in the footage, but now the Canadian committee was unsure how to proceed. J.R. Bowler of the Legion inquired as to the film, writing that he had heard that 'the abdication of King Edward VIII may necessitate certain alterations.'[19] This was unchartered territory, and rumours circulated that the Government had cancelled the picture because it did not want to cause further embarrassment to the Royal Family.[20] Believing these stories, an angry Canadian wrote to Prime Minister William Lyon Mackenzie King, asking indignantly, 'is it the intention of Canadian authorities to pretend that Edward never existed?'[21] However, these rumours proved false, and the modifications were relatively minor, with DND eventually inserting a photo of new King George VI at the beginning of the film.[22]

During this time, there were many other discussions over the content of the film between all the partners. While it was chiefly an official record crafted by the Government to be used for the purposes of commemoration and remembrance, given that *Salute to Valour* was a multi-party initiative, there were other opinions to be considered than that of the politicians or serving personnel in Ottawa. A conflict emerged around the film's different purposes: DND wanted an official record and commemorative object and Columbia Pictures, the distributor, wanted to make something theatrically viable. This disagreement came to a head at the first screening of the film in February 1937. This version was over an hour long with half the film devoted to the Vimy unveiling and the rest set in Canada, the trip overseas, the visit to the battlefields, and Britain. Speaking from the perspective of commercial viability, D.H. Coplan of Columbia Pictures was very pleased with the scenes of the pilgrimage in the various locations, writing that 'the whole story of the Vimy Pilgrimage is presented most dramatically and in the main it shapes up even better than I expected, particularly the last part of the picture showing the pilgrims in England, Scotland and Paris.'[23] However, he had major concerns about the rest of content, mainly the unveiling ceremony. Columbia Pictures suggested reducing the running time drastically to 35 minutes, no longer qualifying it as a feature-length picture, with most of the cuts made to the unveiling ceremony 'where the interest is not sufficiently sustained.'[24] As the ceremony mostly comprised speeches, Coplan felt that it would not hold the audience's attention. He also suggested removing the French portion of King Edward's speech and to keep it only for Quebec and Eastern Ontario showings. Noting the duelling purposes of the film – between the desire of commercial success and the film as a full record of the unveiling and a tool for commemoration – he brought back the suggestion of making 'an exhibition version along the lines that I suggest and another and longer version for the record and for non-commercial showings in which the various factors you deem necessary can be incorporated.'[25] This seemed an ideal solution, but DND wanted the commercial version to reflect the 'message' of the official and longer version. DND refused to compromise and, in fact, recommended adding new scenes, such as the inclusion of Canada's wartime prime minister, Sir Robert Borden, speaking at the departure of the pilgrims from Montreal, Quebec, as there were some complaints that he had been left out of the ceremony for partisan purposes.

Badgley had the difficult task of massaging these conflicting opinions and meeting contested expectations. 'I have been through the entire film,' wrote

Badgley, 'foot by foot, with a view to ascertaining how and where the film can be shortened to meet these requirements.'[26] He recommended reducing the length of the film as per most of Columbia Pictures' suggestions, by shortening the speeches. At the same time, he was able to accommodate the new footage of Borden that DND requested and the film was trimmed to 50 minutes. DND approved most of Badgley's recommendations except the cutting of the King's speech in French, remarking 'the film being of such great historical value, King Edward's speech should be left in both languages.'[27] Much like the official histories crafted by DND, this commitment to create an official audio-visual record of the unveiling means that the footage was carefully crafted and selected to formulate a message that would have been sanctioned and approved by the government.[28] But the commercial distributor's opinion carried a heavy weight, and DND and the Legion were out of their element. Badgely was caught in the middle as he tried to please all.[29]

Salute to Valour was finally completed on 1 April 1937. DND hoped to release it before 9 April, Vimy Day, but the wheels of government turned at their own pace.[30] It was not until 21 April 1937, that DND and the Legion signed a Memorandum of Agreement that provided the Legion with exclusive distribution rights for ten years.[31] According to the agreement, no more than eight copies were provided to the Legion for exhibition, and they could make no alterations, apart from translation or additional narration to make the film more appropriate for distribution in other locations. All copies remained the property of DND as an official record as well as commemorative object, and it had the right to exhibit the film in non-commercial venues. However, the agreement incorrectly described the film as feature length. The film had an estimated running time of 50 minutes, short of what a feature length picture would normally run, and this inexactitude later caused problems for both the Legion and DND.

A premiere in Toronto at Shea's Hippodrome was organised for 9 July 1937, just under one year after the unveiling. The Legion sent out over 1,200 circulars as well as invitations advertising the gala event to pilgrims and Legion members. The premiere was set to be more than just the first public showing of the film; it was another opportunity to commemorate Vimy. The premiere combined both solemn acts of remembrance with vibrant pageantry, with the Queen's Own Rifles military band playing and ex-servicemen participating in a parade.[32] In anticipation of the event, J.A. Gunn of the Canadian Legion wrote, 'I am simply delighted the premiere will mark another mile post in Canadian history.'[33] These were high hopes. Further demonstrating the importance of the premiere as a commemorative event, the Canadian Broadcasting Corporation radio system broadcast the proceedings nationally.

With the loss of *Salute to Valour* in the 1967 fire, it is difficult to know exactly what viewers at the time witnessed on the film screen. Nevertheless, a reconstruction of the film's scenario is possible through the textual records in the archival fonds of DND at Library and Archives Canada (LAC) as well as contemporary newspaper accounts of the motion picture.[34] The film followed the journey of the pilgrims, but it was more than just a travelogue. The role of the film was to give Canadians the opportunity to relive this act of commemoration and remembrance, and perhaps even add new meaning to the event. With around half a million surviving veterans of the war and millions of additional family members, for those who could not travel overseas to see the monument and mourn their lost comrades and loved ones, this film served as a powerful audiovisual memorial. There were some 66,000 Canadians killed during the First World War, and two decades later, many Canadians were still grieving.[35] The film began with the departure of troops from Canada in 1914, and the juxtaposition of the armada of soldiers from the First Contingent played nicely against the 'armada of remembrance': the sailing of the pilgrims in five ocean liners in July 1936.[36] The film next presented combat footage from the Battle of Vimy Ridge with significant attention paid to its geographical place in France, setting it up as the site of the future monument. Additional shots of the vast cemeteries where tens of thousands of Canadians lay buried along the Western Front created a sombre mood. The focus of the picture was the unveiling ceremony. Many dignitaries' speeches were interspersed with frequent pans of the thousands of Canadian veterans in the crowd watching and waiting for that crucial moment when King Edward VIII pulled back the Union Jack flag that draped over the central sculptured figure, Canada Bereft, the grieving mother representing Canada who mourns for her lost sons. While the Last Post played, the narrator broke in with a description of the scene. Much of this was powerful and moving, but according to one viewer, the narration at the important moment of the Last Post was unnecessary and 'I feel sure that the majority of the audience would like to join with the multitude assembled there, in hearing that salute to their loved ones, in perfect silence.'[37] After the ceremony, the film followed the pilgrims to England where they visited the Tomb of the Unknown Soldier and attended a garden party at Buckingham Palace, travelling to Scotland where they visited the grave of Earl Haig, Commander of the British Expeditionary Force on the Western Front, before returning to France where there were events 'recalling the war and honouring the men who died.'[38] Although it has been possible to reconstruct the general outline of the film from the textual records and newspaper accounts, it has not been possible to reconstruct the message of *Salute to Valour*. The previous government film, *Lest We Forget*, was infused with antiwar themes, especially the message of the First World War as a costly and destructive clash that should be avoided. This may have been similar to *Salute to Valour*, as many of the speeches at the unveiling warned of a remilitarised Europe, with the rise of Nazism and the Spanish Civil War soon to break out. But without the film, its unique perspective of the event, its place in the arc of memory and commemoration, has disappeared.

The premiere was a success, with much acclaim and coverage, but there was a problem. LaFlèche, upon seeing the film at the premiere, was 'extremely surprised to note that the production had been cut to such an extent that I can only say that the result is not warranted and is unacceptable.'[39] The film shown at the premiere was not the one that the committee had approved. This version was shorter and many of the scenes with speeches were missing or significantly reduced, including the King's speech in French. Badgley, who had not attended the premiere, was equally astonished to hear this and stated that 'no changes have been made in the negative of the film from its approved original form, and all prints that have so far been made by the Motion Picture Bureau have conformed exactly to the print of the film' approved by the Department. However, Badgley then revealed that there had been a private meeting, without representation from DND, with the Legion and D.H. Coplan of Columbia Pictures of Canada, which he had also attended, although he was quick to note that his attendance was 'in a purely non-official, advisory capacity.'[40] Coplan advised them that after a pre-screening with the theatre owners, the theatres 'had turned the picture down because of its length and the inclusion of too many speeches which tended to slow down the action.'[41] If there were to be any theatre bookings, they needed to shorten the film by cutting down the speeches and picking up the pace. Coplan, obviously realising that the film had no chance for theatrical exhibition in its current form and hoping for the best reviews of it after the premiere, must have altered the version of the film that the CGMPB had provided them, re-cutting it in a fashion that he thought would appeal most to the theatres. This suggests that there were different versions of the film in existence in contravention of the agreement that the Legion and DND had signed. The DND approved picture was about 50 minutes and the new version probably about 35 minutes, likely matching Coplan's initial recommended cuts. That the theatre owners, through Coplan, could unilaterally take such action indicates the strength they wielded. The public was not aware of this controversy and it is not clear if the films that were touring the country were the 'unauthorised version' of *Salute to Valour* or the DND-approved one. More than likely, the Columbia Pictures edited version is the one that circulated.

The Legion staged premieres with commemorative events like the one in Toronto throughout the country, with the film eventually playing in 144 theatres. Given *Salute to Valour*'s short length, theatres paired it with a feature film to provide an evening's worth of viewing. This was the general format in the 1930s with multiple short films exhibited with a longer main feature. The combinations varied from city to city. In Montreal, *Salute to Valour* played alongside *Varsity Show*, a comedy about an annual college stage show production, and in Calgary, it was shown with *Thunder in the City*, a romantic drama of an American salesman in Britain.[42] This must have made some of these events difficult to function as acts of commemoration but newspapers indicate the premieres often included sing-alongs with wartime music, military parades, and musical performances.[43]

The desire to commemorate the Battle of Vimy Ridge and to bear witness to the unveiling of the monument through the motion picture went beyond Canada. There were requests for international showings, from as far away as Australia. The Government turned down these appeals because of the ten-year exclusive distribution contract that it had signed with the Legion.[44] However, a limited audience in the United States of America saw the film, after the Legion branch in California had been 'asking, begging and pleading for release of the pictures by the Canadian government,' and they eventually received permission to show both *Salute to Valour* and *Lest We Forget* to its members in a not-for-profit format.[45]

While there appeared to be large audiences and much critical acclaim, the film did not turn a profit for the Legion. In fact, it did not even break even. The final cost of the film was about 12,000 Ca$ and the Legion, after recouping the costs of advertising the picture, remitted approximately 2,000 Ca$ to DND. The lower than expected proceeds for the distribution of the film was directly linked to the lower rental fees assigned to short films.[46] While the Legion was disappointed that they would not be generating any funds from the distribution, thus enabling them to offer programs or care for veterans, the high command pointed out that 'this situation results very largely, if not entirely, from the fact that the Department failed to carry out its covenant to produce a feature length film.[47] The Legion tried to negotiate with DND over the profits, but there was not much to fight over and eventually both sides cut their losses. That said, Bowler of the Legion, perhaps concerned as to how his past correspondence and complaints about the agreement might appear, was also quick to point out that the 'financial return was never at any time the primary consideration. It regarded the film as one which all Canadians ought to see, and is very happy to have played some part in making this possible.[48] Perhaps more important than the rental fee and the agreement with the DND was the arrangement that the Legion had negotiated with Columbia Pictures. A copy of this agreement has not been located but it is likely that the Legion did not receive a percentage from the ticket sales and thus did not collect from this side of the profit.[49]

Theatres were still showing *Salute to Valour* in 1940, four years after the unveiling.[50] This marked the last theatrical showing of the picture and the Legion and Columbia Pictures returned any copies of the film in their possession to the CGMPB.[51] There is no other mention of the film in the existing archival records of DND and the custodial path of the film from this point is murky.

LAC, then known as the Public Archives of Canada (PAC), is the repository for the archival records of the Canadian government, including DND. While PAC had briefly established a cinematographic division in the 1930s, it was unable to provide suitable space for these film collections as the film stock used at this time was composed of flammable nitrate. Instead, the

CGMPB provided ad hoc storage to PAC and other government departments. The National Film Board of Canada (NFB), headed by John Grierson, was established in 1939 and initially existed alongside the CGMPB, before absorbing it in 1941. The importance of film and archives became a significant issue at the end of the Second World War when DND was looking for storage for its massive army film collection shot during the war.[52] PAC acquired these films and stored them with the NFB. Unfortunately, most of these early films were inadequately stored, and although there were attempts to raise awareness of this problem of audiovisual preservation and to establish a national film archive, this came too late.[53] The catastrophic fire in 1967 destroyed much of Canada's early non-fiction film, including, it is thought, the existing copies of *Salute to Valour*.

Though a complete production of *Salute to Valour* has not survived, it is possible to locate remnants of the film, especially footage of the unveiling, by following the history of the record and its custodial path. As the current Government of Canada's film agency, the NFB continues to maintain a stock footage library and it is common practice to include in it footage from previous productions that have re-sale value. This includes footage that was used in previous CGMPB productions as well as other government films in the NFB's possession, although these film clips are often unidentified and decontextualised. Research into these holdings revealed six clips depicting the unveiling ceremony and the pilgrim's trip through the Western Front, with about 50 minutes located.[54] The only contextual information available is that the clips were shot in 1936 and are from a previous NFB production, but, given that the NFB completely absorbed the CGMPB and its records in 1941, it is highly probable that this is an incorrect provenance and this is footage from *Salute to Valour*. When records are managed by a new agency, they are sometimes reframed within the lens of the current government agency and descriptive information linking this to its original production title or producer is often lost.[55] For this reason, the fate of archival records and their custodial paths hold vital meaning for archivists, and increasingly so for historians.[56] There is a growing awareness that while archivists describe, preserve and make available the records that are contained in archival holdings, they should also be concerned about the records that have not survived. Historians, too, should be aware that archives contain countless records, but that even more often there are records that never find their way to an archive, as they may be destroyed, mislabelled, or misplaced. While these remaining clips can provide important visual evidence of the vast crowds, the Canadian dignitaries and the King at the unveiling, they cannot replace the finished production. *Salute to Valour* was an important commemorative object for the First World War generation. It depicted the commemorative process in 1936 and served as the official record of the Vimy unveiling and pilgrimage. It was also a cultural manifestation, albeit an audiovisual one, of this act of commemoration. It provided a tangible record through moving image and sound of an ephemeral event that would otherwise be remembered or expressed through static scrapbooks, post-cards, or snapshots. Like other films in the travelogue genre, this motion picture had the power to connect audiences through time and space, and it was hoped that *Salute to Valour* could place its audiences in France, in a way that only the motion picture can, at the Vimy memorial as it was being unveiled.[57] The film extended the reach of the commemorative event by in-cluding in its audience the many Canadians who could not travel overseas.

Although *Salute to Valour* was intended to serve as a 'permanent' record-ing of the event, even if it had survived, it is not certain that the film would have resonated and appealed to modern-day audiences. This is likely too much to expect from a black and white film released in 1937. But audiovis-ual records make for complex commemorative tools because they can be copied, altered and repurposed into new objects of remembrance. While one would likely not divide a commemorative medal into pieces, take apart a scrapbook or disassemble a monument, moving image and sound records are continually transformed. There is evidence of this repurposing in April 2017, when more than 25,000 Canadians returned to Vimy Ridge as part of a pilgrimage to mark the 100th anniversary of the battle. The event was broadcast live on three national networks in Canada and some of the surviv-ing audiovisual footage from 1936, the remnants from the stock shot library and clips from commercial newsreel stories, were replayed in this modern act of commemoration.[58] While the loss of *Salute to Valour* is a significant reminder of the fragility of early film, these remaining film clips infused the 100th anniversary commemorations, linking the past to the present, creat-ing a new moving picture remembrance in the digital age.

In 1937, a reviewer in *The Globe and Mail*, one of Canada's national news-papers, described *Salute to Valour* as 'the last sad link in the long chain of remembrance which stretches backward over nearly a quarter of a cen-tury.'[59] The battle, the monument, and the pilgrimage were all a part of this commemorative action. The film was created to be the culmination of remembrance. Like the memorial itself, this act of remembrance through the film was intended to be preserved for all time. But it was not to be that 'final link', not only because of the lack of permanency in the motion pic-ture record but also because there would be many more layers of memory around Vimy and the memorial in the decades to come.[60] The loss of *Sa-lute to Valour* is a sad and ironic end to a film that was created as an act of commemoration for a commemorative event that documented a monument commemorating Canada's fallen. It is a reminder that commemorative acts and cultural products marking remembrance are not permanent in form or meaning, and that without foresight and preservation, they can be lost. While *Salute to Valour* is gone, some of its footage remains. It allows gener-ations of Canadians to re-imagine the pilgrimage and to see themselves as not the final link in the chain but part of a process of commemoration and remembrance that situates the Vimy legend within the context of our gener-ation and those to come.

Notes

1 Cook, *Vimy*; Cook, *Shock Troops*, 142–8; and Hayes et al., *Vimy Ridge*.
2 Brown and Cook, 37–54.
3 The Menin Gate is engraved with the names of Canadian soldiers whose bodies were lost on Belgian soil.
4 Cook describes the evolution of the Vimy legend in *Vimy*.
5 Ibid., 249–63.
6 "The Films that Burned," *The Ottawa Journal*, August 3, 1967, 6.
7 Library and Archives Canada, Ottawa, RG24, C-8320, Letter from LaFlèche to Major J.G. Parmelee, February 18, 1936.
8 Ibid., Memorandum of Agreement between DND and Legion, April 21, 1937.
9 Cook, "Canada's Great War on Film," 5–20.
10 LAC, RG24, C-8320, Estimate of cost of sound motion picture film Vimy Pilgrimage, May 29, 1936.
11 Ibid., Letter from LaFlèche to M.L. Jack, March 16, 1937.
12 Ibid., Letter from LaFlèche to Captain Badgley, March 8, 1937.
13 "The Vimy Broadcast," *The Legionary*, October 1936, 7.
14 LAC, RG24 C-8320, Letter from Alex Ross, to Colonel LaFlèche, August 15, 1936.
15 Ibid., Letter from LaFlèche to Ross, August 31, 1936.
16 Ibid., Letter from J.R. Bowler to Colonel R.J. Orde, October 26, 1936.
17 Ibid., Letter from Judge Advocate General to Mr. Bowler, December 16, 1936.
18 Brigadier-General Alex Ross, "Dominion President's Notes – A Monthly Survey," *The Legionary,* September 1936, 18–19.
19 LAC, RG24, C-8320, Letter from J.R. Bowler to Colonel R.J. Orde, December 19, 1936.
20 Bloom, Chester, "Windsor and Wally too Prominent in Vimy Film," *Winnipeg Free Press*, February 22, 1937, 2. The Wally in the headline was Wallace Simpson.
21 LAC, RG24, C-8320, Letter to W.L. Mackenzie King from M.L. Jack, March 1, 1937.
22 Ibid., Letter from LaFlèche to Captain Badgley, January 13, 1937.
23 Ibid., Letter from Coplan to LaFlèche, February 23, 1937.
24 Ibid.
25 Ibid.
26 Ibid., Letter from Badgley to Lt. Col. L.R. LaFlèche, March 2, 1937.
27 Ibid., Letter from LaFlèche to Captain Badgley, March 8, 1937.
28 Cook, *Clio's Warriors*, 4.
29 For other studies about Canadian government film some which touch on conflicting approaches to productions, see Morris, *Embattled Shadows*, 127–74; Druick, *Projecting Canada*; Khouri, *Filming Politics*; Geller, *Northern Exposures;* Klotz, "Shooting the War"; Travers, "Canadian Film"; and Cook "Canada's Great War on Film." A more recent study is Clemens "Framing Nature and Nation."
30 LAC, RG24, C-8320, Memorandum re: Unveiling of the Vimy Memorial Motion Picture film from LaFlèche, April 1, 1937.
31 Ibid., Memorandum of Agreement between DND and Legion, April 21, 1937.
32 "Salute to Valour," *Globe and Mail*, July 7, 1937, 8 and "Salute to Valour" *The Legionary*, August 1937, 8–9, 28.
33 LAC, RG24, C-8320, Telegram from J.A. Gunn to Major General C.F. Constantine, July 8,1937.
34 There is no script for the film but there are some shot lists as well as correspondence describing the various iterations of the production in LAC, RG24, C-8320. The archival records along with the detailed descriptions in the newspaper

articles, most notably from the *Globe and Mail* were used to reconstruct the content of the picture.

35 Vance, *Death So Noble*.
36 Young, Roly, "Rambling with Roly," *The Globe and Mail*, July 10, 1937, 8.
37 "One Jarring Note," *The Globe and Mail*, July 15, 1937, 6.
38 "Vimy Memorial in Picture," *The Globe and Mail*, June 22, 1937, 6.
39 LAC, RG24, C-8320, Letter from LaFlèche to Captain Badgley, July 12, 1937.
40 Ibid., Letter from Captain Frank Badgley to LaFlèche, July 21, 1937.
41 Ibid.
42 "At the Princess" *The Montreal Gazette*, October 6, 1937, 3; "Bad Man, New Lady," *The Calgary Daily Herald*, October 13, 1937, 14.
43 "Chant War Songs for Palace Sing," The *Calgary Daily Herald*, October 13, 1937, 14 and "Picture to be seen by Distinguished Party," *Ottawa Citizen*, November 4, 1937, 14.
44 LAC, RG24, C-8320, Letter from F.C. Badgley to L.R. LaFlèche, October 25, 1938.
45 Untitled, *Oakland Tribune*, September 20, 1938, 18.
46 LAC, RG24, C-8320, Letter from Parmelee to LaFlèche, November 2, 1937.
47 Ibid., Memorandum re: Salute To Valour, November 28, 1939.
48 Ibid., Letter to Colonel DesRosiers from Bowler, December 14, 1939.
49 In a single week of showing in Montreal, *Salute to Valour* paired with *Varsity Show*, generated sales of $8500 "Theatre Receipts –Cont'd," *Motion Picture Herald*, October 23, 1937, 70.
50 LAC, RG24, C-8320, Letter to Lt. Colonel H. DesRosiers from J.R. Bowler, April 11, 1940.
51 Ibid., Letter from J.R. Bowler to Lt. Colonel H. DesRosiers, July 28, 1941.
52 Cook, "Shrouded History,"137–8.
53 Lemieux, "A Film Archives," 14.
54 It is likely that this 50 minutes may comprise footage shot by the CGMPB and not used in the production as well as footage from the commercial newsreels compiled by the CGMPB. National Film Board of Canada Archives, Shot ID 26101-26106.
55 Cook, "Shrouded History," 143–7.
56 For more on archives and film see Druik and Cammaer, eds. *Cinephemera*; Lemieux, "A Film Archives," and Cook, "Shrouded History." For more on archives and memory creation see Cook, ed., *Controlling the Past*; Cook, "We Are What We Keep" and Nesmith, "Reopening Archives."
57 Peterson, *Education in the School of Dreams*.
58 CBC News - Battle of Vimy Ridge 100th anniversary commemoration
59 Young, Roly "Vimy Ridge to be Shown in Tableau," *The Globe and Mail,* June 19, 1937, 4.
60 Cook, *Vimy*.

Bibliography

Battle of Vimy Ridge 100th anniversary commemoration (CBC News program originally broadcast April 9, 2017; accessed 09–17–2019) https://www.youtube.com/watch?v=FSerGABNyL4.

Brown, Eric and Tim Cook. "The 1936 Vimy Pilgrimage." *Canadian Military History* 20, no. 2 (2011): 37–54.

Clemens, Michael D. "Framing Nature and Nation: The Environmental Cinema of the National Film Board, 1939–1974." PhD diss., McMaster University: 2018.

Cook, Terry. ed. *Controlling the Past: Documenting Society and Institutions: Essays in Honor of Helen Willa Samuels*. Society of American Archivists: 2011.

Cook, Terry. "'We Are What We Keep; We Keep What We Are': Archival Appraisal Past, Present and Future." *Journal of the Society of Archivists* 32, no. 2 (2011): 173–89, doi:10.1080/00379816.2011.619688.

Cook, Tim. "Canada's Great War on Film: *Lest We Forget* (1935)." *Canadian Military History* 14, no. 3 (2005): 5–20.

Cook, Tim. *Clio's Warriors: Canadian Historians and the Writing of the World Wars*. UBC Press: 2006.

Cook, Tim. *Shock Troops: Canadians Fighting the Great War, 1917–1918*. Penguin Canada: 2008.

Cook, Tim. *Vimy: The Battle and the Legend*. Penguin Canada: 2017.

Cook, Sarah. "Shrouded History: The Canadian Film and Photo Unit, Records Creation, Reuse, and the Recontextualizing of 'Lost' Audiovisual Heritage." *Archivaria* 83, (Spring 2017): 125–48.

Druick, Zoë and Gerda Cammaer, eds. *Cinephemera: Archives, Ephemeral Cinema, and New Screen Histories in Canada*. McGill-Queen's Press: 2014.

Druick, Zoë. *Projecting Canada: Government Policy and Documentary Film at the National Film Board*. McGill-Queen's Press: 2017.

Geller, Peter. *Northern Exposures: Photographing and Filming the Canadian North, 1920–45*. UBC Press: 2004.

Hayes, Geoffrey, Andrew Iarocci and Mike Bechthold, eds. *Vimy Ridge: A Canadian Reassessment*. Wilfrid Laurier University Press: 2007.

Khouri, Malek. *Filming Politics: Communism and the Portrayal of the Working Class at the National Film Board of Canada, 1939–46*. University of Calgary Press: 2007.

Klotz, Sarah. "Shooting the War: The Canadian Army Film Unit in the Second World War." *Canadian Military History* 14, no. 3 (2005): 21–38.

Lemieux, David. "A Film Archives for Canada." *The Moving Image* 2, no. 1 (Spring 2002): 1–23, https://www.jstor.org/stable/41164571.

Morris, Peter. *Embattled Shadows: A History of Canadian Cinema, 1895–1939*. Queen's University Press: 1978.

National Film Board of Canada Archives (Shot ID 26101–26106; accessed 05–07–2019), http://images.nfb.ca/images/pages/en/index.html.

Nesmith, Tom. "Reopening Archives: Bringing New Contextualities into Archival Theory and Practice." *Archivaria* 60, (Fall 2005): 259–74.

Peterson, Jennifer Lynn. *Education in the School of Dreams: Travelogues and Early Nonfiction Film*. Duke University Press: 2013.

Travers, Tim. "Canadian Film in the First World War." In *The First World War and Popular Cinema: 1914 to the Present*, edited by Michael E. Paris, 96–110. Rutgers University Press: 2000.

Vance, Jonathan F. *Death So Noble: Memory, Meaning and the First World War*. UBC Press: 1999.

Index

Note: As commemoration is discussed consistently throughout the collection, it is not individually listed in this index. *Italic* page numbers refer to figures and page numbers followed by "n" denote endnotes

George 99; as victims 41, 46–48, 49, 109–10; *see also* sepoys; veterans
sport 3, 9, 11, 56–68, 98, 105; A-league soccer 61; Australian Rules football 56–68; cricket 60, 62, 64, 65, 66; during wartime 62–63; Melbourne Cricket Ground (MCG) 58, 59, 62; militarism and 64–67; National Rugby League (NRL) 60–61; netball 61; rugby union 61, 62; trans-Tasman competition 60–61
Syson, Ian 63

Thomson, Alistair 43, 47
Television New Zealand (TVNZ) 80–82; *Kaleidoscope* 78–79; Martin, Allan 80, 81
Twomey, Christina 47

veterans 25, 47, 59–60, 67, 80, 105–10, 143, 149–51, 154; Black, Ernest 108; Canadian Legion 107–109, 150, 151, 153, 155–56; Kentner, R.G. 106–107; Returned and Services Association (RSA) 81, 83–84, 117; Returned Services League 61; Simpson, Harold 106; Wagner, Ben 109; *see also* soldiers

Victoria Cross: heroism and 42–44; recipients 29, 31, 41, 43, 44, 48, 61–62, 81
Vimy Ridge 106, 149; centenary and 158; commemoration of 7, 11, 12, 149, 150, 151, 152, 153, 154, 156, 157–58; pilgrimages to 149, 150, 151, 157, 158
Voices Against War *see* centenary projects
Vonthoff, Tony 47–48

Wadia, Nina 30
Waitangi, Treaty of 84
Walsh, Melissa 58, 63
Ward, Stuart 46
Warsi, Baroness Sayeeda 21–22, 28, 31, 36–37n43
Weir, Peter *see Gallipoli* (1981)
Weitzel, R.L. 132
Wells, George 107
Weta Workshop 74, 81, 85; Jackson, Sir Peter 13; Taylor, Sir Richard 74, 85, 87
William, Duke of Cambridge 27
Williams, Doc 81
Winter, Jay *see* memory
Woolf, Virginia 33

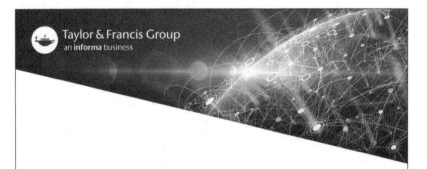